Art, Desire, and God

Expanding Philosophy of Religion

Series Editors:

J. Aaron Simmons, Furman University, USA
Kevin Schilbrack, Appalachian State University, USA

A series dedicated to a global, diverse, cross-cultural, and comparative philosophy of religion, Expanding Philosophy of Religion encourages underrepresented voices and perspectives and looks beyond its traditional concerns rooted in classical theism, propositional belief, and privileged identities.

Titles in the series include:

Philosophical Hermeneutics and the Priority of Questions in Religions, by Nathan Eric Dickman

Philosophies of Religion, by Timothy Knepper

Diversifying Philosophy of Religion, edited by Nathan R. B. Loewen and Agnieszka Rostalska

Collective Intentionality and the Study of Religion, by Andrea Rota

Philosophies of Liturgy, edited by J. Aaron Simmons, Bruce Ellis Benson and Neal DeRoo

Art, Desire, and God
Phenomenological Perspectives

Edited by
Kevin G. Grove, Christopher C. Rios,
and Taylor J. Nutter

BLOOMSBURY ACADEMIC
LONDON • NEW YORK • OXFORD • NEW DELHI • SYDNEY

BLOOMSBURY ACADEMIC
Bloomsbury Publishing Plc
50 Bedford Square, London, WC1B 3DP, UK
1385 Broadway, New York, NY 10018, USA
29 Earlsfort Terrace, Dublin 2, Ireland

BLOOMSBURY, BLOOMSBURY ACADEMIC and the Diana logo are trademarks of
Bloomsbury Publishing Plc

First published in Great Britain 2023

Copyright © Kevin G. Grove, Christopher C. Rios, Taylor J. Nutter and Contributors, 2023

Kevin G. Grove, Christopher C. Rios and Taylor J. Nutter have asserted their right under
the Copyright, Designs and Patents Act, 1988, to be identified as Editors of this work.

For legal purposes the Acknowledgments on p. viii constitute an extension
of this copyright page.

Cover design by Louise Dugdale
Cover image: Sheila Gallagher, Plastic Paradisus (2013), melted plastic mounted on
armature, 53 × 47 in.

All rights reserved. No part of this publication may be reproduced or transmitted
in any form or by any means, electronic or mechanical, including photocopying,
recording, or any information storage or retrieval system, without prior
permission in writing from the publishers.

Bloomsbury Publishing Plc does not have any control over, or responsibility for,
any third-party websites referred to or in this book. All internet addresses given in
this book were correct at the time of going to press. The author and publisher regret
any inconvenience caused if addresses have changed or sites have ceased to exist,
but can accept no responsibility for any such changes.

A catalogue record for this book is available from the British Library.

A catalog record for this book is available from the Library of Congress.

ISBN: HB: 978-1-3503-2715-3
ePDF: 978-1-3503-2716-0
eBook: 978-1-3503-2717-7

Series: Expanding Philosophy of Religion

Typeset by RefineCatch Limited, Bungay, Suffolk
Printed and bound in Great Britain

To find out more about our authors and books visit www.bloomsbury.com
and sign up for our newsletters.

Contents

List of Colour Plates vii
Acknowledgments viii

Introduction *Kevin G. Grove, Christopher C. Rios, Taylor J. Nutter* 1

Part 1 Embodied Experience in Art and Film

1 Call and Response: Negation and the Configuration of Desire
   Férdia J. Stone-Davis 13
2 Making Sense in the Midst of Non-Sense: Félix Ravaisson and
   George Rickey as a Way Forward for Emmanuel Falque *Tyler Holley* 29
3 Perspective in Nicholas of Cusa and the Rise of the Transcendental
   Subject *Nathan D. Pedersen* 43
4 Desirous Seeing: Sol LeWitt, Vision, and Paradox
   Daniel Adam Lightsey 59
5 Memory and Desire for God in Terrence Malick's *To the Wonder*
   Jake Grefenstette 71
6 Life in the Heart of Cinema: Michel Henry's New Phenomenology
   and Cinematic Form *Joseph G. Kickasola* 87

Part 2 Carnal Encounter

7 Scandal in the Cornaro Chapel: Desire for God and *The Ecstasy of
   St. Teresa* *Martha Reineke* 103
8 Art and Desire in the Song of Songs *Richard Kearney* 119
9 The Touch of God: Woundedness and Desire in James Baldwin and
   Jean-Louis Chrétien *Thomas Breedlove* 131

Part 3 Incarnate Performance

10 Of God and Trout Fishing: A Phenomenology of *Ree*ligious Life
    J. Aaron Simmons 149
11 The Prescription of Liturgy for the Problem of Blindness in the
    Thought of Jean-Luc Marion *Christina George* 163

| 12 | Beauty, Sacrament, and the Road to Emmaus *Wendy Crosby* | 173 |
| 13 | The Saturated Flesh of Christ: Christology, Aesthetics, and Subjectivity in Jean-Luc Marion and M. Shawn Copeland *David de la Fuente* | 187 |

| List of Contributors | 205 |
| Index | 207 |

List of Colour Plates

Plate 1 George Rickey, *Two Open Triangles Up Gyratory*, 1982, stainless steel. Raclin Murphy Museum of Art, University of Notre Dame, Gift of the George Rickey Foundation, 2009.046.001 © 2023 George Rickey Foundation, Inc. / Licensed by Artists Rights Society (ARS), New York.

Plate 2 Sol LeWitt, *Serial Project I (ABCD)* (1966), baked enamel on steel units over baked enamel on aluminum, 20 in. × 13 ft. 7 in. × 13 ft. 7 in. The Museum of Modern Art, New York, Gift of Agnes Gund and purchase by exchange, 515.1978.a-ssss. © 2023 The LeWitt Estate / Artists Rights Society (ARS), New York. Digital image, The Museum of Modern Art, New York/Scala, Florence.

Plate 3 Bernini, *Agony and Ecstasy of St. Teresa*, seventeenth-century marble, Getty Images 115623504. Credit: Mondadori Portfolio / Contributor.

Plate 4 Sheila Gallagher, *Plastic Lila* (2013), melted plastic on armature, 81 × 64.5 in. Crystal Bridges Museum of American Art, Bentonville, AR © 2023 Sheila Gallagher.

Plate 5 Sheila Gallagher, *Plastic Glenstal* (2012–2013), melted plastic mounted on armature, 48 × 81 in. © 2023 Sheila Gallagher.

Plate 6 Sheila Gallagher, *Rasa* (2013), single channel video, Courtesy of September Gallery © 2023 Sheila Gallagher.

Plate 7 Sheila Gallagher, *Plastic Paradisus* (2013), melted plastic mounted on armature, 53 × 47 in. © 2023 Sheila Gallagher.

Plate 8 Milton Avery, *China Christ*, 1946, Oil on canvas. Raclin Murphy Museum of Art, University of Notre Dame, Gift of the Milton Avery Trust, 1992.009 © 2023 The Milton Avery Trust / Artists Rights Society (ARS), New York.

Acknowledgments

We would like to express our gratitude to all of those who helped in the preparation of this volume. In particular, we are grateful to the Templeton Religion Trust, through *Art Seeking Understanding*, for its support both of this volume and an earlier conference during which these papers were tested and refined. This project was further made possible by the American Society for Aesthetics and the University of Notre Dame, namely the Departments of Philosophy and Theology, the Institute for Scholarship in the Liberal Arts, the Keough-Naughton Institute for Irish Studies, the Nanovic Institute for European Studies, and the Snite Museum of Art. Additionally, we would like to thank the following individuals: Kimberly Hope Belcher, Peter Casarella, Monica Caro, Kristen Garvin-Podell, Bridget Hoyt, Robin Jensen, Timothy Matovina, Jeff Speaks, and Julie Van Camp.

Introduction: Incarnate Experience

Kevin G. Grove, Christopher C. Rios, Taylor J. Nutter

This book explores phenomenologically the way in which the incarnate subject, broadly conceived, experiences art, desire, and God. Augustine's soaring words to God for this experience were "Late have I loved you, Beauty so ancient and so new."[1] The chapters ahead take up this task through analyses of embodied experiences, carnal encounters, and incarnate performances, drawing on both a diversity of artistic modes—music, painting, sculpture, film, and poetry—and phenomenological resources.

Investigating the incarnate subject as an intertwined locus of art, desire, and God is itself both an ancient and new project. The issues at stake emerged prominently in the iconoclastic controversies of the Byzantine empire. In response to iconoclasm, John Damascene (but also Theodore the Studite) in the eighth and ninth centuries defended the production of images based on the goodness of matter. For him, when the God who was incorporeal became matter in Jesus Christ—the incarnate subject *par excellence*, within Christianity at least—it opened new possibilities within the material for human expression about the divine.[2] As Damascene saw it, the Christian Gospels were filled with matter—the rock of Calvary, the wood of the cross, the table upon which was given the bread of life—authorized by the incarnation for sacred depiction.[3] Yet, as twentieth-century Orthodox thinker Paul Evdokimov claims, the intersection of desire and God at the point of the icon is neither simple nor static. An iconographer's vision must first pass through a "fasting of the eyes" that is as much ascetic as it is aesthetic.[4] In such a fasting, the iconographer's own desires are questioned, brought beyond the self into relation to others in the church, and fixed on the transcendent through the image of the incarnate Christ. The production of an icon questions and complicates the desire of both the artist and the viewer through reflection upon the divine that is experienced only in the finite.

Christ's incarnation is phenomenologically productive for it both illumines and wounds. This is acknowledged by theologians in addition to phenomenologists. In his essay, "The Feeling of Things, the Contemplation of Beauty," Joseph Ratzinger cites the Byzantine Nicholas Cabasilas to describe this experience: "It is [Christ] who has sent a ray of his beauty into their eyes. The greatness of the wound already shows the arrow which has struck home, the longing indicates who has inflicted the wound."[5] Ratzinger is defending the aesthetic as exploratory of the divine and not—as Christianity's cultural detractors might think—a departure into irrationality. Rather, the incarnation demands attention to contradictions in human love and desire—light and wound, incarnate majesty and dejection, fasting and feasting.[6] As such, the incarnation, Ratzinger claims, opens onto beauty as "the very way in which reason is freed from its dullness and made ready to act."[7] His theological appreciation of phenomenological experience characterizes the chapters in this book in the broadest sense. While the approach of these essays is more phenomenological than theological, they engage art—and in some cases sacred art—in order to take up anew the experiences of desire and God, more specifically, to ponder what expressions of freed reason might emerge from the enfleshed, incarnate subject.

Phenomenological Perspectives: Heidegger and Przywara

Phenomenology, broadly defined as the study of the conditions for the meaningfulness of experience, endeavors to uncover the relationship between the subject and object through an examination of the structures of consciousness and lived experience. Art, desire, and God—or more precisely, aesthetic experience, the experience of desire, and the experience of God—confront phenomenology with a particular difficulty; namely, that the subjects under consideration do not appear in the same sort of presence to the viewer as, say, a table or a book. The aesthetic object is irreducible to the material work of art perceived upon first exposure, just as the object of desire is by definition what is not yet attained.[8] The experience of God is incomplete for the finite creature; even reflections on the incarnate Christ, as aforementioned, both illumine and wound. Addressing this challenge with phenomenological tools is promising but nevertheless highlights disciplinary divergences and ongoing debates concerning method, metaphysics, and the appropriateness of theological subjects. A full treatment of phenomenology is beyond what can be accomplished in a brief introduction, but in order to acknowledge differences and situate the work of the chapters in this book, we highlight two divergent "icons" in modern philosophy.

In many ways, developments in twentieth-century phenomenology have some reference—whether endorsement or rejection—to Neo-Scholasticism.[9] This history cannot be fully recounted here, but accounting for the initial divergence helps to situate the project of this book. To this end, we give two key figures, who were students together for a time in Austria, Martin Heidegger (1889–1976) and Erich Przywara (1889–1972).

Martin Heidegger, early in his career, rejected the Neo-Scholasticism of his youth and problematized the possibility of thinking the transcendent in his 1921 interpretation of Augustine's search for the source of the desire for God in memory.[10] For Heidegger, the possibility of experiencing God and therefore of desiring God was fundamentally aporetic. If transcendent, then God must define rather than be defined by what it means to be. Correlatively, if God is the source of the meaning of being, then God must not be a being that is ever adequately understood. Even more so than the apophatic tradition native to Christianity, Heidegger's interpretation of phenomenological method, which required bracketing metaphysics, rendered the question of all God-talk an irresolvable impasse.[11] To necessarily think from within the gift of the meaning of being is to be unable to think that which gives the meaning of being. Heidegger would approach a resolution to this aporia in his reflections on art, since for him art is possibly disclosive of multiple and diverse meanings of being.[12] The work of art, for him, is not like other things that are always understood within a world of already presupposed intelligibility. Rather, it reveals a world of intelligibility and thus instantiates the gift of meaning that conditions all human understanding. The human being is capable of attending to this gift, then, because the latter makes itself paradoxically present to consciousness as the absent source of all thought and affect. To be open to the revelatory capacity of art is thus to hearken back to the fundamental condition of the possibility of human experience and understanding.

In precisely the opposite manner as Heidegger, Erich Przywara authored his key work on the *analogia entis*, or analogy of being, of Thomas Aquinas.[13] Whereas Heidegger bracketed metaphysics, Przywara claimed that metaphysics and phenomenology could be mutually donative. Przywara's position was that a metaphysics of analogy allowed for the relational consideration of many aspects of reality—being and becoming, unity and plurality, this passing world and that of infinite being.[14] The human person's essence is never the same as existence (as God's is) and thus there is ever a sense of "becomingness" in the creature that is dependent upon or referred to Being. Human life unfolds in a dynamic and ongoing tension between essence and existence which is only ever intelligible by analogy to the fullness of being. Many philosophical problems, for Przywara, are referred to this dynamic. The gap, such as that between a subject and an object of a work of art, can only be described analogically—for it allows simultaneously for the description of likeness and unlikeness. For Przywara, as John Betz describes, the *analogia entis* is at its heart a Christological, indeed incarnational, program. Betz writes of Przywara as grounding an aesthetic:

> The transcendent sublimity of Christ (which is ultimately an identity of beauty and sublimity) is an "in-and-beyond" the immanent beauty of the members of his body, who in turn discover their own ever increasing beauty and glory (2 Cor 3:18)—in realization of their own proper sublimity—in him who is properly infinite, whereby "becoming" is first in truth (Jn 14:6) a moving image of infinite being.[15]

As Betz goes on to show, Przywara's *analogia entis* is in this way itself a form of negative theology. God is both profoundly immanent to the creature and radically transcendent to the same. The incarnation, however, does not sentence the creature to dialectical strife, but signifies the redemption and fulfillment of the becoming that the creature now lives analogously.[16] The ascetic or spiritual practice that defines the analogical structure of the human person's existence, and that does justice to this rhythm between the immanent God within (*Deus interior*) and God known in transcendence (*Deus exterior*), is for Przywara likewise determined by the incarnation. Thus, ultimately, while Heidegger overlooks the centrality of desire in Augustine's search for God in memory, Przywara follows Augustine's doctrine of desire by acknowledging that any adequate theory of knowledge must account for the basic erotic orientation of the human intellect—indeed, the entirety of human being—to the divine.[17] To know truly is to love rightly, but to love rightly is to acknowledge that what one ultimately loves is ever greater than what one knows of the ultimate.

Heidegger and Przywara demonstrate radically different paths. The former rejects metaphysics in order to recover being that had been obscured; the latter embraces metaphysics in order to be able to describe both the likeness and unlikeness in givenness. Both made dramatic impacts on aesthetics after them—including those who embraced them and those who critiqued them. On the Heideggerian side, two turns in phenomenology followed, one towards the aesthetic and the other towards the theological, particularly among French thinkers. (Although there has not been as marked a turn toward desire, one need only consider the writings of Renaud Barbaras, Gilles Deleuze, and Jacques Lacan to witness the interest in the topic.) The phenomenological turn toward the aesthetic is commonly associated with voices such as those of Roman Ingarden, Jean-Paul Sartre, Maurice Merleau-Ponty, and Mikel Dufrenne. The turn towards the theological, on the other hand, is commonly associated with, among others, Emmanuel Levinas, Jean-Luc Marion, Jean-Louis Chrétien, Michel Henry, and more recently Emmanuel Falque. These two paths, however, seemingly never cross—Ingarden, Sartre, Merleau-Ponty, and Dufrenne were decidedly non-theological in their programs, whereas the writings of Marion, Chrétien, and Henry have distinctly theological shades of varying intensity.

Those who came after Przywara developed not only phenomenological insights but also aesthetics in a theological register. Those he directly influenced included Edith Stein, Karl Rahner, Hans Urs Von Balthasar, and Joseph Pieper. Later Catholic figures who have drawn upon Przywara's enduring importance include John Paul II, Benedict XVI, and Francis. The payoff of these thinkers in Christian philosophy and theology is continued reflection on how the incarnate Christ specifically reveals the "beautiful." More contemporary texts within the theological tradition, such as Richard Viladesau's *Theological Aesthetics: God in Imagination, Beauty, and Art*, blend together fundamental aspects of phenomenology and the transcendental thought of these authors.[18]

At this point it might seem impossible that such traditions might converge. Yet, here we note that post-Heideggerian phenomenology after its theological turn became explicitly interested in questions of art and the divine—even if approached non-metaphysically.[19] Furthermore, the history of theological aesthetics has remained engaged and interested in phenomenological descriptions of fundamental aesthetic experience as revelatory of the human and divine relationship. The chapters of this book do not attempt to resolve the tensions within the history as such. Rather, they chart paths forward from their shared intersection in the incarnate subject. The volume is organized in three interrelated parts. The first part, "Embodied Experience in Art and Film," draws upon music, sculpture, film, and painting to develop ways of expressing diverse philosophical and religious aspects characteristic of aesthetic experience as lived by embodied human persons. The second part, "Carnal Encounter," opens further onto the mystical and the wounded aspects of the person's embodied interface with God. Finally, the third part, "Incarnate Performance," proceeds to embodied aesthetic *praxis* on themes in philosophy of religion, theology, and religious studies. These contributions are deliberately interdisciplinary and include scholars of philosophy of religion, theology, religious studies, music, art, and film.

Férdia Stone-Davis's "Call and Response: Negation and the Configuration of Desire" opens Part 1. In this first chapter, Stone-Davis engages the thought of Jean-Louis Chrétien while challenging "liquid modernity" through an analogy of mystical experience and musical experience. Mystical experience and musical experience, she argues, share the quality of creating phenomenological moments of impact, absorption, and *ekstasis* that decenter the self and so dispossess desire. This decentering and dispossession call into question the commodification of desire in the contemporary "liquid modern" context. In this way, Stone-Davis applies a phenomenological analysis of the listening subject that incorporates otherwise frequently overlooked modes of music into her reflection on the subject and desire.

In the second chapter, "Making Sense in the Midst of Non-Sense: Félix Ravaisson and George Rickey as a Way Forward for Emmanuel Falque," Tyler Holley deploys the thought of artist George Rickey and philosopher Félix Ravaisson to resolve what he considers to be an insufficiency at the core of Emmanuel Falque's concept of the "spread body." For Holley, Falque wrongfully restricts the domain of language and therefore underemphasizes the social domain. To correct this, he deploys both Rickey and Ravaisson to join the so-called active and passive bodies, as well as the body and the mind, in a way that Falque's notion of the "spread body" seeks to do, but ultimately unsuccessfully.

Nathan G. Pederson's "Perspective in Nicholas of Cusa and the Rise of the Transcendental Subject," tracks the phenomenological nature of aesthetic experience, particularly during the turn of the modern age and the development of linear or Renaissance perspective. In his reading of Cusanus's *De visione Dei*, Pedersen argues that, through the rise of linear perspective, human desire for the infinite or the unknown transformed from a model of virtue formation to an ocular model bespeaking a nascent transcendental desiring subject. He then applies this conclusion to questions of modern public space and the secular question of how we ethically orient a multiplicity of perspectives. This chapter, incidentally, inserts itself into an ongoing debate between Jean-Luc Marion and Emmanuel Falque on the correct reading of Nicholas of Cusa's text *De visione Dei*.

In chapter four, "Desirous Seeing: Sol LeWitt, Vision, and Paradox," Daniel Lightsey explores Christian theological resonances within the neo-avant-garde work of 1960s minimalist artist Sol LeWitt. To do so, Lightsey places the thought of LeWitt in conversation with the work of Natalie Carnes. Under investigation are the diverse ways that human beings think about the meaning of sight or seeing. The author highlights LeWitt's conceptualist theory and especially his critique of the rationalization of the gaze's desire for control of and access to that which is gazed upon. LeWitt's "conceptual mysticism," Lightsey argues, resembles Carnes' "erotics of sight," which entails an *askesis* ordered to a "gaze of love" that resists captivation without eschewing desire.

The next chapter, "Memory and Desire for God in Terrence Malick's *To the Wonder*," presents the first phenomenologically inflected reflection on cinema found in this volume. Jake Grefenstette thematizes the role that memory plays in Malick's study of love and the divine and shows how *To the Wonder* consists of two narrative arcs. One Bernanos-esque narrative follows a priest in a crisis of divine silence, while the other, Bergman-esque this time, follows the disintegration of a love affair. The subject of *To *the Wonder*, Grefenstette then argues, is the mnemonic character often implicated in studies of love and the divine in Malick films. As Malick's *The Tree of Life* (2011) wields memory to promote a theology of grace, *To the Wonder* interrogates Platonic images of desire in service of a functionally Augustinian phenomenology of memory.

The second investigation of cinema in this volume, "Life in the Heart of Cinema: Michel Henry's New Phenomenology and Cinematic Form," appropriates Henry's thought in order to articulate a deeper understanding of cinematic form. Joseph Kickasola argues that Henry's phenomenology of life opens the possibility of considering the formal components of cinema, such as cinematography and sound design, to be more than secondary ornaments in relation to the structural components of cinema, such as narrative. He illustrates this through an analysis of the opening scene of Krysztof Kieslowski's *Blue*. By deemphasizing the *ek-static* concerns of exposition and character while emphasizing pure, non-intentional experience, Kickasola contends that the opening of *Blue* returns one to a self like to that described by Henry. In this way, a scholar of film studies engages in an interdisciplinary dialogue with phenomenology to arrive at a unique interpretation of the formal components of film as fundamental to cinematic experience inasmuch as they are evocative of what Henry calls life, which will later become the Life of Henry's philosophy of Christianity.

Part 2 begins with Martha Reineke's "Scandal in the Cornaro Chapel: Desire for God and *The Ecstasy of St. Teresa*." In her analysis of Bernini's renowned sculpture, Reineke attributes the discomfort of the statue's evocation of desire voiced by commentators (from Burkhardt to Huxley to Lacan) to features of modernity that create seemingly impassable disjunctions between the erotic and the religious. These disjunctions are reflected in tensions between popular religiosity and the institutional concerns of both the Catholic Reformation and art historians. By situating the *Ecstasy* within its cultural context and offering a phenomenological analysis of the work in conversation with Mieke Bal, Gilles Deleuze, and Maurice Merleau-Ponty, Reineke unapologetically argues for the retrieval of the erotic within the religious while illuminating the religious desire that infused Bernini.

In the following chapter, "Art and Desire in the Song of Songs," Richard Kearney reimagines the Song of Songs alongside the contemporary American-Irish artist Sheila Gallagher's *Ravishing Far/Near* to understand better the phenomenon of divine desire as it is manifest in art as a play between lack and surplus—a desire that descends to the flesh and ascends to the spirit. In an analysis influenced by Paul Ricoeur's thought, Kearney describes desire or *eros* as a promissory note that is concrete yet messianic, indeed carnal, and yet its consummation is always still to come. The Song of Songs is a story of transfiguring *eros* as a making possible of the impossible, a love congress between the human and the divine that opens religion to a poetics of aporetics. Gallagher's work does much the same as it explores divine desire in three wisdom traditions (Christian, Hindu, and Muslim), depicting three gardens as sites for theo-erotic encounter defined by the dynamics of the present with the absent, the here with what is to come. As in the Song of Songs, desire manifested in the work of art is never consummated but calls for multiple hermeneutic readings—anatheistic imaginings—of divine desire in a carnal hermeneutic.

Thomas Breedlove's "The Touch of God: Woundedness and Desire in James Baldwin and Jean-Louis Chrétien" puts Chrétien and Baldwin in conversation to illustrate how the phenomenological motifs of touch, wounding, and desire ineluctably possess political dimensions insofar as they are fundamentally embodied. What is the relation between wounded being as described by contemporary phenomenologist Jean-Louis Chrétien on the one hand, and being wounded, or the rupture and suffering of flesh, on the other? Such is the guiding question in this contribution to trauma studies. Reading Chrétien on the wound through the lens of Baldwin's consideration of touch in its capacity both to reveal and conceal the infinite, Breedlove argues that a phenomenology of divine revelation must consider the reality of wounded flesh alongside the political implications of embodied suffering of people like those whom Baldwin depicts in *If Beale Street Could Talk*.

The third and final part of the volume begins with J. Aaron Simmons's phenomenological reflection, "Of God and Trout Fishing: A Phenomenology of *Reel*igious Life." In this direct application of phenomenology's method of analyzing human experience to everyday life, Simmons looks to trout fishing for what it reveals about the religious, ethical, and aesthetic dimensions of existence. Trout fishing, he argues, is a lived practice of desire for an expected end, and yet it also trains us for living into a future in which those expectations remain unfulfilled—in this way it is a living practice of "faithfulness." By bringing together so-called new phenomenology, trout fishing, and open theism, Simmons insists we can get a better picture of how desire facilitates faithful living in light of embodied vulnerability.

"The Prescription of Liturgy for the Problem of Blindness in the Thought of Jean-Luc Marion," by Christina George, engages the work of contemporary philosopher and theologian Jean-Luc Marion on the topic of the liturgy in order to overcome what she identifies as Marion's consistent severance of the subject from the other. This severance effectively places the self in a position of primacy yet simultaneously blinds it to the possibility of arriving at the real object of its desire. George uncovers a theological phenomenological subject constituted by a desire to see what it desires without violating the purity of its givenness through an analysis of the liturgy, which provides the space for the self's response and approach to the given. Building on Christina M. Gschwandtner's contention that Marion ought to allow for degrees of saturation, George contends that liturgy is a habituating *praxis* by which one grows by degrees into the capacity to see the one whom one previously mistook.

"Beauty, Sacrament, and the Road to Emmaus" sees Wendy Crosby study the work of Jean-Louis Chrétien in order to illuminate the reception of beauty and the sacramental response thereto. To redirect focus to the theme of beauty, which in Chrétien's work takes a seemingly subordinate position relative to the wound, Crosby examines two interpretations of the story of the Road to Emmaus: the painting "Emmaus" by Filipino artist Emmanuel Garibay and the poem "Song on the Road to Emmaus" by Dorothee Sölle. The responses of the travelers depicted in these two works, Crosby argues, highlight the transformation of a wound into beauty and establish a paradigm of hope for an appropriate response from within the subject's wounded world.

In the final chapter, "The Saturated Flesh of Christ: Christology, Aesthetics, and Subjectivity in Jean-Luc Marion and M. Shawn Copeland," David de la Fuente argues that diverse depictions of Christ, artistic and otherwise, and especially those that exceed the phenotypic conventions of depicting Christ as white, offer a renewed vision of the decentered subject. The ethic of love that emerges is one that engages and affirms racial and ethnic differences. De la Fuente's chapter pushes Marion's thought toward new directions by way of a novel incorporation of the work of womanist theologian M. Shawn Copeland to discuss issues of race within Marion's well-known phenomenological framework.

We opened this introduction with reference to Augustine—both an enduring interlocutor for phenomenology as well as himself a keen observer of the intertwined experiences of art, desire, and God. At the height of his investigation of his own life and mind in the *Confessions*, Augustine illustrates the enduring challenge of expressing the experience of beauty ever ancient and ever new. To God, he writes, "You called, shouted, broke through my deafness; you flared, blazed, banished my blindness; you lavished your fragrance, I gasped, and now I pant for you; I tasted you, and I hunger and thirst; you touched me, and I burned for your peace."[20] In the artful poetics of high-classical Latin style, the Bishop of Hippo phenomenologically moves from exterior objects to his own incarnate experience of grace. His desires are both heightened and questioned. God is both to be sought and has come humbly enfleshed to him. Beauty is both ancient and new such that it spurs him onward. Augustine's holding up the predicament of the incarnate subject remains the ancient challenge that the chapters of this book address anew by means of phenomenological perspectives.

Notes

1 Augustine, who begins his *Confessions* with a heart "restless" until it rests in God, is an enduring interlocutor for phenomenology treating desire and experience of the divine. This phrase introduces an inflection point in his *Confessions*, book 10. *Confessions*, trans. M. Boulding (New York: New City Press, 1997), 10.27.38.
2 John Damascene, *On Holy Images*, trans. by Mary H. Allies (London: Thomas Baker, 1898).
3 Damascene, *On Holy Images*, 17.
4 Paul Evdokimov, *The Art of the Icon: A Theology of Beauty*, trans. Steven Bigham (Pasadena, CA: Oakwood, 1989), li.
5 Joseph Ratzinger, "The Feeling of Things, the Contemplation of Beauty," Public Address, August 2002. https://www.vatican.va/roman_curia/congregations/cfaith/documents/rc_con_cfaith_doc_20020824_ratzinger-cl-rimini_en.html. Accessed December 2022.
6 The source of the twentieth-century theological controversy concerning the natural desire for God was ignited by Henri de Lubac's *Surnaturel: Etudes historiques* (Paris: Aubier, 1946). For a thorough treatment of the development of thought on the topic within the Scholastic tradition, see Lawrence Feingold, *The Natural Desire to See God According to St. Thomas Aquinas and His Interpreters* (Ave Maria, FL: Sapientia Press of Ave Maria University, 2010). For a more recent intervention in the debate, see David Bentley Hart, *You are Gods: On Nature and Supernature* (Notre Dame, IN: University of Notre Dame Press, 2022).
7 Ratzinger, "The Feeling of Things."

8 Mikel Dufrenne's *The Phenomenology of Aesthetic Experience* remains one of the most sophisticated accounts of aesthetic experience within the phenomenological tradition. See Mikel Dufrenne, *The Phenomenology of Aesthetic Experience*, trans. Edward S. Casey, Albert A. Anderson, Willis Domingo, and Leon Jacobson (Evanston, IL: Northwestern University Press, 1973), as well as his later works, which expand upon the conclusions reached in this seminal text. For an account of the centrality of desire to life and of the absence of the object of desire, see Renaud Barabaras, "The phenomenology of life: desire as the being of the subject," in *The Oxford Handbook of Contemporary Phenomenology*, ed. Dan Zahavi (Oxford: Oxford University Press, 2012).

9 Francesco Valerio Tommasi, "Phenomenology and medieval philosophy," in *The Routledge Handbook of Phenomenology and Phenomenological Philosophy*, ed. D. De Santis, B. Hopkins, and C. Majolino, 50–63 (Abingdon: Routledge, 2020).

10 See the lecture "Augustine and Neo-Platonism," in Martin Heidegger, *The Phenomenology of Religious Life*, trans. Matthias Fritsch and Jennifer Anna Gosetti-Ferencei (Bloomington: Indiana University Press, 2010).

11 Important contemporary work on Heidegger and theology can be found in Judith Wolfe: *Heidegger's Eschatology : Theological Horizons in Martin Heidegger's Early Work* (Oxford: Oxford University Press, 2013); *Heidegger and Theology* (New York: Bloomsbury T&T Clark, 2014).

12 Martin Heidegger, "The Origin of the Work of Art" in *Basic Writings*, ed. David Farrell Krell (London: HarperCollins Publishers, 2008) and Martin Heidegger, "The Question Concerning Technology" in *Basic Writings*, ed. David Farrell Krell (London: HarperCollins Publishers, 2008).

13 Erich Przywara, *Analogia Entis: Metaphysics—Original Structure and Universal Rhythm*, trans. J. Betz and D. Hart (Grand Rapids: Wm. B. Eerdmans, 2014).

14 For consideration of the *analogia entis* by critics, especially Barth, see Keith Johnson, *Karl Barth and the Analogia Entis* (London: T&T Clark, 2010).

15 John Betz, "Beyond the Sublime: The Aesthetics of the Analogy of Being (Part Two)," *Modern Theology* 22, no. 1 (2006): 1–50.

16 Betz, "Beyond the Sublime: The Aesthetics of the Analogy of Being," 38.

17 See "The Religious Gnoseology of Saint Augustine," in Erich Przywara, *Analogia Entis*, 501–19.

18 Richard Viladesau, *Theological Aesthetics : God in Imagination, Beauty, and Art* (New York: Oxford University Press, 1999).

19 See, for example, Jean-Luc Marion, *Courbet, ou la peinture à l'œil* (Paris: Flammarion, 2014); idem, *In Excess: Studies of Saturated Phenomena*, trans. Robyn Horner and Vincent Berraud (New York: Fordham University Press, 2004), and idem, *The Crossing of the Invisible*, trans. James K. A. Smith (Stanford, CA: Stanford University Press, 2004); Jean-Louis Chrétien, *Hand to Hand: Listening to the Work of Art*, trans. Stephen E. Lewis (New York: Fordham University Press, 2003); and Michel Henry, *Seeing the Invisible: On Kandinsky*, trans. Scott Davidson (London: Continuum International Publishing Group, 2009).

20 Augustine, *Confessions*, 10.27.38.

Part One

Embodied Experience in Art and Film

1

Call and Response: Negation and the Configuration of Desire

Férdia J. Stone-Davis

Introduction

This chapter enquires into the de-centering of the self that occurs in certain musical experiences, where the subject is called into a non-instrumental relation with that which is other. It does so through the analogy of musical experience and mystical experience, exploring the possibility that an "apophatic anthropology" can be said to take place within musical experience.[1] Herein the self is constructed through its de-centering, and desire is dispossessed and thereby reconfigured.

In what follows, I begin by outlining what is meant by "liquid modernity," the context for this chapter. I then present an interpretation of mystical experience informed by two strands of thought, one found in Jean-Louis Chrétien and the other in Michel de Certeau. In the light of this I consider musical experience as that which impacts us, absorbs us and takes us beyond ourselves, before outlining the advantages of considering such experiences as involving an apophasis of anthropology. I suggest that, considered as such, musical experience offers an interruption of the liquid modern mode of being by offering a form of attention that is relational and non-acquisitive. In doing so, I suggest that music can return us to something of our core, something eloquently expressed by Nicholas Lash:

> If human beings are . . . "hearers of the word," it is by utterance, and hence by sound, that we are *constituted*—and constituted to be, in every fibre of our being, turned towards, attentive to the voice that makes us and that calls us home.[2]

Liquid Modernity

This chapter is set within a narrative that sees a movement from the pre-modern to the modern world or, otherwise put, from an "enchanted" to a "disenchanted" world.[3] Although there are different understandings about what disenchantment entails exactly,[4] it is clear that in broad terms it involves a flattening out of the epistemic frame, such that meaning is no longer located objectively, outside of the self, but is situated within the subject and the subjective.[5] This shift has been helpfully articulated by Charles Taylor through the juxtaposition of the "porous" and the "buffered' self.[6] In broad terms, the shift gestured towards by these categories signals a process whereby things are reduced to their relation to the subject, specifically to the power of reason and faith in its progress. That is, whereas formerly meaning is received from outside of the self by virtue of the fact that the world has significance aside from and prior to any interaction with it, it becomes the case that a boundary is cultivated that keeps the self "buffered" from the outside world such that it is able to distance and disengage from things outside the mind as well as generate its own purpose and meaning.[7]

Further to this move from the pre-modern to the modern, and the changing relationship between the world and the individual subject, there is another moment to be identified, one that entails a shift beyond the modern to a state identified by Zygmunt Bauman as the "liquid modern." What makes modernity liquid, for Bauman, is "its self-propelling, self-intensifying, compulsive and obsessive 'modernization,' as a result of which, like liquid, none of the consecutive forms of social life is able to maintain its shape for long."[8] As a result, social forms of meaning "cannot serve as frames of reference for human actions and long-term life strategies because of their short life expectation."[9] Thus, "change is *the only* permanence, and uncertainty *the only* certainty," since modernity—with its emphasis on the power of reason and faith in its capacity to improve the human situation—entails the pursuit of a "'final state of perfection'... an infinity of improvement, with no 'final state' in sight and none desired."[10] Strategies for meaning-making are thus episodic rather than long-term.[11] This episodic character shapes individual approaches to life, such that "each next step needs to be a response to a different set of opportunities and a different distribution of odds," and a "swift and thorough *forgetting* of outdated information and fast ageing habits" becomes more important for the next success "than the memorization of past moves and the building of strategies on a foundation laid by previous *learning*."[12] The emphasis of liquid modernity on impermanence and uncertainty has significant consequences for desire which strives for episodic meaning, is driven by need towards consumption, and thereby becomes focused on self rather than self in relation to other.

This said, we must be careful not to suggest that the subject is completely self-determining within this framework. This would be to underestimate the storied nature of human existence, that is, our entanglement in existing narratives and the resources these provide us with, consciously and unconsciously.[13] Bauman implicitly acknowledges this:

> It [short supply of patterns, codes and rules to which one might conform] does not mean that our contemporaries are guided solely by their own imagination and resolve and are free to construct their mode of life from scratch and at will, or that they are no longer dependent on society for the building materials and design blueprints.[14]

What it does mean, however, is that narratives are more lateral than vertical, that the individual bears "the burden of pattern-weaving," and that "the responsibility for failure" falls primarily on the individual's shoulders."[15]

Consequent upon this lateral strategization, and the fact that culture tends to consist of "offers, not prohibitions; propositions, not norms," is that the self in its search for meaning becomes leveraged by a system of meaning-making that is necessarily driven by the short-term and is largely grounded in a narrative that values processes of consumption.[16] To clarify how so, it is worth pausing to consider the kind of desire Bauman has in mind. For Bauman, the desire at work in consumer culture is characterised in terms of need and lack,[17] and is driven by the temporary possibility of fulfilment (given the episodic character of meaning-making). This kind of need-based desire is explained well by Emmanuel Levinas:

> To be cold, hungry, thirsty, naked, to seek shelter—all these dependencies with regard to the world, having become needs, save the instinctive being from anonymous menaces and constitute a being independent of the world, a veritable subject capable of ensuring the satisfaction of its needs, which are recognized as material, that is, as admitting of satisfaction.[18]

In short, if I am hungry, I eat; if I am thirsty, I drink—these are desires that can be satisfied, literally, though consumption. Bauman is clear that the distinctive mark of consumer society and its culture "is not . . . consumption as such; not even the elevated and fast-rising volume of consumption."[19] Rather, what sets consumer society apart from its precursors is that consumption is removed from biological and social survival, thereby removing set points at which satiety is reached and further consumption is no longer necessary.[20] Bauman is clear that what makes consumer culture distinct is:

> the emancipation of consumption from its past instrumentality that used to draw its limits—the demise of "norms" and the new plasticity of "needs," setting consumption free from functional bonds and absolving it from the need to justify itself by reference to anything but its own pleasurability.[21]

These processes of consumption are relentless and all-encompassing since, as Bauman explains, their "chief concern is to prevent a feeling of satisfaction . . . and in particular to counteract their perfect, complete and definitive gratification, which would leave no room for further, new and as yet unfulfilled needs and whims."[22] Thus, Bauman explains: a liquid modern, consumer-oriented economy relies "on a surplus of its offerings" that in turn depends on the obsolescence of items and services (an obsolescence both in terms of longevity but also appeal). The impetus behind this economy is to sufficiently arouse consumer desire, however, working blindly—since the desire of the consumer is multiple and cannot be known for sure and in advance— attempts to do so are numerous and often involve costly mistakes.[23]

Within the narrative of the liquid modern consumer context, then, the subject's capacity for meaning-making is turned on its head, as desire, understood as lack, is commodified as it grasps after the temporarily new and best, the temporarily satisfying. Here, seeking after is rendered perpetual in a negative sense, and fulfilment is postponed in both the present and future tense. As we shall see, however, the absence of satisfaction need not be understood in this way.

Mystical "Event"

In the light of this condition in which we arguably find ourselves collectively, what is the significance of examining music through analogy with mystical experience? There are certain phenomenological similarities that ground the comparison, which itself in turn might point towards a different mode of being, one that can offer some remedy to the liquid modern condition by tendering an experience of a different, more fruitful way of finding meaning and interacting with that which is other than the subject—a mode of being that reconfigures desire as lack into desire as abundance.

Recognizing that attempts to speak about mystical experience in abstract terms risk collapsing the particular into the general, fallaciously presuming that there is *a* thing called mystical experience, I draw upon two streams of thought that are helpful in suggesting ways forward for a fruitful dialogue with musical experience (which, likewise, is not singular in nature). Within both streams of thought, as we shall see, there is a clear sense of being-in-relation. Specifically, being acted upon, of being completely engaged and thereby of being taken to the brink of ourselves where we experience something other and are transformed not through the satisfaction of something lacking but through the experience of something non-reducible and incapable of being possessed, since abundant. Similar moments can be identified within certain music events.

Before proceeding, however, I would like to make one important qualification to my language, for having said that I will speak about musical and mystical *experiences*, in effect I am talking, rather, about musical and mystical *events*. The reason for this language shift is threefold. One, to speak of event is to remind us of the particularity and dynamism of experience—its *happening* rather than its *being*. Two, going further than other recent treatments of event, which understand it simply as that which is marked out from the ordinary in some way,[24] the conception of event I have in mind is more like Slavoj Žižek's, wherein, he says, "at its most elementary, event is not something that occurs within the world, but it is a change of the very frame through which we perceive the world and engage in it."[25] Three, drawing attention to this change in perspective indicates something about the mode of attention involved in a particular experience, namely, one that makes possible a profound transformation and extends beyond the moment, or series of moments.

Chrétien

The first stream of thought that points us towards a dialogue with musical experience is provided by Jean-Louis Chrétien and a central motif that runs throughout his works, namely, call and response. Chrétien offers two observations about this motif. The first is that "I" am *called into being*, and the second is that "I" am *already and always in response*. This dynamic of call and response operates at two distinct levels. At one level, it points towards an originary call, an "*excess* of the encounter with things, other, world, and God."[26] In doing so, that which calls remains resistant to anything that might be said of it and remains beyond any particular response one might make. For this reason, listening does not simply involve listening to what is said but, rather, "to what it is, in the world or, in other words, to which his words are replying—what is calling his words, requesting them, menacing them or overwhelming them."[27] In this sense, listening and responding necessitate an attention not only to what is heard but to what the heard itself responds to. It thereby opens a space of plurality and hospitality:[28]

> Every voice, hearing without cease, bears many voices within itself because there is no first voice. We always speak to the world, we are always already in the act of speaking, always in the world still, so that the initiative to speak always comes calibrated with past speech, with a charge to speak, which it accepts and takes on without having given rise to it.[29]

The second observation follows from the first, for just as I am called into being, so I am constituted in and through this response, and transformed in the process. This observation recognizes that we are called into being in different ways and by different kinds of experience, ones that address our whole being, body and soul.[30] Importantly, the possibility of transformation emerges from the integral asymmetry of the dialogue. This asymmetry is twofold for, on the one hand, what is heard is not heard in its totality (it is always inescapably more)[31] and, on the other hand, our response is always belated[32] and never entirely adequate.[33] This is ontologically significant. As Chrétien notes, "the way the response falls short constitutes neither a contingent deficit nor a regrettable imperfection in the response that we give.... It is the very event of a wound by which our existence is altered and opened," he continues, "and becomes itself the site of the manifestation of what it responds to."[34] This falling short by necessity invokes "chorus and polyphony":[35] "The response accomplishes its unsubstitutable singularity only in giving itself into a community and thus making appeal to other voices. This is not because they complete that response, but because the fault is closed only at the same time as our mouths."[36] The response to the call is thus a space of hospitality but also a site of intimacy. The call does not leave me "intact"; it opens a "space in me to be heard" and shatters "something of what I was before I felt myself to be called."[37] Thus, for Chrétien: "To listen is to be opened to the other and transformed by the other at our most intimate core. Intimacy, in these ways of thinking, is neither escape nor shelter, but rather the place of broader exposure."[38] As we shall see, this place of broader exposure and wounding, generated by a response to a preceding call that always eludes comprehension, is fruitful not only in terms of thinking about mystical events, but also musical events.

De Certeau

The second stream of thought arrives from Michel de Certeau. His treatment of mysticism resonates with Chrétien's account of call and response, and offers something analogous to the sense of hospitality built into the latter's structure. Thus, in relation to mystical experience, De Certeau says:

> The event imposes itself. In a very real sense, it alienates. It pertains to the same order as ecstasy: that is, to that which transports one outside oneself.... [S]uch a "birth" draws from man a truth that is his without coming from him or belonging

to him. Thus, he is "outside himself" at the very moment that a Self is asserted. A necessity is aroused in him, but under the sign of a melody, a spoken word, or a vision coming from elsewhere.[39]

Mystical experiences, in short, operate through a dynamic of call and response. They are "expressions overflowing with the excess of a presence that could never be possessed."[40] Otherwise put, they involve the "discovery of an Other as essential or inevitable that defines this relationship."[41] These discoveries are "indissociable from a place, a meeting, a reading, but not reducible to the means that convey them."[42] For de Certeau, the presence of that which is other stands at the centre of the mystical, and, as in Chrétien, seems to hold together distinct forms of otherness, including not only the originary other, but the community of others within which one is necessarily situated, thereby creating sites of hospitality. It is thus that, speaking of mystical texts, de Certeau notes the importance of the "dialogic spaces" they create.[43] Writing about mystics of the sixteenth and seventeenth centuries, he says:

> Since it was no longer possible to presuppose the same cosmos that was experienced in times past as a (linguistic) encounter between Divine Speaker and His faithful respondents, it was necessary to *produce* the conventions needed to circumscribe the places where one can "hear" [*entendre*] and where one can "come to an understanding with" others [*s'entendre*]. An essential sector of mystic thought attempts to explain and obtain the conditions allowing one to "speak to" [*parler à*] or "speak with" [*se parler*].[44]

Within these spaces, a plurality of voices is brought together, including the voice of the absolute (the Divine), the voice of the institution (the Word of God), and the voice of the author.[45]

Just as for Chrétien, the language of transformation is key for de Certeau. Talking about "mystical life," de Certeau suggests that it is "comprised of experiences that initiate or transform it."[46] These "moments," he says, are like "throwing open a window onto one's dwelling; they give a new sense of ease, allow a breath of fresh air to enter one's life."[47] The elusiveness of the experience is vital, since it reflects something of its ineffability, but also of its unexpected nature and transformative capacity. It has the character of revelation:

> There the unbelievable and the obvious coincide. It is a transformation and a revelation. It is impossible to identify the event with a particular instant in time because of what it awakens in the memory and because of all the life experience [*le vécu*] that emerges in that particular moment. By the same token, it is also impossible to reduce it to the product of a long preparation, since it happens unexpectedly, as a "gift," and is unforeseeable.[48]

Explaining further, de Certeau notes that the mystic can say "It happened *there*" because "he keeps engraved in his memory, the smallest circumstances of that instant." However, at the same time, the mystic must also say, "It was not *that*," because "for him the experience has to do with something other than a site, an impression, or a certain knowledge."[49] The language of "trace" captures something of this, as it refers to the impact of "the fissure of an Absence or a Presence" upon other experiences and understandings.[50] Indicating that "the event cannot be reduced to its initial form," it suggests, for de Certeau, that the mystical event "calls for a beyond to what was only a first unveiling. It opens up an itinerary."[51] The mystical life, therefore, is not "circumscribed in the particular forms of a privileged instant," nor is it constituted by the repetition of a mystical experience.[52] Rather, the mystical life is processual; it "is begun when it recovers its roots and experiences its strangeness in ordinary life—when it continues to discover in other ways what has occurred that first time."[53]

Musical "Event"

The musical event has the capacity to create a particular interrelationship between subject and object, self and world, that can be cast in terms of impact, absorption and ekstasis,[54] and furthermore can be said to involve a mode of attention suggestive of that which we have seen in relation to mystical events. These are not isolated moments but points of interaction that occur throughout the musical process as a result of the self acting, as well as the self's being acted upon. Herein an attunement takes place or, otherwise put, a resonance. This resonance, as we shall see, invokes the transformative site of hospitality and intimacy noted in relation to the mystical.

To elucidate these moments, whether performed or listened to, music—as event—issues a call to us.[55] It *impacts* us physically, striking our ear drums but also reverberating in our bodies, more or less subtly. It catches our attention and invites us to enter into its sound. Depending on how we engage with it (since there are many different ways to do so), we can respond to it and become *absorbed* by it, entering completely into its time, space and flow. Here, we *face outwards*, being in some sense brought to the "brink" of ourselves. The concept of "threshold" (from the Latin *limen*) gives flesh to this. A threshold is a point at which transition occurs. However, that which is most significant about thresholds is not the *moment of crossing*, but the *relation* that manifests at the *instant before that crossing*, since it is here that binaries such as "inside" and "outside," "subject" and "object," are transcended as they are held in tension. A site of hospitality and intimacy is formed.

To illustrate this, let us consider music production, which comprises a succession of physical actions that manipulate wave vibrations: the lengths of channels of air and pieces of string are altered through the impression of the human body. This manipulation runs reciprocally for the sound yielded in turn has an impact on the player, who responds to it. An "attunement" takes place between player, instrument, sound and music, since the physical body becomes one with the instrument and with the sound produced. In this way, the player is brought to a threshold where subject and object, inner and outer meet. Importantly, attunement is not an isolated moment. It is, rather, a process identifiable within different levels of playing and within accompanying modes of attention that move from the mechanical, on the one hand, as one masters bodily movement in relation to achieving a desired sound, to the musical, on the other, where one is freer to become involved in music's shape and internal movement. Here, details are situated within phrases that are then placed within the musical whole, understood as pointing both forwards and backwards "intentionally" within a larger musical structure, which itself is called into being by other sounds, other musics.

The reception of music is as physical an act as that of its production. The aural space is singular in nature and discloses the porosity of the boundary between subject and object. For the distance between them is eliminable. It is thus that the aural experience can be contrasted with the visual. In visual experience, we see discrete things in certain places at particular times. Physical items are thus bounded, for example, two distinct things cannot be in the same place at the very same time, and I experience things as "here" or "there." By contrast, aural experience is more encompassing; although I might hear a sound as generated by a source and thereby as coming from a particular "here" or "there," my experience of the sound is not reliant on this, and indeed can far exceed it, as in the case of music, the foundation of which is the peeling away of sound from source and its consequent ability to create a "field of force" into which I am taken.[56] It is due to the permeability of the boundary between subject and musical object that we are caught up in it. Whether in performance or reception, music calls to us, invites response, and enables us to be taken outside of ourselves so that our experience is reshaped and structured as we are taken into the musical time of what we experience.

To further understand the attunement involved in the music event, the idea of threshold is worth unpacking further, for music can be cast as a threshold practice, since its mode of being is fundamentally bound up with thresholds and is characterized by openness. We can illustrate three ways in which this is so.[57] One, music is integrally connected to sensory thresholds—unlike the relationship between other media and the human senses, the effect of sound is immediate and to a degree unstoppable. The aural threshold is easily trespassed, so to speak. Two, music can be said to operate as a threshold itself, since it is only ever in transition and relies on process and change. This can be seen in the aspects that constitute musical experience, including the dissipation of sound and its organization as it moves through time and space, held together even in its eventual absence. Three, through the moments of impact, absorption and ekstasis that occur within the course of attunement, there is no subject and no object, no inside and no outside, there is only threshold, the point at which the two meet. In this sense, the proximity of the subject to and its dependence upon that which is other is brought to the fore, as is the intransigence of the other. This other cannot be dominated and is not there to simply be acquired and possessed. That is, it never yields or gives itself completely and is abundant in character. More than this, the other makes a demand: utterances (musical and otherwise) are performed and act upon us, they offer an interpellation. They address us, in some sense they call us into being and constitute us in doing so. Thus, value does not derive simply from the self but, rather, is something received and responded to. Meaning and value are in process but are not instrumental. Simultaneously, they are an end in themselves but are not thereby definitive or unambiguous. In these terms, the analogy of the musical and the mystical set Bauman's statement that "change is the *only* permanence, and uncertainty the *only* uncertainty" in a new light.[58] They also, concomitantly, challenge the premising notion of desire as configured in relation to lack, a lack that can be satisfied, even if temporarily.

Apophasis of Anthropology

As we have seen, the alignment of musical and mystical experience arises fundamentally from certain phenomenological similarities that they share, which indicate the situation of desire within an experience that is taken as an end in itself rather than as instrumental, not as lack but a place of abundance. Moreover, they both offer a transformation that is to some degree conceptually ungraspable with an extension beyond its duration. But can we be more specific about what can be constructively offered by musical experience within the context of liquid modernity, within which desire is impelled ever onwards by the promise of various illusory necessities and fulfilment is deferred in both the present and future tense? To attempt this, it is helpful to turn our attention to the idea of detachment found in Meister Eckhart or—as explained by Denys Turner—the idea of an apophasis of anthropology.

In Sermon 52, Eckhart considers the meaning of the verse "Blessed are the poor in spirit, for theirs is the kingdom of heaven." He suggests that a poor man is he who "wants nothing, and knows nothing, and has nothing."[59] In reflecting on each of these three aspects of poverty, Eckhart points towards the ways in which humans tend to form attachments that distract us from our fundamental connection to God. The soul, Eckhart notes, tends to cling to things and is incapable of maintaining a "healthy distance" from them.[60] Thus, human actions have a tendency to become self-oriented. Eckhart says:

> See, all those are merchants, who restrain themselves from major sins and would love to be good people and do their good works to give God the honour, works such as fasting, vigilance, prayer and alike, hence lots of good work, but they do all of this, so that the Lord recompenses them and God gives something they would like back to them.[61]

Will to action obscures the end of action. In the light of this, the goal of detachment is to enable a person to be "so free of all things and all works, both interior and exterior, that he might become a place only for God, in which God could work."[62] Detachment is, then, a reciprocal movement in which humans leave "things" and undergo a self-emptying. However, this detachment is not negation but a fulfillment of being, since in and through it an individual is filled with God's presence (although, importantly, God's limitlessness means that this "filling" is also without end).[63] As Turner explains, "detachment" is not an experience, but "the strategy of dispossessing desire of its desire to possess its objects and so to destroy them" such that a "proper relation" can be set in place wherein desire has "reverence" for its object, rather than seeking to appropriate it.[64] In this way detachment stands as the condition of possibility of love and results not in deficiency but an excess that is neither exhaustive nor exhaustible.

Certain music events provide a strategy for detachment and an opportunity for modelling a different way of being in the world, one that provides a point of orientation that transcends commodity and use (since music always remains to some degree resistant to appropriation and expectation), and has the potential to reconfigure desire. It does this on (at least) three levels. One, by taking us out of ourselves and taking us into its musical time and space, music can lift us beyond self-preoccupation. Two, music can take us beyond our usual form of interaction with things we encounter; we can delight in the absolute "for nothingness" of musical experience. Three, by using the desire elicited by and formative to music's power, music can shape and reshape desire—at a basic level by fulfilling, subverting, deferring or refusing musical expectation (or expectations of music). In doing so, music has the potential to provide not only a modelling of, but an exercise in, attention and attentiveness to that which is Other. This can extend beyond an experience's duration and may even serve as an impetus to re-evaluation and transformation of other (more ordinary) modes of engagement. As such, music can draw us back to the dynamic of call and response that constitutes our being. It gestures in this way towards an understanding of desire that is not based on lack, as in liquid modernity, but on abundance, and is thereby not simply driven by need towards consumption. Rather, it is oriented metaphysically. Such a view of desire and abundance is characterized by Levinas as a "hollowing out," that which in our terms has been cast as apophasis. He says:

> Outside of the hunger one satisfies, the thirst one quenches and the senses one allays, exists the other, absolutely other, desired beyond these satisfactions, when the body knows no gesture to slake the desire, where it is not possible to invent any new caress. This desire is unquenchable, not because it answers to an infinite hunger, but because it does not call for food. This desire without satisfaction hence takes cognizance of the alterity of the other. It situates it in the dimension of height and of the ideal, which it opens up in being.[65]

Conclusion

The shift from enchantment to disenchantment and from the porous to the buffered self is bound up with issues of perception and the flattening of the epistemic frame, such that the subject is cast as the sole meaning-giver. This is complexified by Bauman's diagnosis of the liquid modern where the constructed social frames of meaning become increasingly unstable—because they are fluid—and meaning is pursued within the market context. Here, meaning is strategized in a different way as it becomes perpetually deferred: it relies upon the orientation of desire towards commodities, the allure of which is necessarily transient. In turn, desire itself is commodified, as an attitude of acquisition and usefulness is encouraged and proliferates. In setting mystical experience alongside musical experience by virtue of their shared phenomenological moments of impact, absorption and ekstasis, and by casting them as event, or experiences, with a capacity to transform the frame through which we perceive and engage with the world, I have suggested that the mode of attention that music is capable of eliciting forms an interruption of the liquid modern mode of being. It does so by offering an experience that is relational and non-acquisitive, one that reconfigures desire in terms of abundance rather than lack, thereby recalling us to our human nature which is constituted always in response to the Other.

Notes

1 Denys Turner, *The Darkness of God: Negativity in Christian Mysticism* (Cambridge: Cambridge University Press, 1995), 168.
2 Nicholas Lash, *Holiness, Speech, and Silence: Reflections on the Question of God* (Aldershot, UK: Ashgate, 2004), 92.
3 Max Weber's idea of *Entzauberung* (disenchantment) is articulated in Max Weber, "Science as a Profession [*Wissenschaft als Beruf*, 1920]," in *Max Weber: Essays in Sociology*, edited by H. H. Gerth and C. Wright Mills (New York: Oxford University Press, 1946), 129–56.
4 Meijer, Michael and Herbert De Vriese, eds., *The Philosophy of Reenchantment* (New York/London: Routledge, 2021) offers a range of interpretations of disenchantment, and proposals as to what enchantment might entail (both theistic and atheistic).
5 Disenchantment understood as an epistemic flattening is suggested by two things: (1) within the domain of religion, Weber highlights the movement away from ecclesial sacraments (through which one is assisted in one's progression towards salvation) towards rationalized ethical action (through which one attests to one's own predestination); (2) within society, Weber points to increasing rationalization and intellectualization, for what was previously attributable to the supernatural becomes explicable by more mundane means uncovered through rational and scientific enquiry. In brief, this means "the knowledge or belief that if one but wished one *could learn it at any time* . . . it means that principally there are no mysterious incalculable forces that come into play, but rather that one can, in principle, master all things by calculation." Weber, *Max Weber: Essays in Sociology*, 139. See Férdia Stone-Davis, *Musical Beauty: Negotiating the Boundary between Subject and Object* (Eugene, Oregon: Wipf & Stock, 2001), 178–81.
6 Charles Taylor, *A Secular Age* (Cambridge, MA: Belknap Press of Harvard University Press, 2007), 27–41.
7 Taylor, *A Secular Age*, 38.
8 Zygmunt Bauman, *Culture in a Liquid Modern World* (Cambridge: Polity Press, 2011), 11.
9 Zygmunt Bauman, *Liquid Times: Living in an Age of Uncertainty* (Cambridge: Polity Press, 2007), 1. Bauman continues: "indeed, a life expectation shorter than the time it takes to develop a cohesive and consistent strategy, and still shorter than the fulfilment of an individual 'life project' requires." Ibid.
10 Zygmunt Bauman, *Liquid Modernity* (Cambridge: Polity Press, 2013), 7.
11 "The future—the realistic future and the desirable future—can be grasped only as a succession of 'nows.' And the only stable, hopefully unbreakable continuity on which the beads of episodes could be conceivable strung together so that they won't scatter and disperse, is that of one's own body in its successive avatars." Zygmunt Bauman, "Consuming Life", *Journal of Consumer Culture*, 1 no. 1 (2001): 22.
12 Bauman, *Liquid Times*, 3.
13 See for example, Rodolphe Gasché, "Entanglement in Stories (Wilhelm Schapp)," in *Storytelling: The Destruction of the Inalienable in the Age of the Holocaust* (Albany, NY: State University of New York Press, 2018), 41–56. Thanks to Amy Daughton for drawing my attention to Schapp.
14 Bauman, *Liquid Modernity*, 25.
15 Bauman, *Liquid Modernity*, 25–26.
16 Bauman, *Culture in a Liquid Modern World*, 13.

17 The idea of desire as lack can be traced back to Plato's *Symposium*, 200A, trans. Alexander Nehamas and Paul Woodruff, in *Plato Complete Works*, ed., with introduction and notes, by John M. Cooper (Indianapolis, IN: Hackett Publishing Company, 1997); see also Simon May, *Love: A History* (New Haven, CT: Yale University Press, 2011), 38–55.
18 Emmanuel Levinas, *Totality and Infinity: An Essay on Exteriority*, trans. Alphonso Lingis (Pittsburgh, PA: Duquesne University Press, 1969), 117.
19 Bauman, "Consuming Life", 12.
20 Bauman, "Consuming Life," 12.
21 Bauman, "Consuming Life," 12–13.
22 Bauman, *Culture in a Liquid Modern World*, 16–17.
23 Bauman, *Culture in a Liquid Modern World*, 15–16. As Hartmut Rosa notes: "For a considerable and growing part of the libido of late modern subjects seems to be directed not toward consuming or using purchased items, but toward the act of purchase as such. Year after year, people in affluent societies buy more books, more music devices, more telescopes, tennis rackets, and pianos, but they read and listen to them, look through and play with them less and less." Hartmut Rosa, *Resonance: A Sociology of Our Relationship to the World*, trans. James C. Wagner (Cambridge: Polity Press, 2019), 254.
24 See e.g., Ansgar Nünning, "Making events—making stories—making worlds: Ways of worldmaking from a narratological point of view," in *Cultural Ways of Worldmaking: Media and Narratives*, ed. Vera Nünning, Ansgar Nünning, and Birgit Neumann (New York: Walter de Gruyter, 2010), 191–214.
25 Slavoj Žižek, *Event: Philosophy in Transit* (London: Penguin, 2014), 10.
26 Jean-Louis Chrétien, *The Unforgettable and the Unhoped For*, trans. Jeffrey Bloechl (New York: Fordham University Press, 2002), 121.
27 Jean-Louis Chrétien, *The Ark of Speech*, trans. Andrew Brown (Oxford: Routledge, 2004), 10.
28 "The first hospitality is nothing other than listening. . . . It is the first hospitality, to be sure, but nobody has ever inaugurated it. No man has ever been the first to listen. We can offer it only because we have always already been received in it." Chrétien, *The Ark of Speech*, 9.
29 Jean-Louis Chrétien, *The Call and the Response*, trans. Anne A. Davenport (New York: Fordham University Press, 2004), 1. Elsewhere, Chrétien says: "The act of speech cannot be thought on the basis of a simple duality of you and me. As soon as you speak to me, we are already all there, even the dead, and those who will one day come also." Chrétien, *The Ark of Speech*, 10.
30 "The various powers of call that we describe are not addressed to a pure transcendental ego but to the whole human being, body and soul. . . . If there is indeed an inner voice, it must belong intrinsically to our fleshly voice, not dwell in a spiritual sanctuary: it must therefore put us in dialogue with our very corporeity." Chrétien, *The Call and the Response*, 3–4.
31 Chrétien, *The Call and the Response*, 30.
32 Chrétien, *The Call and the Response*, 44.
33 Chrétien, *The Unforgettable and the Unhoped for*, 122.
34 Chrétien, *The Unforgettable and the Unhoped for*, 122.
35 Chrétien, *The Unforgettable and the Unhoped for*, 122.
36 Chrétien, *The Unforgettable and the Unhoped for*, 122.
37 Chrétien, *The Call and the Response*, 48.

38 Chrétien, *The Call and the Response*, 63.
39 Michel de Certeau, "Mysticism", *Diacritics* 22, no. 2 (Summer 1992): 18.
40 De Certeau, "Mysticism," 16.
41 De Certeau, "Mysticism," 18.
42 De Certeau, "Mysticism," 17.
43 Michel de Certeau, "Mystic Speech," in *Heterologies: Discourse on the Other*, trans. Brian Massumi, forward by Wlad Godzich (Minneapolis, MN: University of Minnesota Press, 2000), 91.
44 De Certeau, "Mystic Speech," 91. Translator's brackets.
45 "Where should I write? That is the question the organization of every mystic text strives to answer: the truth value of the discourse does not depend on the truth value of its propositions, but on the fact of its being in the very place at which the Speaker speaks (the Spirit, 'el que habla'). . . . In every case . . . divine utterance is both what founds the text, and what it must make manifest. That is why the text is destabilized: it is at the same time *beside* the authorized institution, i.e., the Word of God." De Certeau, "Mystic Speech," 92.
46 De Certeau, "Mysticism," 17.
47 De Certeau, "Mysticism," 17.
48 De Certeau, "Mysticism," 18.
49 De Certeau, "Mysticism," 17.
50 De Certeau, "Mysticism," 19.
51 De Certeau, "Mysticism," 19.
52 De Certeau, "Mysticism," 20.
53 De Certeau, "Mysticism," 20.
54 Stone-Davis, *Musical Beauty*, 158–90.
55 Although distinguishing here between performance and reception, I by no means want to suggest that they are wholly discrete activities. The distinction is simply so that we might analytically consider two modes of engaging with music.
56 Roger Scruton, *Aesthetics of Music* (Oxford: Clarendon Press, 1998), 17. Indeed, consequent on this capability of sound, Scruton posits a strictly acousmatic understanding of music, whereby the material source and origin is of marginal importance to sounds as music, see Scruton, *Understanding Music: Philosophy and Interpretation* (London: Continuum, 2009), chapter 2. For an exploration and critique of Scruton on the acousmatic in terms of the anthropology he proposes, see Férdia J. Stone-Davis, "Making an Anthropological Case: Cognitive Dualism and the Acousmatic," *Philosophy* 90, no. 2 (2015): 263–76.
57 For a more detailed outworking, see Férdia J. Stone-Davis, "Music and World-Making: Haydn's String Quartet in E-Flat Major (op. 33, no. 2)," in *Music and Transcendence*, ed. Férdia J. Stone-Davis (Abingdon, UK: Ashgate, 2015), 125–45, esp. 130–35.
58 Bauman. *Liquid Modernity*, 7.
59 Meister Eckhart, *The Essential Sermons, Commentaries, Treatises, and Defense*, trans. Edmund Colledge, O. S. A. and Bernard McGinn (London: Paulist Press, 1981), 199.
60 Markus Vincent, *The Art of Detachment* (Leuven: Peeters, 2011), 59. "The soul's binding attachment is the web in which she is helplessly entangled, so regretfully strangled that she is kept from performing her work, disabled from attending to the work that she does, and concerned only with herself while trying to do her work without being able to stay distant from it, becoming involved because of her relentless self-love." Vincent, *The Art of Detachment*, 60.

61 Eckhart *Predigten 1: Meister Eckhart by Franz Pfeiffer Leipzig, 1857*, trans C. de B. Evans (1924), 28–31, cited in Vinzent, *The Art of Detachment*, 61. Another translation of Sermon 1 can be found in *Meister Eckhart: Teacher and Preacher*, trans. Frank Tobin, ed. Bernard McGinn, with the collaboration of Frank Tobin and Elvira Borgstadt and preface by Kenneth Northcott (London: Paulist Press, 1986), 239–44.
62 Sermon 52 in Eckhart, *Essential Sermons*, 202; Turner, *Darkness of God*, 172–73.
63 See Vinzent, *The Art of Detachment*, 81; see also Turner, *Darkness of God*, 172.
64 Turner, *Darkness of God*, 183.
65 Emmanuel Levinas, "Philosophy and the Idea of Infinity," in *Collected Philosophical Papers*, trans., Alphonso Lingis (Dordrecht: Martinus Nijhoff Publishers, 1987), 56. For an astute consideration of desire as lack and desire as abundance, see Fiona Ellis, "The Quest for God: Rethinking Desire," in *Passions and Emotions: Royal Institute of Philosophy Supplements* 85 (July 2019): 157–73.

Bibliography

Bauman, Zygmunt. "Consuming Life." *Journal of Consumer Culture* 1, no. 1 (2001): 9–29.
Bauman, Zygmunt. *Culture in a Liquid Modern World*. Cambridge, UK: Polity Press, 2011.
Bauman, Zygmunt. *Liquid Modernity*. Cambridge, UK: Polity Press, 2013.
Bauman, Zygmunt. *Liquid Times: Living in an Age of Uncertainty*. Cambridge, UK: Polity Press, 2007.
Chrétien, Jean-Louis. *The Ark of Speech*. Translated by Andrew Brown. Oxford: Routledge, 2004.
Chrétien, Jean-Louis. *The Call and the Response*. Translated by Anne. A Davenport. New York: Fordham University Press, 2004.
Chrétien, Jean-Louis. *The Unforgettable and the Unhoped For*. Translated by Jeffrey Bloechl. New York: Fordham University Press, 2022.
de Certeau, Michel. "Mysticism." *Diacritics* 22, no. 2 (Summer 1992): 11–25.
de Certeau, Michel. "Mystic Speech." In *Heterologies: Discourse on the Other*, translated by Brian Massumi. Minneapolis, MN: University of Minnesota Press, 2000.
Eckhart, Meister. *Meister Eckhart: Teacher and Preacher*. Translated by Frank Tobin. Edited by Bernard McGinn. London: Paulist Press, 1986.
Eckhart, Meister. *The Essential Sermons, Commentaries, Treatises, and Defense*. Translated by Edmund Colledge, O. S. A. and Bernard McGinn. London: Paulist Press, 1981.
Ellis, Fiona. "The Quest for God: Rethinking Desire." In *Passions and Emotions: Royal Institute of Philosophy Supplements* 85 (July 2019): 157–73.
Gasché, Rodolphe. "Entanglement in Stories (Wilhelm Schapp)." In *Storytelling: The Destruction of the Inalienable in the Age of the Holocaust*, 41–56. Albany, NY: State University of New York Press, 2018.
Lash, Nicholas. *Holiness, Speech, and Silence: Reflections on the Question of God*. Aldershot, United Kingdom: Ashgate, 2004.
Levinas, Emmanuel. "Philosophy and the Idea of Infinity." In *Collected Philosophical Papers*, translated by Alphonso Lingis, 47–59. Dordrecht: Martinus Nijhoff Publishers, 1987.
Levinas, Emmanuel. *Totality and Infinity: An Essay on Exteriority*. Translated by Alphonso Lingis. Pittsburgh, PA: Duquesne University Press, 1969.
May, Simon. *Love: A History*. New Haven, CT: Yale University Press, 2011.

Meijer, Michael and Herbert De Vriese, eds. *The Philosophy of Reenchantment*. New York/London: Routledge, 2021.
Nehamas, Alexander and Paul Woodruff, eds. *Plato Complete Works*. Indianapolis, IN: Hackett Publishing Company, 1997.
Nünning, Ansgar. "Making Events—making stories—making worlds: Ways of worldmaking from a narratological point of view." In *Cultural Ways of Worldmaking: Media and Narratives*, edited by Vera Nünning, Ansgar Nünning, and Birgit Neumann, 191–214. New York: Walter de Gruyter, 2010.
Rosa, Hartmut. *Resonance: A Sociology of Our Relationship to the World*. Translated by James C. Wagner. Cambridge, MA: Polity Press, 2019.
Scruton, Roger. *Aesthetics of Music*. Oxford: Clarendon Press, 1998.
Scruton, Roger. *Understanding Music: Philosophy and Interpretation*. London: Continuum, 2009.
Stone-Davis, Férdia. "Making an Anthropological Case: Cognitive Dualism and the Acousmatic." *Philosophy* 90, no. 2 (2015): 263–76.
Stone-Davis, Férdia. "Music and World-Making: Haydn's String Quartet in E-Flat Major (op. 33, no. 2)." In *Music and Transcendence*, edited by Férdia Stone-Davis, 125–45. Abingdon, UK: Ashgate, 2015.
Stone-Davis, Férdia. *Musical Beauty: Negotiating the Boundary between Subject and Object*. Eugene, Oregon: Wipf & Stock, 2001.
Taylor, Charles. *A Secular Age*. Cambridge, MA: Belknap Press of Harvard University Press, 2007.
Turner, Denys. *The Darkness of God: Negativity in Christian Mysticism*. Cambridge: Cambridge University Press, 1995.
Vinzent, Markus. *The Art of Detachment*. Leuven: Peeters, 2011.
Weber, Max. "Science as a Profession [*Wissenschaft als Beruf*, 1920]." In *Max Weber: Essays in Sociology*, edited by H. H. Gerth and C. Wright Mills, 129–56. New York: Oxford University Press, 1946.
Žižek, Slavoj. *Event: Philosophy in Transit*. London: Penguin, 2014.

2

Making Sense in the Midst of Non-Sense: Félix Ravaisson and George Rickey as a Way Forward for Emmanuel Falque

Tyler Holley

Introduction

Writing after the so-called theological turn within French phenomenology alongside representatives such as Marion, Henry, Chrétien, Lacoste, and others, Emmanuel Falque emerges as something of an iconoclast. He brushes aside many common tropes within this field, arguing for the overcoming of the "overcoming of metaphysics." Consequently, his work is deeply engaged not just with ancient patristic and medieval theologians, but also with philosophers and metaphysicians outside the traditional phenomenological corpus, whose thought he interweaves with a remarkable skill and dexterity. Falque talks about the "backlash" of theology on phenomenology and vice versa, but we could just as well talk about the backlash of Emmanuel Falque on phenomenology.[1] This is evident particularly in his emphasis on the goodness of our facticity and our finitude, in contrast to, for example, Marion's prioritization of the rupture of grace in a bedazzling arrival of revelation.

Some of Falque's most profound contributions to understanding our finitude are found in his book *The Wedding Feast of the Lamb*. There he resists what he calls a "swerve of the flesh" that has come to dominate phenomenology, according to which the lived experience of the subjective body, or the "flesh," has overshadowed the corporality of the objective body, what he calls "body." This flesh/body dualism has replaced the soul/body dualism of the past, with flesh relating to the subjective experience that may be associated with mind or soul, and body associated with the raw material of body.[2] By attending to "body," Falque claims to be able to dimly perceive the passions and drives that precede signification. In our "animality" our body feels the influence of these forces even though they cannot be signified. They are non-sense, even though they are part of our drive for sense.[3] These forces, which at different times he associates with *eros*, the Holy Spirit, Chaos, and the Freudian drive, constitute a vital part of our humanity that phenomenology needs to explore.

There would be much to discuss in a work of such multifaceted and nuanced argumentation. For our part, we can helpfully enter into the range of interconnected issues that Falque presents in this work through his conception of the "spread body." The "spread body" has a passive and an active sense to it. In reference to passivity, the body is spread out in that it is open to the forces and drives that come from our animal engagement with the world. In reference to activity, we are also spread out in that our body is extended and extending in the world through the force of life. This active element of the spread body leads to the development of the "lived flesh" that continues the active movement of life in the realm of sense and subjectivity. In holding up both of these aspects of Falque's concept of the spread body, I argue that there remains an ambiguity about their relation for Falque. Does the lived flesh, along with language and culture, emerge out of the body's raw animal engagement with the world, or is the lived flesh merely superimposed on the body? If the sense of the lived flesh does not somehow express the non-sense of the body, then how can we judge the felicity of lived flesh's sense? Falque's work could lead to a delimiting of the sphere of language to a separate realm that at times may seem merely superimposed. In light of these questions, the work of Félix Ravaisson and George Rickey can provide a way forward for Falque to address these concerns. Ravaisson relates the passivity of the body with the activity of flesh by theorizing force as divine mind and desire rather than as chaos. This substitution allows him to see a relation between the supposed non-sense of the body's sensation and the sense of the flesh's activity. Rickey's kinetic sculptures portray this way forward that Ravaisson lays out. By showing us how forces that bump into a passive body can be translated into an intelligible motion, Rickey allows us to perceive force as a mode of mind rather than chaos.

The Spread Body in Passivity and Activity

By attending to the passive dimension of our spread body, Falque emphasizes the animality of humanity. *Contra* Aristotle, he argues that the human is not primarily a "rational animal" or "political animal."[4] The philosophical tradition has tended to follow Aristotle in considering the human primarily in terms of rationality, rather than considering humanity in terms of one's corporeal engagement with the world that marks one's animality and affectivity.[5] By valuing rationality, particularly the rationality of language, one may miss the sensations and emotions that arise in the phenomenon of the voice. "What makes our community in animality, here and always," Falque claims, "is certainly not speech, or the kind of discourse that requires a shared rationality; it is the 'voice' that 'is but an indication of pleasure or pain, and is therefore found in other animals.'"[6] Unlike the rationality of language, which tends to create a distance of the self from the world, the voice demonstrates our proximity to the world through affectivity and sensation.[7] Before the human begins to analyze the raw experience of the world in terms of rational discourse, one is affected by the world through the body's encounter with it in the form of sensations of pleasure and pain. Therefore, the voice, in the form of "a cry, a groan, a moan, [or] a whimper," brings us to our animal engagement with the world.[8]

After drawing attention to this animal engagement with the world, Falque draws on Schopenhauer in order to claim that man is a "metaphysical animal."[9] The human is a metaphysical animal in that she is led to ponder the nature of the world through sheer wonder at the quality of life, which consists in the constant reception of the world through sensations that sends one careening through momentary pleasures and persistent pains, ultimately leading to *ennui* and suffering. This wonder at the world is brought about by the immediacy of sensations that we feel with our animal engagement with the world. In the spread body, I can experience myself as opened to the world through pure feeling and sensation in the objective body, but this knowledge through feeling, according to Falque, is forgotten through attempts at interpretation through the rational discourse of lived flesh.[10] Thus, he writes that the spread body "brings out our animality ... in the closeness to our own bodies that the words with which we speak (language), and the multiplication of the meanings of the signifier (hermeneutics), have often made us forget."[11] In this passive sense of the spread body, we are attuned to our animality, meaning that we know ourselves to be fundamentally opened to the reception of sensations from the world. We know that we undergo the world in our objective body, and only in the undergoing of sensations do we know our selves in our bodily life. Falque thus demonstrates a certain distrust of language and rational discourse that characterizes the lived flesh. The faculties of rationality occlude the way that we move in the world as a result of sensations and the unprocessed experience of forces.

The passive sense of the spread body flows into its active sense, where we find that sense and consciousness emerge. Falque argues that "animality is the mark of our interior Chaos of feelings, that accumulation of passions and drives that ensures we open up the world by the body rather than by the consciousness."[12] To "open up the world" by our body means to account for the world in terms of our body's engagement with it. He is careful not to reify the spread body into a kind of substance such that we can account for the subjective element of the experience of the lived flesh in some definitive way. There is no *a priori* fixity to the body that brings about a sure mode of thought in the lived flesh.[13] We can only attend to the material and chaotic forces that influence the body and that consequently shape both our thoughts and the way we live in the lived flesh. In this way, the realm of the mind and lived flesh is not added to the body but emerges out of the forces that drive the body. The active spread body is thus the activity that emerges as a result of the body's experience of the world. Falque finds Nietzsche's conception of the will to power helpful here. Contrary to interpretations that emphasize a violent and domineering force, the will to power is, in Falque's words, the ability "to imitate and follow the true *internal power of life* in its capacity to create forms, to seek new modalities for its existence, and to be *always becoming* so as never to remain definitively fixed."[14] The forces at play in the world move the spread body so much so that the it begins to flow with the power of the world, and here lies the truly creative principle of humanity. In the "will to power" humans make themselves. This power or force of life arises from the chaotic flows of the world and leads to the construction of a self. This construction has no governing *a priori* structure in terms of an idea, mind, or anything that resembles a substance or essence; instead, the self arises out of the infinite creative capacity of the will to power that characterizes life.

Falque doubles down on the lack of fixity within force in talking about Deleuze's conception of the "body without organs," ultimately at the expense of language and culture.[15] The organs, according to Falque, prevent us from seeing life as pure flows of power because they confine power and funnel flows into prearranged movements and structures.[16] Unsurprisingly, this gesture de-emphasizes the realm of language and culture, because these realms confine the chaotic forces of the world, or rather they gloss over them, hiding them like a bad paint job. As Falque argues, "Chaos or Tohu-Bohu is the opening of our existence, certainly, but in wanting it to be too 'cosm-etic'—that is, organized into a world (*cosmos*), as also into the beautiful (*cosmetic* products), we come all at once to conceal the world, to disguise it in makeup, even to forget it."[17] The need to get beyond the surface and into the depths, that is, beyond the merely cosmetic into the reality of the chaos of things, suggests that for Falque the linguistic as well as the cultural are merely superimposed, often distractingly so.

Falque's suspicions of the sense and signification of the lived flesh and the tension it creates in his project regarding the relationship between body and flesh, chaos and speech, is particularly evident when he is talking about the erotic.[18] As he understands it, the objective body is what secures the transformative power of sexuality. When a woman encounters a man and vice versa, they encounter their limit, a difference that cannot be brought into a union. This difference allows the body of the woman to be the body of resistance and sensation for the man's body, such that the man becomes himself only in encountering the body of the woman and vice versa. It is the sensation of the body that establishes difference and identity between the two lovers. This difference leads to a desire to become oneself on the body of the other through the experience of sensation in the body. Love here becomes a kind of loving struggle to become oneself. However, in the amorous encounter, Falque argues that there is a desire not for mere consumption, but for the desire of the desire of the other, meaning that what one seeks is not a mere body spread out but a flesh of lived experience that welcomes and embraces. As Falque points out, noting how a doctor's relation to a cadaver differs from his relation to the body of a lover in bed, "[e]verything here is a question of the 'situation' rather than just the body. There is a 'liturgy of eros' in the lovers' night."[19] This reference to a "situation" and the "liturgy of eros" suggests a context of signification that makes the spread body a lover for embrace rather than a cadaver for medical study. The suggestion is that true sexual desire can only exist in the realm of signification, cultural meanings, and language. This reading is supported by the fact that Falque goes on to argue, with Michel Henry, that "desire is only possible in anxiety," meaning that sexuality can only exist in a hermeneutic realm where two lovers strive to read each other reciprocally and where speech necessarily arises to fill gaps in our ability to experience the experience of the other.[20] The erotic experience therefore cannot adequately be accounted for in terms of the sensations of the objective body alone. The subjective realm of the flesh is required. On the one hand, Falque talks about the necessity of the experience of sensation in the bodily encounter in order for a man and woman to become themselves, but, on the other hand, he admits that the sensation of the sexual act can only happen in the cultural world of signs and language ("situation"), when body becomes flesh. So it seems that objective "body" must become subjective "flesh" in order to know itself to be a "spread body" of "lived flesh" for the erotic embrace. The flows of desire or force that arrive through the body must be confined and funneled into the fixed forms of a particular culture's signifying structures in order to really become what they can become.

A series of questions arise from the tension in Falque's thought presented above. Can a philosophy that claims to attend to the body adequately conceive of a body without organs as Falque understands it? It seems that wherever there is body, there we also find organs. Wherever we find force, we also find fixity and funnels. Wherever we find the activity of the body's forces, we also find the confining ideas of mind. Wherever we find body, we also find the lived flesh. Concomitantly, wherever we find the individual passions, we also find society's signifying structures. Part of this tension in Falque's work arises from the hard distinction he draws between the non-sense of the body and the sense of the lived flesh. In placing mind and matter so far apart, the lived flesh seems merely superimposed and arbitrary, a cosmetic addition to an otherwise chaotic force. If this were the case, how do we know what is a good addition and what is a bad addition? These considerations lead us to question whether or not what the body receives is really non-sense or if it is the case that sensations actually make sense.

The Way Forward of Felix Ravaisson

Félix Ravaisson (1813–1900), associated with French Spiritualism, was significantly influenced by Maine de Biran, whose focus on the body would later influence the phenomenology of Merleau-Ponty and Michel Henry, and therefore by association perhaps Falque himself. Like Biran, Ravaisson attends to the way that bodily sensations lead to consciousness, and like the later Henri Bergson (who is himself heavily influenced by Ravaisson) he moves into metaphysical speculation about the nature of consciousness and its relation to the world. Ravaisson, like Falque, sees a productive force in the world that moves through the passive and active senses of the body in order to propel the self to create the self. We receive this force in the sensation of the objective body and act in union with this force through the creative action of the subjective flesh. In this way, Ravaisson's project bears a remarkable similarity to Falque's. However, for Ravaisson, as will become clear, there is no tension in how the passive sensation of the body is related to the social and linguistic action of the flesh, because he theorizes force as a mode of mind and desire rather than as chaos. This metaphysical displacement of chaos with mind and desire allows him to demonstrate that the action of the subjective and linguistic flesh (Falque's "lived flesh") is what the sensation of the objective corporeal body has always been inclined to produce. Additionally, the replacement of mind with chaos allows for a way to think of the activity of the self in terms of a growing union of human and divine action. This final point, it is worth noting, problematizes Falque's insistence throughout his work on the method of finitude.[21]

One of Ravaisson's methods of philosophical inquiry is the inward perception of the act of being. He suggests that one is able to perceive the act of being through the interior act of becoming in desire. As one looks interiorly, they find that they are directed to be in a particular way, either through cultural formation or through the natural needs of animal instincts. The relation between these instinctive and cultural motions of becoming is central to Ravaisson's most widely read work, *On Habit*. To explore the dynamics of human subjectivity he utilizes (in broad strokes) Kant's notion of the active intellect, which synthesizes a multiplicity of sensations into an intelligible unity so as to form an object of thought. In this way, sensation gives way to the perception of an object in the movement of synthesis. This synthesis requires the mind to attend to an object's extension by attending to the "parts" and "limits" of a "continuous quantity" in order to determine its number and to construct a mental image.[22] What is significant for Ravaisson here is the movement that this synthesizing action implies, namely, the interior traversal of extension. The process of knowing anything is not a mere passive registering of phenomena, it is an active motion of the mind. This interior activity gives way to what Ravaisson describes as "an awareness, more or less obscure, of voluntary activity and personality," that underlies this activity of knowledge.[23]

The voluntary activity and personality of the mind in the action of synthesizing is a mysterious force that precedes our awareness and arouses the mind in order to know. In the idioms established by Maine de Biran, Ravaisson articulates how this interior force, moving out of the self, encounters resistance in things and undergoes them by a kind of passion. The internal movement surmounts the resistance of things through "effort," and it is this effort that indicates the free, active movement of self-consciousness and personality. The dynamic of passion and action corresponds to sensation and perception, respectively. In sensation, for Ravaisson, one suffers the impress of the world in a manner that corresponds closely to Falque's passive sense of the spread body, and in perception one takes in the world through a creative action of intellection, which roughly corresponds to Falque's active sense of the spread body. Thus, effort is where sensation and perception, passion and action, meet.[24] Effort is the cause and essence of consciousness as the mixture of passivity and activity. However, its beginning remains mysterious in that the force that initially thrusts the self out of itself to encounter the world through the sensations of the body (which ultimately leads to the perception and action of the flesh) remains unexplained.

Ravaisson takes up the question of the origin of effort later in his essay on habit. Effort must have an origin because it implies some resistance with which a prior force engages. Therefore, he writes, "effort necessarily requires an effortless antecedent tendency, which in its development encounters resistance."[25] This tendency that precedes personality and consciousness is what Ravaisson calls desire. All movement finds "its source and origin in desire," and in this way "desire is a primordial instinct."[26] Desire is a constitutive element of our being, and Ravaisson's conception of it and its relation to being leads him to think of being as a kind of motion in the process of becoming, much like Falque deploys Nietzsche's will to power to understand life.[27] In the human, significantly, this movement of becoming can be experienced in the dynamics of intellection, although all of nature experiences the motion of desire. Thus, in the human, Ravaisson conceives of this driving force of desire as moving through the sensations of the body to form the consciousness of the subjective flesh through effort. Therefore, unlike Falque, Ravaisson does not separate the experience of sensations in the body from the conscious subjectivity that arises in the flesh. Rather, the process of becoming a conscious self in desire includes both the sensations of the body and the subjectivity of the flesh in the same movement of becoming.

Ravaisson is able to overcome the tension between body and flesh in this way because he relates desire to a divine principle. Quoting the seventeenth-century theologian François Fénelon, he makes the remarkable claim that "nature is prevenient grace," and for this reason he affirms that "nature lies wholly in desire, and desire, in turn, lies in the good that attracts it.... It is God within us, God hidden solely by being so far within us in this intimate source of ourselves, to whose depths we do not descend."[28] God hidden within nature, including the human, is the driving force of becoming, and desire is the means by which God moves the raw material bodies of nature in such a way that mind and conscious subjectivity emerge. Much like Falque talks of a "metamorphosis of finitude," we could talk here of a metamorphosis of matter into mind, of sensations into perceptions, or of body into lived flesh.[29] In his later work, *La Philosophie en France au XIXème siècle*, which reads like a manifesto of French Spiritualism, Ravaisson picks up these themes of divine descent in the form of desire and thematizes them in terms of the descent of divine mind.[30] This rearticulation allows him to give a metaphysical explanation of the emergence of consciousness through the force of desire that moves through the body to form the subjectivity of the lived flesh, thereby providing a solution to address the tension within Falque's work.

Following Plotinus and those German idealists influenced by Neo-Platonism (e.g., Fichte and Schelling), Ravaisson asserts that human mind and consciousness emerge from the world because divine mind is diffused through matter. He makes this claim rather tersely when he writes that "nature, one could say, is like a refraction or dispersion of spirit."[31] In another place, he states that "nature is an edifice of thoughts."[32] Put otherwise, nature contains diffusely what is simple and unified in the absolute mind. This diffusion ensures that the experience of moving through life is akin to regathering the deposits of divine mind and bringing them into a stronger concentration and reflection in the higher degree of mind that is human consciousness.[33] Through the movement of life, which is the process of becoming for the human self, the human mind partially gathers from dispersed elements what the infinite concentrates totally in itself. This diffused mind is what we find even in sensation, or the passive body, and the mind's interior action of perception discussed above restores the intelligence of the supposed non-sense of sensations. In contrast to Falque, Ravaisson thus thinks of sensations as a mode of mind and not as non-sense. Flavors, smells, sounds, and colors are simply "lower modalities" of mind.[34] Ravaisson describes this regathering of mind through the reception of sensation as a process of gradually increasing in action.[35]

> According to our experience, the mainspring of the interior life is therefore intellectual thought or action which, from a state of diffusion and confusion in which it has in a way only a virtual existence, takes place, recalls, is brought back, by a continual movement of recomposition in the unity of consciousness, to active existence, and from a state of sleep and dream returns incessantly to the waking state.[36]

In the waking up of mind, we gradually perceive a dim awareness of the end and fulfillment of nature, which is an order of beauty to which we are to progressively give expression through action. The more we receive from the emergence of mind, the more we desire this end so that "from the depths of our being, elementary movements emerge, of which the desired movement is the end and the accomplishment."[37] The movement from the sensations of the passive body to the linguistic activity of the subjective flesh is a result of the same movement of desire that is metaphysically grounded in God who has diffused his mind into creation. This is suggested by the increasing movement described above. In the process of this increasing activity, the human can perform the end towards which nature is directed because she is "a special generating principle" or a "genius" that "produces nothing, can do nothing except through the superior virtue, in which [humanity] participates, of the universal God, who is absolute good and infinite love."[38]

Like Ravaisson, Falque also emphasizes that an increasing activity, understood as the creative potential of the will to power, leads to the construction of a self. That said, as discussed above, he is unable to account for the relation of the body and the lived flesh with his description of the active and creative self. Ravaisson's notion of genius can resolve this tension by showing how the self is creative through reception. Because the sensations of the passive body signify a reception of divine mind for Ravaisson rather than of chaos, the activity of the genius is a making sense out of the dimly perceived sense of sensations rather than a cosmetic and superimposed addition of sense to non-sense. Thus, to be a genius is not to possess a supreme intelligence, but rather to be connected to the supreme reason and creativity of God through bodily mediation. As Ravaisson writes, "If reason is properly the character of man, there is in genius something that passes man, something which in fact has always been called divine."[39] Although the archetypal example of genius may be the artist who supremely manifests the creative principle, genius characterizes all human rationality because all thinking requires this creative dimension that is a result of union with God. Because the human person, and *a fortiori* the genius, participates in God and the divine mind has been diffused in nature, the human person contains a creative principle that may be experienced through discovery.[40] As she moves through life, she discovers mind in matter and only comes to phenomenal awareness of this mind through the interior act of creative imagination that characterizes genius. Ravaisson can thus say both that "[g]enius … consists above all in inventing, in *creating*," and that it is "everywhere, always, the genius who *discovers*, because [s]he is in immediate communication with the absolute, with the divine."[41] In this way the genius is able to blend creative action and passive reception, creation and discovery, only because she participates in the absolute. Unlike Falque, for whom the will to power signals an unfixed creative potential, Ravaisson sees the creative power of the genius as synonymous with reception from a divine source because the creativity of the self that is moving in desire, that is, the subjective flesh, is grounded in the reception of divine mind rather than chaotic forces.

It is important to note that the descent and dispersion of mind into all matter, as well as the elevation of humanity through genius, is not arbitrary for Ravaisson. These ideas establish significant parallels with the Christian conceptions of salvation and incarnation that have made Christianity historically compatible with Neo-Platonic modes of thought. The divine mind had to be diffused into the furthest degree of matter so that it could exist as being on the way back to itself in the process of nature and human life's becoming. Likewise, the Triune God has descended into creation and has descended all the way into death, becoming body without spirit, mere dust—the furthest degree from the fullness of life. For this reason, God in Christ can lead all souls, even those in the farthest degree of matter back to the highest degree of Trinitarian life. As Ravaisson writes, "God is descended by his Son, and descended thus without descending, into death, so that life may be born out of it, and a very divine life. 'God became man so that man might be made God.' The spirit, lowering itself, became flesh; the flesh will become spirit."[42] In another place, Ravaisson makes clear that the divine descent into matter that forms the metaphysical ground for the movement of all nature towards the fullness of mind takes place as a kind of sacrifice and self-gift:

> [Creation] is the unity of God projected, by a sort of immolation, of sacrifice, in the diffusion of the expanse, then, by the development of the divine powers, in these successive orders, where complexity and the unity are growing together, inorganic things, organized beings, and finally intelligent and free people, returning and bringing everything back to themselves.[43]

The movement of creation that reaches a kind of climax in genius has been that to which the movement of desire has always been leading.[44] All things in nature, by virtue of the divine mind within them, contain a desire for their fulfillment and their reintegration in God. Because the genius follows the movement of all things she is overcome with desire and love. She is "outside of herself" in the mind that she has received from her environment and she moves wholly in their love that has become hers. She experiences a "love which is like a god in man, animating the soul itself, love carrying thought high."[45] This process of love and desire unfolds in her bodily engagement with the world and leads to the linguistic and cultural sense-making of her lived flesh.

George Rickey's Kinetic Sculpture

As shown above, both Félix Ravaisson and Emmanuel Falque speculate on the nature of force. For both thinkers, this force moves through the passive body of sensation and leads to the activity of the subjective or lived flesh. However, Falque's work suffers from a certain tension regarding the relation between these two elements of the spread body. If force is chaos and chaos is what we experience in sensation, then we need to account for how sensation, which appears to have no sense, can lead to activity of the lived flesh, which seems to be full of sense. Ravaisson's metaphysical replacement of chaos with divine mind and desire moves the conversation forward for Falque, and begins to offer an account of how body and lived flesh, mind and matter, can be related. Sensations contain intelligence that is only received by performative and creative action. This creative action is the initial force of mind in the sensations of the body reproduced at a higher level in the action of the flesh.

One artist in particular shows the mediation between Falque and Ravaisson that I draw here (Plate 1). Like Falque and Ravaisson, George Rickey is attuned to the forces and movements of nature in a manner that is illuminating for the present discussion. In his work, he claims to attend to nature, particularly the way that nature is constantly in motion and flux. He points out that

> Nature is rarely still. All the environment is moving, at some pace or other, in some direction or other, under laws which are equally a manifestation of nature and a subject for art. The artist finds waiting for him, as subjects, not the trees, not the flowers, not the landscape, but the waving of branches and the trembling of stems, the piling up or scudding of clouds, the rising and setting and waxing and waning of heavenly bodies.[46]

By attending to nature's motion, Rickey attempts to learn the "language" of motion, which has its own morphology, vocabulary, and syntax.[47] This language does not consist in phonemes and morphemes, but styles of motion like gyrations, scudding, twisting, swaying, swirling, and so forth. Learning this language does not fix the kinetic artist arbitrarily into confined mechanical rhythms. Unlike the work of other kinetic artists, which utilize machine driven movement and mechanical repetition, Rickey creates structures that dance on the threshold of the mechanical while remaining at the whims of nature's flux. As a result, he demonstrates a delicate balance between pre-arranged flexibility and spontaneous motion. At the same time, his attention to the forces of nature does not send him towards purely chaotic motion. He criticizes both the reduction of kinetic structures to "the mere dangling of objects in the wind," which would cause a sculpture to represent the merely senseless and chaotic, and the "tendency toward monotony and the obvious" inherent in the mechanical kinetic structures that arbitrarily confine a sculpture to a pre-established routine.[48] In finding the balance between these two extremes, he learns a language that he then translates into the idiom of engineering.

The concerns of Falque and Ravaisson are situated between the same extremes. Falque, for his part, wants to avoid arbitrary confinement in linguistic and cultural categories, while Ravaisson wants to avoid conceiving of the motion of force as senseless chaos. Rickey steers a path between these two concerns in portraying a language of motion. Like Ravaisson, who articulates force, desire, and divine mind as moving through bodily sensations in order to double itself in a higher form of consciousness, Rickey creates sculptures that receive the forces of the world and performatively doubles them in a new idiom. His poetry of motion, as it were, is a careful tension of activity and receptivity. In receiving the forces of gravity and wind, his work does not reproduce them identically, as when a tumbleweed roles wherever the wind wishes or when an apple falls from a tree, obeying without much objection the forces of gravity and wind. For the kinetic sculptures of Rickey, there is a kind of poetic response and sympathy with these forces. Wind and gravity often provide the dominate forces. However, the sculptures themselves contain weights and counter-weights, gyrations and bearings that seem to actively and poetically double and construe external forces through movements that are in some sense brought about by external forces on the "body" of the sculpture, as well as by internal additions animated by the pre-arranged flexibility and fixity within the sculpture itself. Again, like

Ravaisson's conception of genius, who gathers mind from her environment in order to perform it in herself, Rickey's sculptures align themselves with the movement of external forces and in so doing create their own performative movement. They repeat and elaborate in their own idioms the motions of the external force. In this way, Rickey's sculptures exemplify the dynamic of Ravaisson's genius. They move in the specific way that they do because external forces have been confined to a particular mode of fixed expression, as when a southern wind is translated into a spinning or gyrating activity, and in that expression, what appears to be non-sense takes on a kind of sense. Rickey's sculptures are not like Deleuze's "body without organs," where fixity would inhibit flow. Rather, each structure contains a degree of fixity that allows the flow to be perceived as a dancing structure. It would not be a stretch to say that, for Rickey, engineering perfects nature, although not in a crassly mechanical repetition so indicative of modernity. Engineering here provides a vocabulary for nature's expression in an elaboration that simultaneously elevates nature to a realm of mind and spirit.

Rickey's work assumes that the external forces that bump into his sculptures can be translated into a beautiful display through the "spread body" of his sculptures. As his sculptures become "actors" in movement, they necessarily act out the force that gave rise to their motion. His sculptures thus suggest that force is not necessarily chaos, but has a language that we may learn to speak, if not in propositional assertions, then in performative expression. Rickey claims to learn this language through his art. If we take Ravaisson and Rickey seriously and apply their thought to the human person as a spread body of both passive reception of sensations and active experience of subjectivity, we may see the human subject as a kind of kinetic sculpture who receives the forces at play in reality and ceaselessly articulates them in her own idioms through language and culture, but this can only be the case if force is not senseless chaos. We may be able to make sense in the midst of what appears to be non-sense if the force behind all things is the divine mind and desire that gives sense to all things and grounds our own sense-making.

Conclusion

Falque's work contributes to the growing emphasis on the need to consider the corporal dimension of our existence. However, his thought contains a tension at the heart of the relation between body and lived flesh in his elaboration of the notion of the spread body. This tension results from the claim that what the body receives in its engagement with the world is non-sense and chaos. As I have shown, the art of George Rickey and the philosophy of Félix Ravaisson offer a way forward. Both suggest that the sensations of the world can make sense and can give way to sense-making. For Ravaisson, this claim is tied to a larger metaphysical picture that prioritizes the descent of divine mind and desire, in contrast to Falque, who prioritizes chaos. However, as Falque makes clear in his works, the chaos of our existence can be "metamorphosed" by the resurrection and incarnation.[49] Here Falque is speaking phenomenologically, but if we place this conception into a metaphysical register, we may say that the Incarnation has always already turned chaos into the order of the Good. This is the path opened up by

Ravaisson, a path which Falque could surely take, a path which he seems to already implicitly desire.

Notes

1. See particularly, Emmanuel Falque, *Crossing the Rubicon: The Borderlands of Philosophy and Theology*, trans. Reuben Shank (New York: Fordham University Press, 2016).
2. Emmanuel Falque, *The Wedding Feast of the Lamb: Eros, the Body, and the Eucharist*, trans. George Hughes (New York, NY: Fordham University Press, 2016), 1–4.
3. In other places, he also talks about our bodily engagement with the chaos of the world as something we cannot know. See Emmanuel Falque, "The Extra-Phenomenal," *Diakrisis Yearbook of Theology and Philosophy* 1 (2018): 9–28; and Emmanuel Falque, *Nothing to It: Reading Freud as a Philosopher*, trans. Robert Vallier and William L. Connelly (Leuven, Belgium: Leuven University Press, 2020).
4. Falque, *The Wedding Feast of the Lamb*, 84–90.
5. Falque, *The Wedding Feast of the Lamb*, 87.
6. Falque, *The Wedding Feast of the Lamb*, 87, citing Aristotle, *Politics*, trans. Benjamin Jowett (Oxford: Clarendon, 1885), 1:1.2.
7. Falque, *The Wedding Feast of the Lamb*, 88.
8. Falque, *The Wedding Feast of the Lamb*, 88.
9. Falque, *The Wedding Feast of the Lamb*, 90–99.
10. Falque, *The Wedding Feast of the Lamb*, 97.
11. Falque, *The Wedding Feast of the Lamb*, 98.
12. Falque, *The Wedding Feast of the Lamb*, 100.
13. Falque, *The Wedding Feast of the Lamb*, 108.
14. Falque, *The Wedding Feast of the Lamb*, 110.
15. See Gilles Deleuze and Felix Guattari, *Anti-Oedipus: Capitalism and Schizophrenia*, trans. Robert Hurley, Mark Seem, and Helen R. Lane (Minneapolis: University of Minnesota Press, 2010), 9–16.
16. Falque, *The Wedding Feast of the Lamb*, 113.
17. Falque, *The Wedding Feast of the Lamb*, 114.
18. The same may be argued with respect to his understanding of the Eucharist, which is so closely tied to the body and the erotic relation between man and woman. See particularly Falque, *The Wedding Feast of the Lamb*, 129–30.
19. Falque, *The Wedding Feast of the Lamb*, 162–63.
20. Falque, *The Wedding Feast of the Lamb*, 166–72.
21. See Falque, *Crossing the Rubicon*, 121–28, and Emmanuel Falque, *The Metamorphosis of Finitude: An Essay on Birth and Resurrection*, trans. George Hughes (New York: Fordham University Press, 2012), 30–40. Barnabas Aspray has shown this element of Falque to be a major feature of his work in Barnabas Aspray, "Transforming Heideggerian Finitude?: Following Pathways Opened by Emmanuel Falque," in *Transforming the Theological Turn: Phenomenology with Emmanuel Falque*, ed. Martin Koci and Jason Alvis (Lanham, MD: Rowman & Littlefield, 2020), 163–74.
22. Félix Ravaisson, "Of Habit," in *Félix Ravaisson: Selected Essays*, ed. Mark Sinclair (London: Bloomsbury Academic, 2016), 37–38.
23. Ravaisson, "Of Habit," 38.

24 Ravaisson outlines this theory also in Félix Ravaisson, "Contemporary Philosophy," in *Félix Ravaisson: Selected Essays*, ed. Mark Sinclair (London: Bloomsbury Academic, 2016), 73–74. This essay was originally published in 1840, two years after his essay on habit.
25 Ravaisson, "Of Habit," 46.
26 Ravaisson, "Of Habit," 47.
27 This notion of being as desire is thematized by Mark Sinclair as "being inclined." Sinclair's book is the most significant work on Ravaisson in English. His main point is in continuity with mine because, as he points out, desire and inclination are used synonymously in Ravaisson. Mark Sinclair, *Being Inclined: Felix Ravaisson's Philosophy of Habit* (Oxford: Oxford University Press, 2019), 43.
28 Ravaisson, "Of Habit," 51.
29 Falque, *The Metamorphosis of Finitude*, 41–90.
30 See Jean-Louis Vieillard-Baron, "Le Manifeste Spiritualiste de Ravaisson: Le Rapport Sur La Philosophie En France Au XIXe Siècle," *Revue Philosophique de La France et de l'Étranger* 144, no. 1 (2019): 39–48.
31 Félix Ravaisson, *La Philosophie En France Au XIXe Siècle*, 2nd ed. (Paris: Hachette, 1885), 271. Hereafter PeF.
32 Félix Ravaisson, "Philosophical Testament," in *Félix Ravaisson: Selected Essays*, ed. Mark Sinclair (London: Bloomsbury Academic, 2016), 300–301.
33 Ravaisson, PeF, 271.
34 Félix Ravaisson, "On the Teaching of Drawing," in *Félix Ravaisson: Selected Essays*, ed. Mark Sinclair (London: Bloomsbury Academic, 2016), 162.
35 Significantly, this increase in activity is also the same dynamic that we see in his essay "On Habit."
36 Ravaisson, PeF, 260.
37 Ravaisson, PeF, 259.
38 Ravaisson, PeF, 260; Ravaisson, "Philosophical Testament," 312.
39 Ravaisson, PeF, 213–14.
40 For a possible Schellingian influence of overlapping themes of genius, art, and the identity of nature and mind in Ravaisson, see Sinclair, *Being Inclined*, 115–25. Although, Sinclair does not mention Ravaisson's use of genius, he does relate Ravaisson's notion of habit to Schelling's conception of genius.
41 Ravaisson, PeF, 213, 157. Emphasis mine
42 Ravaisson, PeF, 280.
43 Ravaisson, PeF, 35–36.
44 Ravaisson also saw this movement towards union with the divine within ancient and pagan sources. His two essays on Greek art are attempts to show the longing of the ancients to be reunited to the divine, a longing that is only fulfilled in Christianity. See Félix Ravaisson, "Greek Funerary Monuments," in *Félix Ravaisson: Selected Essays*, ed. Mark Sinclair (London: Bloomsbury Academic, 2016), 229–42; Félix Ravaisson, "The Venus de Milo," in *Félix Ravaisson: Selected Essays*, ed. Mark Sinclair (London: Bloomsbury Academic, 2016), 189–229.
45 Ravaisson, PeF, 214.
46 George Rickey, "The Morphology of Movement: A Study of Kinetic Art," in *The Nature and Art of Motion*, ed. Gyorgy Kepes (New York: Braziller, 1965), 110.
47 Rickey, "The Morphology of Movement," 106–7, 113–14.
48 Rickey, "The Morphology of Movement," 94.
49 Falque, *The Metamorphosis of Finitude*, 41–90.

Bibliography

Aristotle. *Politics*. Translated by Benjamin Jowett. Vol. 1. Oxford: Clarendon, 1885.

Aspray, Barnabas. "Transforming Heideggerian Finitude?: Following Pathways Opened by Emmanuel Falque." In *Transforming the Theological Turn: Phenomenology with Emmanuel Falque*, edited by Martin Koci and Jason Alvis, 163–74. Lanham, MD: Rowman & Littlefield, 2020.

Deleuze, Gilles, and Felix Guattari. *Anti-Oedipus: Capitalism and Schizophrenia*. Translated by Robert Hurley, Mark Seem, and Helen R. Lane. Minneapolis: University of Minnesota Press, 2010.

Falque, Emmanuel. *Crossing the Rubicon: The Borderlands of Philosophy and Theology*. Translated by Reuben Shank. New York: Fordham University Press, 2016.

Falque, Emmanuel. "The Extra-Phenomenal." *Diakrisis Yearbook of Theology and Philosophy* 1 (2018): 9–28.

Falque, Emmanuel. *The Metamorphosis of Finitude: An Essay on Birth and Resurrection*. Translated by George Hughes. New York: Fordham University Press, 2012.

Falque, Emmanuel. *Nothing to It: Reading Freud as a Philosopher*. Translated by Robert Vallier and William L. Connelly. Leuven, Belgium: Leuven University Press, 2020.

Falque, Emmanuel. *The Wedding Feast of the Lamb: Eros, the Body, and the Eucharist*. Translated by George Hughes. New York, NY: Fordham University Press, 2016.

Ravaisson, Félix. "Contemporary Philosophy." In *Félix Ravaisson: Selected Essays*, edited by Mark Sinclair, 59–83. London: Bloomsbury Academic, 2016.

Ravaisson, Félix. "Greek Funerary Monuments." In *Félix Ravaisson: Selected Essays*, edited by Mark Sinclair, 229–42. London: Bloomsbury Academic, 2016.

Ravaisson, Félix. *La Philosophie en France au XIXe Siècle*. 2nd ed. Paris: Hachette, 1885.

Ravaisson, Félix. "Of Habit." In *Félix Ravaisson: Selected Essays*, edited by Mark Sinclair, 31–58. London: Bloomsbury Academic, 2016.

Ravaisson, Félix. "On the Teaching of Drawing." In *Félix Ravaisson: Selected Essays*, edited by Mark Sinclair, 159–88. London: Bloomsbury Academic, 2016.

Ravaisson, Félix. "Philosophical Testament." In *Félix Ravaisson: Selected Essays*, edited by Mark Sinclair, 295–336. London: Bloomsbury Academic, 2016.

Ravaisson, Félix. "The Venus de Milo." In *Félix Ravaisson: Selected Essays*, edited by Mark Sinclair, 189–229. London: Bloomsbury Academic, 2016.

Rickey, George. "The Morphology of Movement: A Study of Kinetic Art." In *The Nature and Art of Motion*, edited by Gyorgy Kepes, 81–115. New York: Braziller, 1965.

Sinclair, Mark. *Being Inclined: Felix Ravaisson's Philosophy of Habit*. Oxford: Oxford University Press, 2019.

Vieillard-Baron, Jean-Louis. "Le Manifeste Spiritualiste de Ravaisson: Le Rapport Sur La Philosophie En France Au XIXe Siècle." *Revue Philosophique de La France et de l'Étranger* 144, no. 1 (2019): 39–48.

3

Perspective in Nicholas of Cusa and the Rise of the Transcendental Subject

Nathan D. Pederson

Whether for good or ill, there is something world-building in our art, in the human capacity to imagine and represent. Martin Heidegger makes this, in fact, decisive for our age: "The fundamental event of modernity is the conquest of the world as picture.... Within this, man fights for the position in which he can be that being who gives to every being the measure and draws up the guidelines."[1] Particularly important here is *perspective*, not merely as an artistic technique but as a whole theory of seeing and being. This chapter explores this notion using the thought of Nicholas of Cusa, or Nicholas Cusanus, a fifteenth-century German philosopher and theologian who reflects upon perspective in a way that marks the very threshold of our age.[2] I focus on Cusa's *On the Vision of God* (*De visione Dei*), in which a picture or icon of an all-seeing face is central to what is at stake in Cusa's perspectivism, an omnivoyant that engenders an experience in which Cusa, reflecting on God's gaze, confesses "because you [God] regard me, I am."[3] Of particular interest is a disagreement between Jean-Luc Marion and Emmanuel Falque over the phenomenological nature of perspective, specifically as it pertains to whether Cusa describes an icon (Marion) or a Renaissance picture (Falque). The question is how this Cusan confession of "seeing oneself seen" speaks of both genuine subjectivity and genuine sight of the other, and whether it is about the immediacy of vision or the hermeneutical detour of vision. I show, however, that there need not be a sharp divide here, as a hidden relation between these various tensions is at play. To this end, I focus on the development of modern perspective, wrestling with the relation between Cusa's perspectivism and Renaissance linear perspective. From there, I offer an archeology of the subject that explores the phenomenological nature of aesthetic experience marking the turn to our own modern age. Modern perspective, this chapter argues, is articulated within and upon—though ultimately negates—the notion of mystical darkness, along with its themes of the mirror and enigma. In Cusan perspective we see a laying bare of the conceptuality that makes possible the birth of the modern, transcendental subject. More specifically, we see how *through the rise of linear perspective, darkness comes to represent a negation of otherness at the center of modern subjectivity*. This reveals malformed networks of desire in the formation of the nascent transcendental desiring subject and the modern public space it creates, as "darkness" more broadly is signified negatively at the modern turn with the rise of colonialism. I conclude by gesturing towards how we might reorient our subjectivity and its perspective in view of forging a genuinely pluralistic society.

Cusan Perspective as Situated within Mystical Darkness

Central to this chapter's analysis is a key point of Cusa's thought: how, in Karsten Harries' words, perspective "is used to undermine the traditional idea of a center."[4] While we have to examine the relation between Cusan and linear perspectives to see the extent to which this is truly the case, we must first make clear how Cusa founds his perspectivism upon the notion of mystical darkness, mirror, and enigma, even while ultimately hiding such darkness within perspective's apparatuses. An examination of *De visione Dei,* and specifically the "darkness of God," brings us to "the focal point of Cusanus' speculation."[5] Cusa writes this text in 1453 to a group of German monks wrestling with the specific way to divine contemplation, proposing to help them uncover mystical wonders. "[B]y means of a very simple and commonplace method," Cusa argues, he will "attempt to lead [them] experientially into the *most sacred darkness*."[6] To enter this mystical darkness, Cusanus suggests a dramatic thought-exercise: the monks should hang on the wall an all-seeing picture or icon which he has provided them, and each should move around it separately in various directions (some from East to West and others vice-versa). Through this experiment, the monks experience a gaze that is simultaneously unchanged and changeable as the vision of the all-seer follows each brother individually *at the same time and all at once.* They discern this as they hear each other's testimony while crossing paths in their semicircular ambulation around the image.[7] The omnivoyant image, bearing a logic of the "coincidence of opposites," thus facilitates an impossibility which catalyzes an experience of God's absolute vision, a transcendental vision which is the essence of God's love, providence, grace, and even creative power. As Cusa would have it, at one and the same time the monks learn of the uniqueness of their perspective, of their perspective's relativity in the face of other perspectives, and of its transcendence as they grasp the absolute power of sight.

At the core of this experiment in Cusan perspectivism is a reliance on the all-seeing face as a similitude or figure to contemplate infinity as if "in a mirror, in an icon, in an enigma."[8] In this contemplation, one ultimately "must leap beyond every knowledge and concept" to enter into the "cloud, mist, darkness, or ignorance," into "a certain secret and hidden silence beyond all faces where there is no knowledge or concept of a face."[9] Issuing forth from this place is Cusa's testimony of "seeing oneself seen," his confession to and of God, "because you regard me, I am."[10] In the mirror of this mystical darkness, awakening to God's gaze, one gains the vision of God and "sees all things openly and nothing remains hidden to this person."[11]

This experience reflects the broader Cusan notion of *docta ignorantia* or "learned ignorance," a new mode of thought that reflects Cusa's claim of the absolute disproportionality between the finite and the infinite, the human and God.[12] Reflecting on approaching the infinite God, Cusa writes:

Does not whoever ascends above the end enter into what is indeterminate and confused and thus, with respect to the intellect, into ignorance and obscurity, which belong to intellectual confusion? The intellect, therefore, must become ignorant and established in darkness if it wishes to see you. But what, my God, is intellect in ignorance if not learned ignorance?[13]

God is like an infinite sphere which has its center everywhere and circumference nowhere such that center and circumference actually coincide. This means something for our own pursuit of knowledge, according to Cusa: our own center or viewpoint only *appears* to be absolute or fixed; in fact, a natural center has been lost as all viewpoints, proportionality, and distances are relativized in the infinite.

To become learned about one's ignorance, therefore, is to become aware, in one and the same experience, of one's perspective as unique and yet as infinitely relativized by the perspectives of others. Yet this experience of the coincidence of opposites catalyzes mystical knowledge of the divine. Truth is always just out of our finite reach; we reason through the similitude or figure (like the infinite circle) in which we are able to grasp after infinite truth only by leaping over (even as we go through) the finite figure.[14] In *De visione Dei* this similitude is the enigmatic mirror of the all-seeing face, a figure that leads one in learned ignorance to absolute vision. As we awaken to the impossible-made-possible of God's gaze upon us and upon all, we see—and as we see, we *are*. Falque therefore marks this as the "birth of egoity."[15] More generally, Peter Sloterdijk here points out Cusa's influence upon the nascent modern age as it pictured God as "lender of eyesight [... and] of subjectivity."[16] This transition—or perhaps better, this *disjunction*—from perspective to transcendent selfhood by way of the mirror of mystical darkness is the secret of the birth of modern subjectivity and the modern public space it forges.

The Relation of Cusan Perspective to Linear Perspective

To understand what is at stake in placing the birth of the modern subject here upon this discourse of mystical darkness, we need to explore the relation between Cusan and Renaissance linear perspective. The nature of this relation is disputed. On the one hand, Hans Belting, among others, argues that Cusan perspective "is the counter-position to the perspective picture, which is constructed to serve only one focal point and seeks to make that view absolute."[17] Similarly, Michel de Certeau argues in a detailed manner how Cusa's perspectivism avoids linearity.[18] In such a view, Cusan perspective is a type of nonlinear or "reverse" perspective which resists the monocular, controlling gaze of the subject. Common in such perspective is the simultaneous showing of multiple viewpoints or planes of vision (similar, the argument goes, to the experience engendered by Cusa's all-seer); for example, a table might be shown simultaneously from the side and from above (to better show its contents).[19] On the other hand, scholars like Charles Carman find intimate similarity between linear and Cusan perspective in the ability to invoke "the presence of an infinite manifest to all viewers."[20] Undoubtedly, the juxtaposition in Cusa's text of *a de-centering of one's perspective* and *a centralizing of subjectivity as one gains absolute vision* argues for a complex relationship between Cusan and linear perspective. I argue that *these two apparently contradictory aspects are just what hold Cusan and linear perspective together.* Particularly, this happens through the use of the mirror at the center of both Cusan and linear perspective.

Arising most prominently among the artists of Renaissance Italy, the new artistic technique of linear perspective was developed out of scientific discourses on optics (including that of Islamic scientist and philosopher Alhasen),[21] especially out of the theory and use of the mirror in ancient optical theory (or catoptrics) and its concern with the similarity between the eye and the mirror regarding dynamics of accuracy and distortion in representation.[22] In what becomes a new way of seeing the world as a whole, Renaissance perspective ultimately sought to represent space as ruled by mathematics, "a fully rational—that is, infinite, unchanging and homogeneous—space," which it was able to achieve by intersecting the visual pyramid with a planar cross section.[23] This technique engendered a "new kind of picture [which] simulated a three-dimensional space that viewers then appropriated for themselves with their gaze."[24] An especially important figure is Leon Battista Alberti, who in his *De Pictura* (1435) codified and circulated this new perspective more broadly in Europe, discussing it in terms of a "window" into nature meant to frame a world perfected and mastered by geometry.[25] Belting explains that in this way Alberti was attempting to usurp the theological symbol of the singular eye for his own vision instead of God's. The full force of this new technique was such that, as a kind of "disembodied eye," the viewer "standing in front of a picture painted in linear perspective could feel—and wanted to feel—the same dominance toward it that people attributed to God's relationship with the world."[26] Yet this seeing-through "window" perspective does not completely leave behind the matter of the mirror from which it arose, even if its claim to transparency is in tension with the mirror's potential to overturn vision. We can unravel this puzzle by focusing more directly on the constitutional origin point of linear perspective.

In 1425, ten years before Alberti's text, Filippo Brunelleschi would create a precise picture of the Florence baptistry.[27] Through a specific technique with a mirror, Brunelleschi's viewers were able to compare the representational accuracy of the picture to the actual building. Antonio Manetti, writing in the 1480s, provides the most complete account of how Brunelleschi used the mirror in his demonstration: the mirror operated in concert with a hole placed at the backside of the picture, the mirror held in one hand in front of the viewer at a distance and the picture in the other hand held up against their face, though from its backside; this hole corresponded to the picture's vanishing point on the frontside, a hole specifically carved so one could fit their eyeball in the backside of the picture as they gazed through the hole at the mirror they held in front of them to view the picture in its reflection. Standing in the right place, they could then remove the mirror, still looking through the hole, to compare the actual baptistry with the picture's reflection they had just seen.[28] Only through this operation of the mirror, argues Hubert Damisch, was the "[now modern] subject [able] to obtain self-confirmation" of the drawing's representational precision.[29] Moreover, Damisch writes, "the point of view and the vanishing point [of the picture] *coincide on the plane of projection.*"[30] The mirror at the center of perspective, which makes the entire apparatus operative, did not merely allow the subject to confirm the accuracy of representation and measure out the world. More importantly, we must realize that the vanishing point in the perspective painting represented infinity: thus, upon this plane of projection made possible by the mirror, we find the coincidence of the gaze of infinity with our very own gaze.[31] *Through the operation of the mirror, we are caught in, and constituted by, the gaze of infinity as we see ourselves being seen.* While here the "vanishing point has the value of a look of the Other," and thus presents a decentering gaze, it is at the same time a gaze "that constitutes me as viewer,"[32] as my own gaze is made possible as it coincides with and thus inhabits the omnivoyant gaze. Through the technique of linear perspective, then, one is able to gaze into the deepest mystery of reality, forging modern subjectivity by co-opting the potentiality and productivity of the mirror's enigmatic darkness. The self is now that which *maps out* the secret unknowns of the universe through transcendent vision.

In view of this historical recounting (and especially Damisch's argument), we have in linear perspective, as in Cusan perspective, the juxtaposition of two seemingly opposed logics, namely, of an enigmatized observer who gains absolute vision. But the fact and nature of this relationship is obscured in linear perspective, and the dark spot of the modern subject's transcendental vision—that is, its foundation in the enigmatic— is left un-reflected. The careful and more revealing conceptuality of Cusan perspective lays open how Renaissance linear perspective is built upon but hides within itself nonlinear perspective and shows that this specifically has to do with how it deals with darkness or enigma, represented in the notion of the mirror.

The Phenomenological Stakes of Cusan Perspective

In order to understand how the mirror figures more exactly in Cusan perspective itself, we must first raise perspective more clearly to its phenomenological importance. Marion and Falque's debate surrounding Cusa's *De visione Dei* facilitates this examination. Their disagreement about the nature of the omnivoyant is well-known; what is significant, for us, is the phenomenological claims that follow from their argument regarding whether a subjectivity moored in *seeing oneself seen* (and the genuine vision of the other required here) is a matter of immediacy or of a hermeneutics of intersubjectivity. While Marion and Falque claim to show two possible (and diverging) paths of modern perspective's trajectory toward subjectivity, I argue we can navigate this sharp dispute by surfacing the importance of the mirror in relating linear and nonlinear perspective. Moreover, this exploration raises the stakes of perspective, shifting from a more historical register to a more phenomenological register: *how we see fundamentally shapes who we are.* This makes the mirror's operation at the core of modern perspective something that *concerns us* in our own subjectivity.

For Marion, Cusan perspective is connected to the all-seeing icon of the face of Christ and thus to God's absolute sight as condition for human sight. Marion particularly focuses on connecting the conceptuality of the icon in Cusa to the "possibility of seeing the other," expressed in Cusa's focus on *seeing oneself seen*; this is a matter of the icon because it is a matter of the genuine crossing of gazes.[33] In the case of the icon's "double gaze," as with Cusa's omnivoyant, the viewer's own gaze is overturned because the icon "sees so originally and so completely the one who looks at it that [the icon] overturns the order of intentionality and makes itself felt precisely through the experience of receiving a gaze that is absolutely concentrated on each of the spectators. To see an icon amounts to seeing oneself seen by it."[34] This is precisely the transition Marion makes from Cusa's conceptuality of God's iconic gaze to a model of an iconic gaze of the other: the other becomes visible as other and not merely as object "to the precise extent that, with his *invisible gaze, he sees me*."[35] An iconic phenomenology, Marion suggests, provides an escape from the "linearity" of the idolizing, objectifying gaze which traps one within the horizon of the object and prohibits genuine sight of the other.[36] God's absolute gaze, though universal, is fundamentally one of love and care, and on these terms, he argues, "the *visio Dei* is freed from the horizon of objectity and no one can or should be able, strictly speaking, to idolize it."[37] Thus is opened the possibility of inhabiting a loving gaze and so the possibility of properly seeing the other.

While Marion's phenomenology of the icon, with its immediacy of vision, puts the transcendental possibilities for subjectivity in the best light, the problem is whether this configuration of the icon negates the enigmatic mirror that gives it power to grant genuine vision. Marion writes that the icon grants an exit from objectity through a shifting of horizons that happens "right away, at once, without transition or mediation."[38] By linking, however, the icon so closely with God's absolute vision and with such an experience of immediacy, Marion hides the hermeneutical moment within the phenomenological moment, the interpretation of perception within the immediacy of sight. A whole history and operation—which I have traced above, and which is fundamentally concerned with overcoming the mediation of darkness—haunts any claim to immediacy of sight that modern perspective and its subjectivity claim for themselves. Any absolute gaze, *in its factical manifestation,* is an authoritarian panopticon, *one* perspective masquerading as the *universal* perspective. Such transcendental vision does not untie the enigma that marks the divide between seeing the other as object or as truly other, but only reinscribes the aporia on a higher plane.

Falque, like Marion, considers the notion of *seeing oneself seen* and the problem of genuine sight of the other to be central to Cusan perspective. Reflecting on Cusa's all-seer, Falque writes of Cusan perspective: "The objectivity of seeing—seeing both things and the world—is substituted here by the subjectivity of the seen—of the self and the other."[39] Vision is *only* counter-vision as "[e]goity is born of alterity, in a counter-intention of seeing."[40] Falque, however, problematizes Marion's iconic conceptuality, troubling the claim to immediacy of vision as he focuses on the hermeneutical and intersubjective nature of sight. He does this, in particular, by relating Cusa's omnivoyant to the mirror in Renaissance perspective painting.

Referencing Jan van Eyck's *Giovanni Arnolfini and his Wife* (1434), Falque writes of the rise of the all-seeing gaze in the "new perspective" of Renaissance paintings, specifically connecting this motif to the "new use of 'mirror' ... as it is attested in the aesthetics of the fifteenth century and as it is also in use by Nicholas of Cusa in his theology," which, Falque claims, *marks the rupture that overturns the order of vision*. He continues: "a world takes place in the mirror, which, far from merely reflecting, attracts us to it, to the point of containing another reality that I do not see."[41] Unlike what happens in the icon, argues Falque, where the observer is engulfed, "the invention of 'reverse perspective' in the Renaissance . . . allows for the 'including the one looking with the represented space.'"[42] While this seems to be inaccurate (it is *linear* perspective that marks the Renaissance), we realize with Falque that Cusa, like his contemporary perspectivist theorists, uses the mirror or all-seer to intimately relate linear and nonlinear perspective in complex ways. In any case, according to Falque, this new "inclusive" space created by the Renaissance perspective painting through its conceptuality of the mirror is already and necessarily communal and intersubjective as it engenders the birth of the self *as one is seen by others in filial community*. Falque writes: "The inverted mirror of the One who truly sees me in him constitutes me as subject in the accusative (me) or in the vocative (to me)."[43] Accordingly, the crux of Cusa's experiment, argues Falque, is the "revelation of the witness" who "reveals the validity of the revealed to me," because otherwise the reality of the All-Seer would have been impossible.[44] Thus the experience is less about God and more about my neighbor in whose perspective I have to trust.[45] The danger here, of course, is whether all verticality (or the infinite) has collapsed into an immanent horizontality with its own kind of linearity.

These two thinkers, in the end, highlight both the complexity of Cusan perspective and its phenomenological importance. Their commentary does not so much clarify but rather reveals an ambiguity in Cusa's conceptuality of perspective, showing both its linear and nonlinear aspects. Both Marion and Falque struggle with constructing a phenomenology out of a Cusan perspective which escapes linearity. Falque, however, shows more promise in this as he pays attention to the hermeneutics of the mirror and what it means for the intersubjectivity of vision. As we ourselves (who now experience a certain *malaise* in the midst of modernity's failures) seek to put into question the transcendental subject, Falque shows us a way forward with Cusa's conceptuality. It must become our concern to wrestle with how an all-too-immediate phenomenological vision is tied up in, but seeks to negate, a hermeneutics of the mirror that is at stake in the intersubjectivity of *seeing oneself seen*. Until we first release any nonlinear perspective from its linear strictures, its full potential is not easily activated. Thus we must examine Cusan perspective more closely as it lays open the apparatus that modern, transcendental subjectivity founds itself upon, so that we can understand how linear perspective co-opts the power of the mirror.

In Focus: Cusan Perspective and the Mirror

The mirror, for Cusa, stands as a nodule of the logic of the coincidence of opposites fastened within created reality, thereby catalyzing the transition from finitude to the infinite. Again, the idea is that a similitude or figure is used to "leap beyond" towards an absolute or the infinite. Here de Certeau highlights the Cusan tension between "observation" and "intuition": "These two forms of 'seeing' constantly intersect . . . Their point of coincidence lies in *the visible figure in which the gaze grasps the invisible element active within the figure*. This instrument for the passing (*transsumptio*) from one 'seeing' to the other is the *mirror*."[46] Through the mirror the mind makes the mystical transition from the "visible places" and "'perceptible image' offered to 'the eye'" to the vision of "formal relations and their possible developments."[47] Finite reason eventually gives way to a flash of infinite insight.

Such a mystical transition is possible because, according to Cusa, "visible things are truly images of invisible things and … from creatures the Creator can be seen in a recognizable way *as if in a mirror or in an enigma*."[48] But this means we must "reject things that … are attained through the senses, the imagination, or reason" in order to reach the absolute.[49] We proceed from an image with "transumptive proportion to which the unknown is investigated," which happens best through "mathematicals" that have "incorruptible certitude."[50] Cusa provides a helpful summary:

> [W]e must first consider finite mathematical figures along with their attributes and relations; then we must transfer these relations to corresponding infinite figures; and finally we must, at a still higher level, apply the relations of the infinite figures to the infinite simple, which is entirely independent even of every figure. *And then, as we labor in the dark of enigma, our ignorance will be taught incomprehensibly how we are to think of the Most High more correctly and more truly.*[51]

Laboring "in the dark of enigma"—discovering in the crucible of the mirror of mystical darkness one's perspective, only to then hide one's perspective in order to overcome it—is the secret history of modern thought. The initial discovery of knowledge-as-perspective gives birth to a decidedly scientific-spirited trajectory and "a demand for liberation from the distorting power of perspective … [as] objectivity requires freedom from particular points of view."[52] Cusa engenders *a thought birthed out of recognition of one's perspective that, at the same time, reveals a higher logic through which one overcomes one's perspective.*

At stake here is a re-orientation of "form" amidst the ascendency of the creative power of the mind. Cusa's thought becomes illustrative of what Giorgio Agamben refers to as the "'artistic machine' of modernity," where, beginning in the Renaissance, there was a transition from the "working" (*energeia*) of artwork as being outside of the artist and within the art produced, to the artist who now "possesses his *energeia* in himself and can thus affirm his superiority over the work."[53] Instead of the artist showing form in displaying the interconnectedness of being through the exercise of "habit," there was now a collapse of form into mere efficient causality. This represented a move away from ontology toward the power of subjectivity, away from being *informed* by being to *informing* being itself. This transition had to do more broadly with the rise of Nominalism at the end of the Middle Ages, which affected the disintegration of the "ontotheological synthesis," in the words of Louis Dupré. Nominalists "effectively removed God from creation," Dupré writes, as the "divine became relegated to a supernatural sphere separate from nature, with which it retained no more than causal, external link."[54] As form lost the ontological function of mediating the participation between the finite and the infinite, it eventually became associated with the expressions of the human mind.[55]

Indeed, for Cusa not only is the mind important, but *the mind itself functions like a mirror* as "[t]hrough its capacity for measuring, numbering, and representing, [it] accomplishes everything" as an image of the divine mind.[56] Seeking a new immanence for God in the wake of Nominalism, Cusa insisted on the direct and absolute immanence of God in all the universe and called for a new way both of thinking and of approaching the world. For Cusa, the infinite now envelops the finite as a "virtual reality" of sorts; the "leap" to the infinite is necessary because such virtual reality "is a middle in which we are already participating, which envelops to such an extent that it exceeds every grasp."[57] Amidst the milieu of this virtual reality, the mind is raised to a new, creative power as it is able to forge the abstraction of space necessary to transcend finitude. As Harries describes it, through human freedom expressed in reason, one "can transcend the limitation of the here and now and arrive at a more objective mode of representing the world."[58] The modern subject has dawned, as has the task not to *inhabit* being so as to recognize form in its potentiality (*dynamis*), but to *shape* reality through the copy-making of the mind's eye.

In Cusa, ultimately the mirror functions as *a type of screen*, which brings together the seemingly contradictory ideas in modern perspective of a "looking through" (of a window) and of a turning back of vision (in the mirror). Even Alberti's "window" turned out to be more of a screen, since it was a "rectilinear frame gridded with a network of strings" (which he called a "veil," *velum* in Latin).[59] The veiling nature of Alberti's window-grid already anticipates (or impinges upon) the enigmatic quality of the mirror in nonlinear perspectives. The screen, then, brings both ideas together in the dialectic of *transparency* and *opacity*. Through its straining, obstructing, or (re-)directing function, a screen only secondarily serves the transparency and openness of the window. As the screen or veil grows in opacity (almost toward solidification, maximizing this obstructing function), it transmogrifies its seeing-through visibility into the "virtual" visibility of projection (as with a movie screen). In terms of Cusan perspective and the trajectory it enlivens, the enigma of the mirror absorbs into itself, under the dense veil of mystical darkness, a kind of substantive opacity and becomes a solid screen. While purporting to retain its transparent seeing-through and world-opening qualities, the Cusan mirror comes to operate according to a kind of transparency saturated with mental ideation. Cusa's mirror-as-screen captures the nuance of depth and variability into its fair and flat surface, re-arranging it according to the transcendental logic which befits a homogeneous and rational conception of space.

The Rise of "Colonial Desire"

Cusa's effort to loosen and indeed to *sever* the participatory relation between the finite and the infinite through the notion of perspective affected no less than the now more technical suturing of the rift through the formation of *a new center of transperspectival subjectivism*. This engendered a kind of techno-artificing of the subjective perspective of the finite in order to reach the infinite by way of mere causal link.[60] Such a re-orientation of the relationship between finitude and infinitude, crafted upon the discourse of the mirror-as-screen, empowered *a desire to unriddle the enigma, to capture the unknown through what one can measure*. So, for someone like Alberti, perspective in painting "promises something like a mastery of nature through mathematical representation."[61] Ultimately the newly freed mind "is moved to measure by the desire to measure itself and its own capacity."[62] Like one gaining the vision of God in the Cusan experiment, the "eye-subject ... becomes absorbed in, 'elevated' to a vaster function, proportional to the movement which it can perform" through the measuring mind as it spans and expands the abstract and homogenous world created through the symbol of linear perspective—a world "constituted not only by this eye but for it."[63]

But as Belting notes, the subject's "impulse to see—his visual drive—leads into uncertain territory."[64] Marion refers to such "uncertain territory" as a "counter-world" that the screen creates. While a mirror can, ideally, open a world, Marion argues a screen does not represent an "opening of a world but rather an (en)closure of it." He continues: "the screen substitutes for the things of the world an idol constantly repeated for viewers, an idol multiplied without spatial or temporal limits, in order to attain the cosmic scope of a counter-world." Such a counter-world is normed by *the desire to see* (*libido vivendi*), "which satisfies itself with the solitary pleasure of the screen, [and] does away with love by forbidding sight of the other face—invisible and real."[65] Everything is filled up merely as the product of what one wants to see and comes to form an economy of commerce, distribution, and commodification. While linear perspective and its disembodied seeing subject claims to *open* a world in screening out any kind of mediation (desires, finitude, body, and so on), instead it *encloses* our subjectivity back upon itself, engendering "a phantasmatization of objective reality (images, sounds, colors)"[66] fueled by the repression of otherness.

Yet an *actual* world, our modern world, comes to birth in linear perspective. This "conquest of the world as picture"—in Heidegger's words—is already a colonial world because it is a world constitutionally normed by both the mirror-turned-screen and the *libido vivendi*. As such, it is crafted through the negation of darkness, now not just of mystical darkness but of unknown lands and dark-skinned peoples. This is not merely a philosophical line of thought. Cusa and his close friend Paolo Toscanelli, as well as Alberti, shared a great interest in geography and accurate cartography. In point of fact, as Harries explains, Toscanelli "is rumored to have been the author of the chart that first encouraged Columbus to seek the East by going west."[67] And Cusa, in his *Compendium*, explicitly paints a picture of humankind, and by analogy the Creator, as a geographer.[68] My examination, however, puts into question what was at stake in this exercise of trying to clarify the horizon and seek a new world: whether or not this seeking to unriddle the enigma (of unknown, dark lands) was a matter of hiding "alternative" perspectives (that is, native ordering of space) within linearity. Walter Mignolo, for example, writes that "the process of putting the Americas on the map ... was at the same time a process of concealing the Amerindian's representation of space."[69] One could, however, argue with Cary Nederman, reflecting on Cusa's *De Concordantia Catholica*, that Cusa himself did not envision such an "imperial reach"; that, in fact, "Cusanus's emphasis on the 'historicity' of secular political life, and hence of the inescapable diversity of systems of rule, may indeed be viewed as a recurring theme in his social thought."[70] Nevertheless, Cusa's "one religion in a variety of rites" envisions "a decidedly Christian unity of belief in matters of salvation."[71] The uneasiness with darkness and the unknown in the phenomenological domain inevitably finds its way to the ethical and political domain.

Imagining a New Public

On the most charitable interpretation, Cusa is still a threshold figure, caught between mystic and modern, a figure who conceptualizes the apparatus of modern perspective but does not fully seize on it. Accordingly, we can still find in his thought certain fissures that chasten the transcendental status of subjectivity. One could argue, for example, that Cusa's discovery of the moment of selfhood as fundamentally perspectival is an awakening to a particular socio-political and historical awareness that eventually critiques modernity's hubris. Furthermore, we can witness in Cusa's work the secret concordance (not yet entirely a *discordance*) between interpretation and intuition, hermeneutics and phenomenology, the enigma and the *ego*.[72] Consider how Cusa ends his *De visione Dei*, where he writes: "each intellectual spirit sees in you, my God, something which must be revealed to the others if they would attain to you, their God, in the best possible way," as each "reveal[s] their secrets to one another."[73] With such a promise, Cusa's "virtual reality" created within the forging of this secret concordance between enigma and selfhood could be recovered as a type of distanciation or *epoché* necessary to recover subjectivity not as foundation but as task.[74]

Emmanuel Falque's argument, then, must be further explored regarding how Cusa develops perspective in order to build a public or filial space *found only through the multiplicity of perspectives*. Of course, this would amount to stopping Cusa mid-move, before perspective is closed back up into the modern machine. But this points toward the hope of a kind of "trust" of hearing and believing each other in building our future, as we are invited into a new way of seeing. This new way of seeing would be one that challenges an entire history of phenomenology, which explores perception under the aegis of light and clarity, as it would wrestle with how shadow, darkness, and opacity decisively shape our vision of self and other.

Notes

1 Martin Heidegger, "The Age of the World Picture" in *Martin Heidegger: Off the Beaten Track*, ed. and trans. Julian Young and Kenneth Haynes (New York: Cambridge University Press, 2002), 71.

2 Several scholars trace Cusa as a key figure in the turn to modernity. For example, Ernst Cassirer describes Cusa as "the first modern thinker." Ernst Cassirer, *The Individual and the Cosmos in Renaissance Philosophy*, trans. Mario Domandi (New York: Angelico Press, 2020), 10. Not intending to adjudicate such debates here, I focus on the central claim of the importance of perspective for Cusa. Concerning this, see Karsten Harries' approach to Cusa and his convincing argument when he writes, "the history of art, especially the history of the theory of perspective, provides helpful hints" regarding how "the destruction of the medieval cosmos follows from a changed self-understanding, bound up with a new sense of freedom. A passionate interest in perspective and point of view helps to characterize that self-understanding and offers a key to the shape of modernity. That interest in perspective is in turn bound up with theological speculations centering on the infinity of God." *Infinity and Perspective* (Cambridge, MA: MIT Press, 2001), 15 and 19.

3   Nicholas Cusanus, *De visione Dei*, English and pagination as *On the Vision of God,* in *Nicholas of Cusa: Selected Spiritual Writings*, trans. H. Lawrence Bond (New York: Paulist Press, 1997), 4 §10, p. 240.
4   Harries, *Infinity and Perspective*, 39.
5   Cassirer, *Individual and Cosmos*, 33.
6   *De visione Dei*, Preface §1, p. 235. Emphasis mine.
7   *De visione Dei,* Preface §3, p. 236.
8   *De visione Dei*, 4 §10, p. 240.
9   *De visione Dei*, 6 §21, p. 244.
10 *De visione Dei*, 4 §10, p. 240.
11 *De visione Dei*, 7 §25, p. 246.
12 See Nicholas Cusanus, "*De docta ignorantia*," English and pagination as *On Learned Ignorance*, in *Nicholas of Cusa: Selected Spiritual Writings*, 1.1-3 §2–10, p. 88-91.
13 *De visione Dei*, 13 §52, p. 258.
14 *De docta ignorantia*, 1.3 §10, p. 91.
15 Emmanuel Falque, "The All-Seeing: Fraternity and Vision of God in Nicholas of Cusa," trans. Kyle H. Kavanaugh and Barnabas Aspray. *Modern Theology* 35, no. 4 (2019): 771.
16 Peter Sloterdijk, *Bubbles: Microspherology,* in *Spheres, Volume I*, trans. Wieland Hoban (South Pasadena, CA: Semiotext[e], 2011), 576.
17 Hans Belting, *Florence and Baghdad: Renaissance Art and Arab Science* (Cambridge, MA: Belknap Press, 2011), 222–23; see also Taylor Knight, "In a Mirror and an Enigma: Nicholas of Cusa's *De Visione Dei* and the Milieu of Vision," *Sophia* 59 (2020): 114 and 118.
18 See Michel de Certeau, "The Gaze: Nicholas of Cusa," trans. Catherine Porter. *Diacritics* 17, no. 3 (Autumn, 1987): 2–38.
19 For helpful reference here, see: Clemena Antonova, *Space, Time and Presence in the Icon: Seeing the World with the Eyes of God* (New York: Routledge, 2010), 38–67.
20 Charles H. Carman, *Leon Battista Alberti and Nicholas Cusanus: Towards an Epistemology of Vision for Italian Renaissance Art and Culture* (New York: Routledge, 2014), 95. There are, indeed, mediating positions that find both relation and difference, similar to what I myself offer. See, for example, Knight, "In a Mirror and an Enigma," esp. 114 and 121.
21 Knight, "In a Mirror and an Enigma," 115.
22 Samuel Y. Edgerton, *The Mirror, the Window, and the Telescope: How Renaissance Linear Perspective Changed our Vision of the Universe* (Ithaca, NY: Cornell University Press, 2009), 22–27.
23 Erwin Panofsky, *Perspective as Symbolic Form*, trans. Christopher S. Wood (New York, NY: Zone Books, 1997), 28–29.
24 Belting, *Florence and Baghdad*, 211.
25 Edgerton, *The Mirror, the Window, and the Telescope*, 8; Harries, *Infinity and Perspective*, 69–71.
26 Belting, *Florence and Baghdad*, 211–12.
27 Hubert Damisch notes that it was Filarete's *Treatise on Architecture* (1460–1464) that first associated Filippo Brunelleschi and his experiments with the discovery of linear perspective. Hubert Damisch, *The Origin of Perspective*, trans. John Goodman (Cambridge, MA: MIT Press, 1994), 61.
28 On Manetti's text and its explanation, see Edgerton, *The Mirror, the Window, and the Telescope*, 44-53; and Damisch, *The Origin of Perspective,* 115-131.

29 Damisch, *The Origin of Perspective,* 121.
30 Damisch, *The Origin of Perspective,* 121. Emphasis mine.
31 Damisch, *The Origin of Perspective,* 121.
32 Margaret Iversen, "The Discourse of Perspective in the Twentieth Century: Panofsky, Damisch, Lacan," *Oxford Art Journal* 28, no. 2 (2005): 200. Moreover, Edgerton argues that Brunelleschi's demonstration "permitted viewers to believe that they had *penetrated the very 'enigma' of the mirror.*" Edgerton, *The Mirror, the Window, and the Telescope,* 49. Emphasis mine.
33 Jean-Luc Marion, "Seeing, or Seeing Oneself Seen: Nicholas of Cusa's Contribution in *De visione Dei*," trans. Stephen E. Lewis, *The Journal of Religion* 96, no. 3 (2016): 305.
34 Marion, "Seeing, or Seeing Oneself Seen," 314.
35 Marion, "Seeing, or Seeing Oneself Seen," 317.
36 Marion, "Seeing, or Seeing Oneself Seen," 323.
37 Marion, "Seeing, or Seeing Oneself Seen," 325.
38 Marion, "Seeing, or Seeing Oneself Seen," 323.
39 Falque, "The All-Seeing," 762.
40 Falque, "The All-Seeing," 762.
41 Falque, "The All-Seeing," 769–70.
42 Falque, "The All-Seeing," 770.
43 Falque, "The All-Seeing," 771.
44 Falque, "The All-Seeing," 784. See Cusanus, *De visione Dei*, Preface §3, p. 236.
45 Falque, "The All-Seeing," 783.
46 de Certeau, "The Gaze," 8. Emphasis mine.
47 de Certeau, "The Gaze," 9.
48 *De docta ignorantia*, 1.11 §30, p. 100. Emphasis mine.
49 *De docta ignorantia*, 1.10 §27, p. 98–99.
50 *De docta ignorantia*, 1.11 §31–32, p. 100–1.
51 *De docta ignorantia*, 1.12 §33, p. 102. Emphasis mine.
52 Harries, *Infinity and Perspective*, 45.
53 Giorgio Agamben, *Creation and Anarchy: The Work of Art and the Religion of Capitalism*, trans. Adam Kotsko (Stanford, CA: Stanford University Press, 2019), 7–8.
54 Louis Dupré, *Passage to Modernity: An Essay in the Hermeneutics of Nature and Culture* (New Haven, CT: Yale University Press, 1993), 3.
55 Dupré, *Passage to Modernity,* 40–41.
56 Graziella Federici Vescovini, "Nicholas of Cusa, Alberti and the Architectonics of the Mind," in *Nexus II: Architecture and Mathematics*, ed. Kim Williams (Fucecchio, Italy: Edizioni dell'Erba, 1998), 167
57 Knight, "In a Mirror and an Enigma," 136; see also Ibid., 126–28.
58 Harries, *Infinity and Perspective*, 118.
59 Edgerton, *The Mirror, the Window, and the Telescope*, 126–27.
60 Regarding the change in the relation between finitude and infinitude from being normed by the notion of participation to being normed by mere "causal, external link", see Dupré, *Passage to Modernity*, 3. Regarding the notion of "techno-artificing" (my phrase), Harries writes of the sentiment of modernity: "Artifice will gain us back that clarity of vision Adam lost. Technology will help us undo the results of the Fall." Harries, *Infinity and Perspective*, 106.
61 Harries, *Infinity and Perspective*, 16.
62 Vescovini, "Nicholas of Cusa, Alberti and the Architectonics of the Mind," 165.

63 Jean-Louis Baudry, "Ideological Effects of the Basic Cinematographic Apparatus," in Philip Rosen, ed., *Narrative, Apparatus, Ideology: A Film Theory Reader* (Columbia, NY: Columbia University Press, 1986), 292.
64 Belting, *Florence and Baghdad*, 214
65 Jean-Luc Marion, *The Crossing of the Visible*, trans. James K. A. Smith (Stanford, CA: Stanford University Press), 53–54.
66 Baudry, "Ideological Effects of the Basic," 292.
67 Harries, *Infinity and Perspective*, 68–69.
68 Cusanus, *Compendium*, English and pagination as *Nicholas of Cusa on Wisdom and Knowledge*, trans. Jasper Hopkins (Minneapolis: The Arthur J. Banning Press, 1996), 8.22–23, p. 1398.
69 Walter D. Mignolo, "The Darker Side of the Renaissance: Colonization and the Discontinuity of the Classical Tradition," *Renaissance Quarterly* 45, no. 4 (Winter 1992): 820.
70 Cary J. Nederman, "Empire Meets Nation" in *Cusanus: The Legacy of Learned Ignorance*, ed. Peter Casarella (Washington, D.C.: The Catholic University of America Press, 2006), 187; for larger context see 184–87.
71 Cary J. Nederman, *Worlds of Difference: European Discourses of Toleration, c. 1100–c. 1550* (University Park, PA: Pennsylvania State University Press, 2000), 87–88.
72 On this point see Paul Ricoeur, *From Text to Action: Essays in Hermeneutics, II*, trans. Kathleen Blamey and John B. Thompson (Evanston, IL: Northwestern University Press, 2007), 50–51.
73 *De visione Dei* 25 §117, p. 288.
74 See Ricoeur, *From Text to Action*, 40, for the phenomenological *epoché* as a "virtual event."

Bibliography

Agamben, Giorgio. *Creation and Anarchy: The Work of Art and the Religion of Capitalism*. Translated by Adam Kotsko. Stanford, CA: Stanford University Press, 2019.

Antonova, Clemena. *Space, Time, and Presence in the Icon: Seeing the World with the Eyes of God*. Burlington, VT: Ashgate Publishing Company, 2010.

Baudry, Jean-Louis. "Ideological Effects of the Basic Cinematographic Apparatus." In *Narrative, Apparatus, Ideology: A Film Theory Reader*, edited by Philip Rosen, 286–98. New York: Columbia University Press, 1986.

Belting, Hans. *Florence and Baghdad: Renaissance Art and Arab Science*. Cambridge, MA: Belknap Press, 2011.

Carman, Charles H. *Leon Battista Alberti and Nicholas Cusanus: Towards an Epistemology of Vision for Italian Renaissance Art and Culture*. New York: Routledge, 2014.

Cassirer, Ernst. *The Individual and the Cosmos in Renaissance Philosophy*. Translated by Mario Domandi. New York: Angelico Press, 2020.

Damisch, Hubert. *The Origin of Perspective*. Translated by John Goodman. Cambridge, MA: The MIT Press, 1994.

de Certeau, Michel. "The Gaze: Nicholas of Cusa." Translated by Catherine Porter. *Diacritics* 17, no. 3 (Autumn, 1987): 2–38.

Dupré, Louis. *Passage to Modernity: An Essay in the Hermeneutics of Nature and Culture*. New Haven, CT: Yale University Press, 1993.

Edgerton, Samuel Y. *The Mirror, the Window, and the Telescope: How Renaissance Linear Perspective Changed our Vision of the Universe*. Ithaca, NY: Cornell University Press, 2009.

Falque, Emmanuel. "The All-Seeing: Fraternity and Vision of God in Nicholas of Cusa," translated by Kyle H. Kavanaugh and Barnabas Aspray. *Modern Theology* 35, no. 4 (Oct 2019): 760–87.

Harries, Karsten. *Infinity and Perspective*. Cambridge, MA: MIT Press, 2001.

Heidegger, Martin. "The Age of the World Picture." In *Martin Heidegger: Off the Beaten Track*, edited and translated by Julian Young and Kenneth Haynes, 57–85. New York: Cambridge University Press, 2002.

Iversen, Margaret. "The Discourse of Perspective in the Twentieth Century: Panofsky, Damisch, Lacan." *Oxford Art Journal* 28, no. 2 (2005): 193–202.

Knight, Taylor. "In a Mirror and an Enigma: Nicholas of Cusa's *De Visione Dei* and the Milieu of Vision." *Sophia* 59 (2020): 113–37.

Marion, Jean-Luc. *The Crossing of the Visible*. Translated by James K. A. Smith. Stanford, CA: Stanford University Press, 2004.

Marion, Jean-Luc. "Seeing, or Seeing Oneself Seen: Nicholas of Cusa's Contribution in *De visione Dei*," translated by Stephen E. Lewis. *The Journal of Religion* 96, no. 3 (2016): 305–31.

Mignolo, Walter D. "The Darker Side of the Renaissance: Colonization and the Discontinuity of the Classical Tradition." *Renaissance Quarterly* 45, no. 4 (1992): 808–28.

Nederman, Cary J. "Empire Meets Nation." In *Cusanus: The Legacy of Learned Ignorance*, edited by Peter Casarella, 178–95. Washington, D.C.: The Catholic University of America Press, 2006.

Nederman, Cary J. *Worlds of Difference: European Discourses of Toleration, c. 1100–c. 1550*. University Park: Pennsylvania State University Press, 2000.

Nicholas Cusanus. *Compendium*, Eng. as *Nicholas of Cusa on Wisdom and Knowledge*. Edited and translated by Jasper Hopkins. Minneapolis: The Arthur J. Banning Press, 1996.

Nicholas Cusanus. *De docta ignorantia*, Eng. as *On Learned Ignorance*, in *Nicholas of Cusa: Selected Spiritual Writings*. Translated by H. Lawrence Bond. New York: Paulist Press, 1997.

Nicholas Cusanus. *De visione Dei*, Eng. as *On the Vision of God*, in *Nicholas of Cusa: Selected Spiritual Writings*. Translated by H. Lawrence Bond. New York: Paulist Press, 1997.

Panofsky, Erwin. *Perspective as Symbolic Form*. Translated by Christopher S. Wood. New York: Zone Books, 1997.

Ricoeur, Paul. *From Text to Action: Essays in Hermeneutics, II*. Translated by Kathleen Blamey and John B. Thompson. Evanston, IL: Northwestern University Press, 2007.

Sloterdijk, Peter. *Bubbles: Microspherology*, in *Spheres, Volume I*. Translated by Wieland Hoban. South Pasadena, CA: Semiotext[e], 2011.

Vescovini, Graziella Federici. "Nicholas of Cusa, Alberti and the Architectonics of the Mind." In *Nexus II: Architecture and Mathematics*, edited by Kim Williams, 159–71. Fucecchio, Italy: Edizioni dell'Erba, 1998.

4

Desirous Seeing: Sol LeWitt, Vision, and Paradox

Daniel Adam Lightsey

This chapter explores how desire relates to the plural ways humans think through what it means to see. As it participates in the burgeoning conversations regarding constructive Christian theology, the imagination, and the arts, this chapter furthermore delves into the art and thought of Sol LeWitt as well as the contemporary theological work concerning images and desire by Natalie Carnes. The latter's work is vitally important for reflection on theological vision and the logics of desire inherent in human interaction with images. I argue that LeWitt's "conceptual mysticism" can be read as possessing a family resemblance to what Carnes outlines as an "erotics of sight," which disciplines one towards a "gaze of love." These phrases will need to be teased out, but by way of a brief outline, I first examine a sensibility of artistic making arguably most well known as "minimalism," then move on to LeWitt's unique contribution within this sensibility, with specific attention paid to the theme of vision and his so-called conceptual mysticism. Finally, I place LeWitt's thought in relation to Carnes' theological taxonomy regarding desire, sight, and love.

I

"What you see is what you see."[1] Artist Frank Stella's tautological dogma concerning the meaning (or non-meaning) inherent in his work typifies the vigorous debate regarding vision in the 1960s New York avant-garde art scene. As inheritors of a modern epistemological stance, many twentieth-century artists in the North Atlantic were critiquing frameworks of seeing that seemingly prized control and scientific precision. Individual artists as well as whole movements or sensibilities attempted to create avenues of resistance to modern fetishes for objective, unmediated knowledge of an object or work of art. One sensibility that was involved in that tumultuous decade and beyond goes by many names—ABC art, literalist art, primary structures, specific objects, etc.—but arguably is most well-known simply by "minimalism."

Caricatured as "not-art-enough" by some and critiqued by others for its supposed "theatricality," the emergence of 1960s North Atlantic minimalist art stood as a watershed moment in contemporary art history. With an extreme amount of diversity with regard to artists, mediums, styles, modes of production, etc., perhaps the only thing "minimalists" agreed upon was their eschewal of the term itself. As James Meyer argues, "[w]e may conceive 'minimalism' as a critical debate in which the artists were leading participants.... The literalist aesthetic most associated with minimalism held that a work should reveal nothing other than its constitutive materials and manner of construction."[2] While a great amount of scholarship has surfaced connecting artists from this sensibility with various historical, sociological, and ethical concerns, distinctly Christian theological engagement with minimalism has been rather mute. Such taciturnity could be due to certain minimalist artists stressing the strict materialism of their work, seemingly stamping out any trace of referential symbolism, metaphor, or metaphysical truth. For example, Robert Morris, a leading figure in 1960s minimalism, reflected that,

> At thirty, I had my alienation, my Skilsaw and my plywood. I was to rip out the metaphors, especially those that had to do with 'up,' as well as every other whiff of transcendence. When I sliced into the plywood with my Skilsaw, I could hear, beneath the ear-damaging whine, a stark and refreshing 'no' reverberate off the four-walls: no to transcendence and spiritual values, heroic scale, anguished decisions, historicizing narrative, valuable artifact, intelligent structure, interesting visual experience.[3]

However, Morris' caricature of a "Nietzschean carpenter slaying modernist metaphysics"[4] should by no means establish the rule, nor should his seeming materialist bent be seen as a flatly iconoclastic rejection of theological questioning in any straightforward sense.

This chapter represents an inquiry of sorts that takes as its lodestar a kind of "theologically oriented criticism" outlined by artist and art critic Jonathan Anderson. He suggests three broad canopies for theologically oriented criticism, and I situate this chapter under his third canopy: theological questioning of an "artwork specifically dealing with subjects of interest to a theological tradition."[5] However, I would qualify this by adding that I am less experimenting with art criticism *qua* art criticism than entering into dialogue with conceptual features of Sol LeWitt's work that I think merit attention within theology, as well as in philosophy of religion; namely, the connection of vision and desire.[6]

In what follows, I use vision and gaze rather interchangeably while recognizing that there are nuances to each, especially depending on the discipline to which one is attending.[7] Thomas Pfau helpfully describes how vision is not a disinterested, passive act: "to see means prima facie to be involved in, not detached from, the world and, thereby, to grasp ourselves as capable and ethically responsible agents of whatever knowledge may yet eventuate."[8] My use of these terms, therefore, does not reduce them to mere biology or culture, but instead holds a tension between them. There is obviously a plurality of frameworks for seeing the world, often replete with tacit rules, assumptions, and prejudices. As Ola Sigurdson summarizes, "Every gaze is active and so represents a way to see, that is to say, a way to be-in-the-world."[9]

Art historian and critic James Meyer notes that there were "several models of vision asserted ... in the New York avant-garde during the mid-sixties."[10] He names a host of competing models of vision by many inside and outside minimalism during that time. In contrast to "the optical, transcendental visuality of [the hugely influential art critic Clement] Greenberg," as well as Stella's "literalist model" of "what you see is what you see,"[11] LeWitt's work of this time is characterized as "problematiz[ing] vision" or exposing "a vision that failed to grasp its object."[12] This critical debate is in part why some classify the framework of minimalism as an "epistemological disturbance" to modernity.[13] As Hal Foster, for his part, contends, "[m]inimalism threatens modernist practice ... consummates it, completes and breaks with it at once."[14] Although LeWitt explicitly shunned the designation "minimal art," saying that it must be "a secret language that art critics use" and that he has "not discovered anyone who admits to doing this kind of thing," he was nonetheless one of the key figures of this 1960s sensibility.[15] More specifically, LeWitt championed a version of "conceptual art" that placed primacy on the "idea" of the piece of art, (in)famously saying what the "art looks like isn't too important," thereby making "the execution [of the piece of art] ... a perfunctory affair."[16] In short, LeWitt's conceptualism can be summarized as a kind of rule-based proceduralism where he carefully worded his instructions for drafting a piece, but in the actual execution an open-ended range of possibilities could be generated.[17] Charles Haxthausen summarizes: "For LeWitt, the idea was sovereign and absolute, while its material embodiment was relative and contingent, adaptable to multiple iterations in different spaces and dimensions and, over time, even to changes in medium.... It was this very material contingency and ephemerality that guaranteed the sovereignty of the idea."[18]

II

What specifically about LeWitt's work invites the description of problematizing vision? LeWitt famously opens his "Sentences on Conceptual Art" with a rather startling proclamation: "Conceptual Artists are mystics rather than rationalists. They leap to conclusions that logic cannot reach."[19] What kinds of seeing or not seeing does the "conceptual mystic" offer? What forms of vision does a conceptualist leap toward that rationalists and their logic cannot? Little shock that LeWitt does not answer these questions explicitly. One cannot but hear the words of the great Russian philosopher and theologian Sergius Bulgakov's: "in keeping with its spirit and with its internal pathos, art is liable only to *mystical* and religious judgment."[20] However, since LeWitt places much primacy on the intellect of the viewer herself—"Different people will understand the same thing in a different way"[21]—I offer a theologically informed reading of LeWitt's concern regarding vision and desire, one that admittedly takes LeWitt where he probably wouldn't go himself.

LeWitt exploits the ambiguity of the eye and mocks the possessive, spectatorial gaze and its desire for scientific precision. In contrast to Stella's "what you see is what you see" or Donald Judd's "empirical faith" regarding the "given" quality of his structures, LeWitt's works hide more than they reveal, seemingly destabilizing "what can be known in vision, [as well as] the function of desire in its pursuit of this knowledge."[22] As witnessed in a work entitled *Serial Project #1* (1966) (Plate 2). LeWitt's structures subvert the kind of "Cartesian perspectivalism" discussed by Paul Ricoeur: a kind of "vision of the world in which the whole of objectivity is spread out like a spectacle on which the *cogito* casts its sovereign gaze."[23] Instead of this, LeWitt works with shadow and darkness—hiding cubes within cubes or shading cubic structures with heavy shadows—many times either suspending any quick and obvious access to knowledge or explicitly hiding elements of his "projects within other elements where their existence must be completely taken on faith."[24] He suggests the kind logic inherent to *Serial Project #1* in his "Paragraphs on Conceptual Art," written one year after the debut of that work, where he writes: "Conceptual art is not necessarily logical. The logic of a piece or series of pieces is a device that is used at times only to be *ruined*. Logic may be used to *camouflage* the real intent of the artist, to *lull* the viewer into the belief that [she] understands the work, or to infer a paradoxical situation."[25] At issue for LeWitt, therefore, is challenging viewers' possible avaricious spectatorship by opening spaces of visual uncertainty, ambiguity, paradox, and seeming irrationality.

In summarizing pieces such as *Serial Project #1* as an attempt to playfully deny full disclosure for a complete vision and the desire for the same, Meyer compellingly argues that LeWitt reconfigures sight "into a desiring act incapable of grasping its object."[26] However, as we turn to our theologically oriented questioning of the work, one is led to ask: is desirous seeing interminably deferred? Is vision always frustrated? It does not seem so. Desire here in LeWitt's works is not wholly deferred nor forever frustrated, but instead chastened, giving vision a more modest place in the artist's visual calculus upon consideration.[27] LeWitt seems to speak to this in at least two ways. First, when describing his cubes' placement inside other cubes in one work and the viewer's inability to verify the concealed components, LeWitt guarantees that, "in all cases, the hidden elements were actually in place, even if they were not verifiable visually."[28] Is this the kind of leap of faith "conceptual mystics" can make and not the kind made by "rationalists" who seemingly desire a kind of panoptic vision? If so, desirous vision then is not wholly deferred, but disciplined into forms of seeing and not seeing, order and disorder, that must rest in the paradox or ambiguity of the moment. Or, to borrow Stephen Mulhall's idiom concerning the nature of "religious language," LeWitt's exploitation of the ambiguity of the eye can be argued to be "essentially self-subverting," where "the repeated collapse of its affirmations into complete disorder *is* its mode of order."[29]

Second, if a bit more tangentially, LeWitt welcomes misperceptions of his work as they too can be fecund in generating further interpretations or art. LeWitt describes this in his "Sentences on Conceptual Art": "One artist may mis-perceive (understand it differently than the artist) a work of art but still be set off in his own chain of thought by that misconstrual."[30] What's more, as mentioned above, while LeWitt formed strict rules for his many wall drawings, he left ample room for interpretation by the drafters, who in some cases largely did their work without LeWitt present. For example, LeWitt's strict instructions in *Wall Drawing #65* (1971) were: "Lines not short, not straight, crossing and touching, drawn at random using four colors, uniformly dispersed with maximum density, covering the entire surface of the wall."[31] And yet, he fully embraced the contingency of the interpretation of the drafter as well as the architectural restraints for the wall drawings themselves: "The draftsman perceives the artist's plan," LeWitt argued, "then reorders it to his experience and understanding.... The artist and the draftsman become collaborators in making the art."[32] Thus, for LeWitt, the conceptual artist must allow things to be. This "letting be" is not the flex of one's egoistic muscles but, to use Williams' words, a "most extraordinary concentrated suspension of will, so that something is allowed to happen."[33] For LeWitt, the artist must get out of the way of the work, so to speak, not forcibly imposing one's will, but making room for others to help one see.

III

LeWitt's so-called conceptual mysticism shares marked affinities with some recent theological work concerning desire, vision, and human creaturely interaction with images. Natalie Carnes' work concerning the development of an "erotics of sight" can imaginatively extend this reading of LeWitt's chastened, desirous seeing in order to draw out its Christian theological resonances. Carnes describes an "erotics of sight" in *Beauty: A Theological Engagement with Gregory of Nyssa* as "resisting descriptions that cast encounters between beholder and beheld as a static, two-node, abstractable network. It means instead casting this relationship as one embedded in many different nodes as the viewer is drawn deeper into what is beheld."[34] A classic example of this from the Christian tradition would be Augustine's description of seeing and becoming what one sees from book thirteen of his *Confessions*. This kind of eschatological vision is far from the purview of LeWitt, of course, but from a distinctly Christian angle a chastened desirous seeing, such as one finds evoked by LeWitt's work, may be viewed in terms of a (re)formation of the spectator towards an eschatological horizon, albeit through a glass darkly at present. The family resemblance to LeWitt, so to speak, is developed in how Carnes goes on to elucidate an "erotics of sight" that is full of ambiguity, as the "contingencies of desire" cannot be fully accounted for, at least not in an entirely possessive way.[35]

The ambiguity of desire is compellingly mapped by Carnes in another work, *Image and Presence*, where she describes at length how "[d]esire, whether we name it *eros*, *caritas*, or *agape*, leads us into versions of ourselves we do not know and are perhaps afraid to know."[36] Desire, in this vein, is as perilous as it is risky and transformative. There is clearly the risk of deleterious (de)formation as Carnes describes: "The image represents and elicits a desire that terminates in consumption by the viewer. In so giving itself over to consumption—in such readiness for complete absorption to the viewer—the image elicits a desire infected with the lust to dominate and control desire's object."[37] In other words, the viewer's gaze is at risk of making an idol, an illusion, or a mere object of the image, according to Carnes. Furthermore, possessive vision suffers the "dual dangers of exhaustion and perversion" as forms of *libido dominandi* continually haunt our individual and collective gazes.[38]

What, then, would a *faithful desirous seeing* entail? What kinds of *attention* can be cultivated that discipline the chastened vision of the viewer into new forms of seeing that do not end in a form of *libido dominandi*? In the background of my questioning is

Austin Farrer's concern, which he raised in a perceptive essay written between 1943 and 1948 (thus, predating the artists at issue in this essay): "The chief impediment to religion in this age, I often think, is that no one ever *looks* at anything at all: not so as to contemplate it, to apprehend what it is to be that thing, and plumb, if he can, the deep fact of its individual existence."[39] Thus, how does one unlearn habits of inattentive looking? First, to help frame an answer, Maximos Constas' assertion from *The Art of Seeing: Paradox and Perception in Orthodox Iconography* is helpful: "Seeing, of course, is a metaphor for knowing, and there is no knowledge apart from love. Thus the desire to see without being seen, to know without being known, to take without giving, stands in the same relation as love does to an act of violence."[40] Desirous seeing, therefore, is the kind of attention to others that "prompts us to attend to what we see, ... rather than enjoying perspectival dominion over, and thus merely *looking at*."[41] As Simone Weil and Iris Murdoch well attested, real attention toward an-other in the world concerns justice and love.[42] In a similar vein, Carnes generates a helpful designation for this kind of attention and inattention, namely, "the gaze of love" versus "the gaze of contempt."[43] She writes that the "contemptuous gaze believes that its object is fully known; it believes itself to be the master of the object.... [I]t is a gaze ordered to power, expressed as exhaustively knowing, as unmasking."[44] The gaze of love, on the other hand, "delights in the one it beholds" and resists "the will to master the world" by allowing the layers of the one(s) it sees to unfold "in image after image."[45] There is a certain ethos of ungraspability at play here, a recognition that a loving gaze is one that is playfully open to the surprise of seeing or not seeing depending on the ambiguities or contingencies of the moment, whereas the contemptuous gaze supposedly sees the world as effortlessly grasped by the thorax and pinned to a felt board inside a display case (again, care must be taken not to make this distinction too dualistically). Thus, by imbibing this sense of ungraspability, the gaze of love gives "occasion for 'unselfing,'" whereby one's attention is directed, according to Murdoch, "outward, away from self ... towards the great surprising variety of the world, and the ability so to direct attention is love."[46]

Carnes describes the unfolding of multiple images upon images as a kind of "Wittgensteinian iconoclasm," which utilizes "an album of sketches that attempts to loosen the grip a certain picture has on our imagination," this certain picture, according to Carnes, being a tendency "to seek a controlling mastery narrative" of what we see—or, in a different linguistic register, "what you see is what you see."[47] Instead, Carnes uses a "cascade of images" to demonstrate how certain forms of iconoclasm act as a therapy for both faithful and distorted desire and vision of the world.[48] This ethos resembles LeWitt's assertions in "Sentences," where an artist's misperceptions and "misconstruals" can nonetheless be generative—and this is especially relevant with regard to LeWitt's wall drawings, where he anticipated the multiple, open-ended interpretations that his "ideas" could generate once they were being drafted. In their mutual dependency with her drafters as well as the surrounding architecture, a LeWittian conceptualist is constrained by architectural irregularities and ofttimes absurdities.[49] Thus, there is a sense of "reciprocal poiesis" between the conceptualist, the drafter, and the architecture.[50] Furthermore, the artist must "let be" according to the drafter's sense for how the work could be drawn, as well as take into consideration architectural constraints. LeWitt embraced the plural nature his wall drawing instructions could evoke, saying,

> The physical properties of the wall, height, length, color, material, and architectural conditions and intrusions, are a necessary part of the wall drawings.... Imperfections of the wall surface are occasionally apparent after the drawing is completed. These should be considered a part of the wall drawing.... Most walls have holes, cracks, bumps, grease marks, are not level or square and have various architectural eccentricities.[51]

This ethos of ungraspability, working with the grain of contingency and openness to multiple "albums of sketches," allowed LeWitt to view the "boundary between the work and the world [as] both porous and highly contingent."[52] This same ungraspability allows for an overflow of meaning and meaningful responses that pressure totalizing images into a form of desirous-seeing therapy—that is, towards a "gaze of love." As Carnes' Wittgensteinian iconoclasm points out, "When we are overly captivated by an image . . . further images, further interpretations can release us from our thrall without squelching desire."[53] Thus, learning to see through a gaze of love can emancipate one to the kind of intimacy with an-other that is in the pursuit of driving onward in love, to use the words of Maximus the Confessor, "until it is wholly present in the whole beloved."[54]

In the final analysis, I have foregrounded intriguing points of departure between an artistic sensibility little studied to date in the circles of Christian theology and philosophy of religion. We have begun to see how LeWitt's so-called conceptual mysticism possesses fecund insight for Christian reflection concerning desirous seeing. With the aid of Carnes' taxonomy regarding an "erotics of sight," a "gaze of love," and a "Wittgensteinian iconoclasm" that reflects upon a multiple album of images and interpretations, we have witnessed how one might begin to see inroads into certain artistic sensibilities that at first seem antithetical to Christian theological contemplation.[55]

Notes

1 Frank Stella's dogmatic proposal that seemingly forecloses imaginative interpretation was made famous in a 1966 Q & A with Bruce Glaser, later edited by Lucy Lippard. Stella would later amend this dogmatic formulation. For the context of this interview as well as a perspicacious commentary on what was at issue and what was at stake for those involved, see James Meyer, *Minimalism: Art and Polemics in the Sixties* (New Haven, CT: Yale University Press, 2001), 87–93.
2 Meyer, *Minimalism,* 6–7.
3 Robert Morris, "Three Folds in the Fabric and Four Autobiographical Asides as Allegories (or Interruptions)," *Art in America* 77, no. 11 (November 1989): 144.
4 Thomas Crow, *Modern Art in the Common Culture* (New Haven, CT: Yale University Press, 1998), 258n31.
5 Jonathan Anderson, "The (In)visibility of Theology in Contemporary Art Criticism," in *Christian Scholarship in the Twenty-First Century: Prospects and Perils*, ed. Thomas M. Crisp, Steve L. Porter, and Gregg Ten Elshof (Grand Rapids, MI: Wm. B. Eerdmans Publishing Company, 2014), 68. The first two canopies Anderson considers are, first, contemporary artworks made with religious references in their very form, and, second, artworks made by those of religious faith. Anderson rightly considers the third way

the most precarious, stating later in the essay, "We must recognize that theological interpretations are extremely prone to being thin and reductive." Ibid., 72.

6   As alluded to before, this paper focuses on LeWitt's work and places it in conversation with elements of Christian theological thought. Space disallows me from examining here LeWitt as a distinctly Jewish artist, a path that possesses rich veins worth mining, especially given LeWitt's later work for the Congregation Beth Shalom Rodfe Zedek.

7   For acute discussion on the gaze and its various uses in different disciplines, see Marita Sturken and Lisa Cartwright, *Practices of Looking: An Introduction to Visual Culture* (Oxford: Oxford University Press, 2001).

8   Thomas Pfau, "Varieties of Nonpropositional Knowledge: Image, Attention, Action," in *Judgment and Action: Fragments toward a History,* ed. Vivasvan Soni and Thomas Pfau (Evanston, IL: Northwestern University Press, 2018), 280.

9   Ola Sigurdson, *Heavenly Bodies: Incarnation, the Gaze, and Embodiment in Christian Theology,* trans. Carl Olsen (Grand Rapids, MI: Wm. B. Eerdmans Publishing Company, 2016), 171.

10 Meyer, *Minimalism*, 205.

11 Meyer, *Minimalism*, 108. Meyer points out LeWitt's maxim that "what the work looks like isn't too important" to be a "direct challenge to Donald Judd's purely visual aesthetic," as well as to the aesthetic of others, Ibid., 208.

12 Meyer, *Minimalism*, 205.

13 Annette Michelson and Rosalind Krauss, quoted in Meyer, *Minimalism,* 206.

14 Hal Foster, "The Crux of Minimalism," in *Individuals: A Selected History of Contemporary Art 1945–86,* ed. Howard Singerman (Los Angeles, CA: Museum of Contemporary Art, 1986), 162. Furthermore, LeWitt's contribution "to the aesthetic implications of minimalism" was by "examining the differences between conceptual modes of information and the paradoxical changes, permutations, and disorder that occur when a priori intentions are converted into concrete images or objects"; thus, "attend[ing] to the gaps between perception, description, and representation." Kristine Stiles, "Language and Concepts," in *Theories and Documents of Contemporary Art: A Sourcebook of Artists' Writings,* ed. Kristine Stiles and Peter Selz, 2d ed. (Berkeley, CA: University of California Press, 2012), 957.

15 LeWitt, "Paragraphs on Conceptual Art," in *Theories and Documents of Contemporary Art: A Sourcebook of Artists' Writings*, ed. Kristine Stiles and Peter Selz, 2d ed. (Berkeley, CA: University of California Press, 2012), 989.

16 LeWitt, "Paragraphs on Conceptual Art, 989 and 987.

17 Many thanks to Jonathan Anderson for helping me think through this line of thought.

18 Charles Haxthausen, "Thinking About Wall Drawings: Four Notes on Sol LeWitt," *Australian and New Zealand Journal of Art* 14, no. 1 (2014): 42. Furthermore, Kirsten Swenson helpfully points out that LeWitt's œuvre "implied a new agency for the viewer and belief in the primacy of subjective experience and judgment...[which insists] on open-endedness and ambiguity... and embraced the uncertainty and flux of perception," *Irrational Judgments: Eva Hesse, Sol LeWitt, and 1960's New York* (New Haven, CT: Yale University Press, 2015), 9. One could interpret "the primacy of subjective experience" as an embrace of a rather lazy aesthetic relativity, but this need not be the *only* reading. It at least signifies aptly how LeWitt's works complicate any totalizing gaze, especially the seeing of art that tends to baffle immediate impressions.

19 Sol LeWitt, "Sentences on Conceptual Art," in *Art in Theory: 1900–2000: An Anthology of Changing Ideas,* ed. Charles Harrison and Paul Wood (Oxford: Blackwell Publishing, 2002), 849. By "mystic," LeWitt clearly does not have in mind the rich mystical heritage

of certain strands of Christian experience and contemplation (or, if he does, he does not elucidate upon it). However, this should not render his thought here in relation to Christian discourse moot. Instead, it is more interesting to pursue why and how he chose this word instead of another.

20 Sergius Bulgakov, *Unfading Light: Contemplations and Speculations,* trans. Thomas Allan Smith (Grand Rapids, MI: Wm. B. Eerdmans Publishing Company, 2012), 396. Emphasis added.
21 LeWitt, "Paragraphs," 989.
22 Meyer, *Minimalism,* 208 and 108. Meyer argues, "LeWitt found [Judd's] empirical faith problematic," and thus started "to produce an art that troubled vision," 208.
23 Paul Ricoeur, "The Question of the Subject: The Challenge of Semiology," in *The Conflict of Interpretation: Essays in Hermeneutics,* trans. Kathleen McLaughlin (London: Continuum, 2004), 232.
24 Meyer, *Minimalism,* 266. To anticipate our turn to theological sources below, Rowan Williams similarly, although in a different idiom, elucidates, "if we think of the essential hiddenness that the image reminds us of, we must not suppose that being aware of that presence will necessarily make it easier for us to pin down where it is." Rowan Williams, *Ponder These Things: Praying with Icons of the Virgin* (Franklin, WI: Sheed and Ward, 2002), 49.
25 LeWitt, "Paragraphs," 987 and 989, emphasis added.
26 Meyer, *Minimalism,* 205.
27 My assertion is somewhat of a corollary to Haxthausen, who writes something similar concerning LeWitt's view of subjectivity: "LeWitt did not deny that subjectivity enters into the artwork, yet now it has a different, more modest status in its economy." Haxthausen, "Thinking About Wall Drawings," 46. Rye Dag Holmboe agrees: "Rather than eclipse subjectivity *tout court,* then, it would be more accurate to say that LeWitt's work reconfigured what the subject of Conceptual art might look like." Rye Dag Holmboe, "LeWitt, in the Shadow of the Object," *October,* no. 166 (Fall 2018): 116.
28 LeWitt quoted in Swenson, *Irrational Judgments,* 99.
29 Stephen Mulhall, *The Great Riddle: Wittgenstein and Nonsense, Theology, and Philosophy* (Oxford: Oxford University Press, 2015), 59–60. Emphasis original.
30 LeWitt, "Sentences," 992.
31 Susannah Singer, quoted in Haxthausen, "Thinking About Wall Drawings," 55n14.
32 Sol LeWitt, "Doing Wall Drawings" (1971), Artifex Press, accessed September 9, 2020, https://www-artifexpress-com.proxy.libraries.smu.edu/catalogues/sol-lewitt-wall-drawings/artist/info-pages/5edf9ad9ba92dc1c011b4106. This is in part how some interpret LeWitt's so-called "conceptual mysticism." "By imposing strict limits," Haxthausen argues, "by embracing simplicity, one achieves infinite variety and richness." Furthermore, "this mystical faith of LeWitt as relating to his principled acceptance of contingency, of the unforeseeable in the realization of his ideas." Haxthausen, "Thinking About Wall Drawings," 53–54. Thus, an embrace of ambiguity, contingency, paradox, and perhaps irrationality characterizes the kind of chastened vision I am arguing that LeWitt's work imbibes.
33 Rowan Williams, "Creation, Creativity, and Creatureliness: The Wisdom of Finite Existence," in *Being-in-Creation: Human Responsibility in an Endangered World,* ed. Brian Treanor, Bruce Ellis Benson, and Norman Wirzba (New York: Fordham University Press, 2015), 29.
34 Natalie Carnes, *Beauty: A Theological Engagement with Gregory of Nyssa* (Eugene, OR: Cascade Books, 2014), 246.

35 Natalie Carnes, *Image and Presence: A Christological Reflection on Iconoclasm and Iconophilia* (Stanford, CA: Stanford University Press, 2018), 27.
36 Carnes, *Image and Presence*, 24.
37 Carnes, *Image and Presence*, 48–49. Carnes is clearly not arguing that all forms of "consumption" are unfaithful—this would be nonsense if one considers quotidian activities such as eating.
38 Carnes, *Image and Presence*, 49.
39 Austin Farrer, *Reflective Faith: Essays in Philosophical Theology,* ed. Charles Conti (London: Society for Promoting Christian Knowledge, 1972), 37. Emphasis mine.
40 Maximos Constas, *The Art of Seeing: Paradox and Perception in Orthodox Iconography* (Alhambra, CA: Sebastian Press, 2014), 31–32.
41 Pfau, "Varieties of Nonpropositional Knowledge," 285. Emphasis original. Constas believes that a refinement of perception—what I would call a faithful form of desirous seeing—involves attending to and "accept[ing] what is given just as it offers itself to us." This could be described, as it were, as *the first look* of a kind of faithful desirous seeing: dwelling with what gives itself to be known before moving to alter it, to cultivate it at best, or to employ machinations of violent control at worst. To do this requires the abandonment of "old ways of seeing," a disciplining away from "habituated ways of seeing" and "summon[ing] the eye to a new mode of vision." For Constas, as it was so heavily practiced by LeWitt, the key to this new mode of vision is to accept "the positive role played by paradox and contradiction in the deepening of perception." Constas, *The Art of Seeing*, 16, 22, and 27, respectively.
42 Iris Murdoch, *The Sovereignty of the Good* (New York, NY: Routledge, 1971), 33.
43 Much care is needed here. Carnes is not arguing for the same "two-node network" that she critiques in her first work, *Beauty*. Instead, these two kinds of gazes must be read within the slipperiness of desirous seeing: as perhaps two poles of a continuum that we must navigate constantly and of which we never quite reach the end. Thus, as Carnes is at pains to make plain (as is Constas), each of us needs our vision disciplined towards faithfulness and love.
44 Carnes, *Image and Presence,* 176. Concerning the gaze of love, Farrer contends something similar: "It comes from the appreciation of things which we have when we love them and fill our minds and senses with them, and feel something of the silent force and great mystery of their existence." Farrer, *Reflective Faith,* 38.
45 Carnes, *Image and Presence*, 176.
46 Murdoch, *The Sovereignty of the Good*, 82 and 65. Another philosopher concerned with how human creatures direct their attention to an-other, resisting the temptation to live a hermetically sealed individual existence, is Vladimir Solovyov, who warns of how we are so easily ensnared into what Charles Taylor would later describe as a kind of "buffered self": "We are locked in ourselves, impenetrable for the 'other,' and therefore, the other, in turn, is impenetrable for us." Vladimir Solovyov, *Lectures on Divine Humanity,* trans. Peter Zouboff, rev. and ed. Boris Jakim (Hudson, NY: Lindisfarne Press, 1995), 122.
47 Carnes, *Image and Presence*, 158.
48 Carnes, *Image and Presence*, 165.
49 See Holmboe, "LeWitt, in the Shadow of the Object," 111.
50 I have in mind here, although they are of course not univocal, David Bentley Hart's imaginative description of "allegory" as "reciprocal poiesis," in David Bentley Hart, *The Beauty of the Infinite: The Aesthetics of Christian Truth* (Grand Rapids, MI: Wm. B. Eerdmans Publishing Company, 2003), 284n143.

51 Sol LeWitt, "Wall Drawings" (1970/1978), Artifex Press, accessed September 9, 2020, https://www-artifexpress-com.proxy.libraries.smu.edu/catalogues/sol-lewitt-wall-drawings/artist/info-pages/5edf9998ba92dc1b6f1b4107. The generative connections between LeWitt's conceptualist instructions and music—particularly classical music, for which LeWitt possessed an enduring love—are ripe for discussion. As Haxthausen points out, "LeWitt repeatedly compared the wall drawing process to musical composition and performance and was fond of comparing his written instructions for the wall drawings to a 'musical score,' and himself to a 'composer.'" Haxthausen, "Thinking about Wall Drawings," 47.

52 Holmboe, "LeWitt, in the Shadow of the Object," 114.

53 Carnes, *Image and Presence,* 162–63.

54 Maximos the Confessor, *On Difficulties in the Church Fathers, The Ambigua,* trans. Nicholas Constas (Cambridge: Harvard University Press, 2014), 1073C-D, p. 87.

55 Thanks to Celeste Jean, Tim Basselin, Jonathan Anderson, Steve Long, Chris Dortch, Garrett Flatt, Christina Carnes Ananias, Bo Helmich, Natalie Carnes, Jeremy Begbie, Trevor Hart, Janet Soskice, Matthew Milliner, and Thomas Pfau for their helpful insights and suggestions throughout the development of this project.

Bibliography

Anderson, Jonathan. "The (In)visibility of Theology in Contemporary Art Criticism." In *Christian Scholarship in the Twenty-First Century: Prospects and Perils*, edited by Thomas M. Crisp, Steve L. Porter, and Gregg Ten Elshof, 53–79. Grand Rapids, MI: Wm. B. Eerdmans Publishing Company, 2014.

Bulgakov, Sergius. *Unfading Light: Contemplations and Speculations.* Translated by Thomas Allan Smith. Grand Rapids, MI: Wm. B. Eerdmans Publishing Company, 2012.

Carnes, Natalie. *Beauty: A Theological Engagements with Gregory of Nyssa*. Eugene, OR: Cascade Books, 2014.

Carnes, Natalie. *Image and Presence: A Christological Reflection on Iconoclasm and Iconophilia*. Stanford: Stanford University Press, 2018.

Constas, Maximos. *The Art of Seeing: Paradox and Perception in Orthodox Iconography*. Alhambra, CA: Sebastian Press, 2014.

Crow, Thomas. *Modern Art in the Common Culture*. New Haven, CT: Yale University Press, 1998.

Farrer, Austin. *Reflective Faith: Essays in Philosophical Theology*. Edited by Charles Conti. London: Society for Promoting Christian Knowledge, 1972.

Foster, Hal. "The Crux of Minimalism." In *Individuals: A Selected History of Contemporary Art, 1945–86*, edited by Howard Singerman, 35–68. Los Angeles, CA: Museum of Contemporary Art, 1986.

Hart, David Bentley. *The Beauty of the Infinite: The Aesthetics of Christian Truth*. Grand Rapids, MI: Wm. B. Eerdmans Publishing Company, 2003.

Haxthausen, Charles. "Thinking About Wall Drawings: Four Notes on Sol LeWitt," *Australian and New Zealand Journal of Art* 14, no. 1 (2014), 42–57.

Holmboe, Rye Dag. "LeWitt, in the Shadow of the Object." *October* 166 (Fall 2018): 105–26.

LeWitt, Sol. "Doing Wall Drawings." Artifex Press. https://www-artifexpress-com.proxy.libraries.smu.edu/catalogues/sol-lewitt-wall-drawings/artist/info-pages/5edf9ad9ba92dc1c011b4106 Accessed September 9, 2020.

LeWitt, Sol. "Paragraphs on Conceptual Art." In *Theories and Documents of Contemporary Art: A Sourcebook of Artists' Writings*, edited by Kristine Stiles and Peter Selz, 2d ed., 987–91. Berkeley, CA: University of California Press, 2012.

LeWitt, Sol. "Sentences on Conceptual Art." In *Art in Theory: 1900–2000: An Anthology of Changing Ideas*, edited by Charles Harrison and Paul Wood, 000–000. Oxford: Blackwell Publishing, 2002.

Maximos the Confessor, *On Difficulties in the Church Fathers, The Ambigua,* trans. Nicholas Constas (Cambridge: Harvard University Press, 2014).

Meyer, James. *Minimalism: Art and Polemics in the Sixties*. New Haven, CT: Yale University Press, 2001.

Morris, Robert. "Three Folds in the Fabric and Four Autobiographical asides as Allegories (or Interruptions)." *Art in America* 77, no. 11 (November 1989): 142–51.

Mulhall, Stephen. *The Great Riddle: Wittgenstein and Nonsense, Theology, and Philosophy*. Oxford: Oxford University Press, 2015.

Murdoch, Iris. *The Sovereignty of the Good*. New York: Routledge, 1971.

Pfau, Thomas. "Varieties of Nonpropositional Knowledge: Image, Attention, Action." In *Judgment and Action: Fragments toward a History*, edited by Vivasvan Soni and Thomas Pfau, 269–301. Evanston, IL: Northwestern University Press, 2018.

Ricoeur, Paul. "The Question of the Subject: The Challenge of Semiology." In *The Conflict of Interpretation: Essays in Hermeneutics*, translated by Kathleen McLaughlin, 232–62.

Sigurdson, Ola. *Heavenly Bodies: Incarnation, the Gaze, and Embodiment in Christian Theology*. Translated by Carl Olsen. Grand Rapids, MI: Wm. B. Eerdmans Publishing Company, 2016.

Solovyov, Vladimir. *Lectures on Divine Humanity*. Translated by Peter Zouboff, revised and edited by Boris Jakim. Hudson, NY: Lindisfarne Press, 1995.

Stiles, Kristine. "Language and Concepts." In *Theories and Documents of Contemporary Art: A Sourcebook of Artists' Writings*, edited by Kristine Stiles and Peter Selz, 2d ed, 955–70. Berkeley, CA: University of California Press, 2012.

Sturken, Marita and Lisa Cartwright. *Practices of Looking: An Introduction to Visual Culture*. Oxford: Oxford University Press, 2001.

Swenson, Kirsten. *Irrational Judgments: Eva Hesse, Sol LeWitt, and 1960's New York*. New Haven, CT: Yale University Press, 2015.

Williams, Rowan. "Creation, Creativity, and Creatureliness: The Wisdom of Finite Existence." In *Being-in-Creation: Human Responsibility in an Endangered World*, edited by Brian Treanor, Bruce Ellis Benson, and Norman Wirzba, 23–36. New York: Fordham University Press, 2015.

5

Memory and Desire for God in Terrence Malick's *To the Wonder*

Jake Grefenstette

Introduction: *Anamnesis*

Terrence Malick's *To the Wonder* (2012) comprises parallel narratives: one arc follows a priest in a crisis of divine silence, the other the disintegration of a love affair.[1] These respective Bernanos- and Bergmanesque stories have robust literary and cinematic precedents; the film's categoric uniqueness lies in the emergent onus to identify points of intersection of two familiar tales. The most serious engagements to date have posited transcendence or love as key to *Wonder*'s cipher. David Calhoun, for instance, advances a transcendent inheritance surveyed from Plato via Kierkegaard;[2] Julie Hamilton construes the film as a phenomenology of love;[3] Roger Ebert, in the final review before his death, formulates the priest's relationship to Christ as, analogously, that of "a sort of former lover."[4] Alongside these productive currents, this essay argues that *Wonder*'s two arcs are commensurated by a mutual preoccupation with memory. I accordingly explore *Wonder*'s treatment of memory, specifically the memory of vocational security (marital and sacerdotal) symbolized in the image of Mont-Saint-Michel Abbey. In assuming this emphasis, we see that as much as *The Tree of Life* (2011) wields memory to promote a theology of grace, *To the Wonder* interrogates Platonic images of desire in service of a functionally Augustinian theology of memory. In this interrogation, Terrence Malick's *To the Wonder* comes into focus as a film that does its own form-specific phenomenological work: it is a filmic description of *what it is like* to find love, to forget love, to struggle to recover the memory of love and love's divine grounding. After exploring various phenomenological approaches to memory and their consequences in married life and the priesthood, Malick's *Wonder* stages an ultimate conversion from a Platonic to an Augustinian conception of memory.

Beginning with a poetic prelude on *anamnesis*, *To the Wonder* lays the theological groundwork for the rest of the film's treatment of memory. "Newborn," begins a voice, "I open my eyes." This first only to darkness, but then: "A spark. I fall into the flame." Every facet of *Wonder*'s opening sequence is an intertextual representation of memory as a mode of return. The spark-flame image conjures Empedoclean, Stoic-Christian, and Platonic-Christian genealogies; among these, the film's (often verbatim) Platonic intertexts suggest an anamnestic self-universe relationship iterated in dialogues like the *Philebus*.[5] Over an expository montage of the film's lovers, Hanan Townshend's score functions as a kind of musical recollection, as the opening "Awareness"—a flurry of open fifths on strings and woodwinds—enacts a literal return to the standard notes of pre-concert orchestral tuning.[6] Following this visual and auditory "tune up," the yet unidentified lovers approach Mont-Saint-Michel.[7] Townshend's music proceeds on orchestral logic as the pre-act tuning dissolves into the first prelude of *Parsifal*. The score thus accords with the mnemonic theme: Malick here imbeds an intertext which introduces Wagner's *Namenlose*, "nameless one," a hero who struggles to recall his provenance.

Beyond merely taking memory as the musical and intertextual subject, *Wonder*'s opening presents itself as an audio-visual approximation of memory. Following Jean-Luc Godard and other New Wave precursors, Townshend's music is fittingly fragmentary: as in films like Godard's *Le Mépris* (1963), *Wonder*'s ethereal score tends alternatively towards indistinction or else reiterated motifs. Emulating memory, minute audio and visual fragments recur in both music and jump-repeat shots. Orchestral music is diminished to minimal harmonies on strings, evoking a nebulous sense of having heard the music somewhere before. On the visual front, the couple's ur-cinematic train journey is captured between 35mm film and a Super-8 emulator, which, in contrast to Emmanuel Lubeski's later sequences in "hyper-real" 65mm and "alienat[ing]" digital Red, appear (as the cinematographer describes them) contextually nostalgic.[8] From the very outset, *Wonder*'s plot is—significantly—challenging to follow, the object of its nostalgia obscure. In this difficulty, the audience must accord with the characters in reconstructing action through imported memories of known romance archetypes. From these early moments of exposition, *Wonder* makes clear that it does not comprise a linear love story; it rather suggests a story that is remembered by means of return, of coming continually into being.

If Malick's slogan of a film about "radiant zig-zag becoming" seems initially obstruse, the first minutes of *Wonder* triumph as experiential disambiguation.[9] By these filmic mechanisms, *Wonder* is staged as a kind of phenomenological record of memory that encourages reflection upon the very experience of film viewership. The cinematography, the score, the characteristically oblique character interactions—all these contribute to Malick's sense of *what it is like* to recollect love's origins. The obliqueness of its telling requires the audience to import cinematic and real-life precedents to render the story sensible, thus posing to the audience the same question posed to the characters: what grounds the memory of this love? Or, following Malick's Augustinian, trans-*œuvre* questions: where does this love come from? And what is this love? This first turn of *Wonder*'s narrative, framed thusly as a mnemonic prelude together with its *Parsifal* backing, finds the film's two lovers, Neil (Ben Affleck) and Marina (Olga Kurylenko) face-to-face with a theological answer to these questions. Literally inhabiting "The Wonder" or "The Marvel" (the famous "*la Merveille*" building of Mont-Saint-Michel Abbey), the two experience rightly ordered love in a place of vocational security. In the abbey desire and memory accord, and love of lover discloses divine love. It is here that Marina speaks the title of the film—climbing the steps *à la Merveille*, "to the Wonder"—suggesting, propositionally, a movement towards, a continual becoming towards God.

After this early episode of ascent, however, Malick's film changes focus to the experience of coming down the mountain: *Wonder* is henceforth structured as an inverted romance, narrativizing movement *from* this early nexus of human and divine love. After the couple descends the abbey to Perelandran syzygy tides below, the action of the film unfolds along character intentionalities towards the memory of their experience of the divine.[10] As in the *Philebus*, where memory "provides the impulse towards the objects of desire," Neil and Marina's future relationship flourishes only when oriented to *la merveille* as a thing both past and phenomenally present in memory.[11] In this way, the story of the film—as with all love stories before it—remains that of the journey *à la merveille*, to the origin of things, even in chronological subsequence.

On this formulation, Malick's opening sequence establishes the theological stakes of the relationship between desire and memory. Either memory and the desire it founds are enduringly present, as in Augustine; or else memory is something ephemeral, subject to Cartesian doubt, and Affleck's Neil (with Socrates' interlocutor in the *Philebus*) is within his rights to shore up extra-marital pleasure against oblivion.[12] Similar to the grace-nature dyad sustained by the parents in *Tree of Life*, Marina and Neil come to inhabit respective advocacies for the memory and pleasure pitted against each other in the *Philebus* and, in turn, in Augustine.[13] As with *Tree of Life*, this formulation is neither reductive nor narratively deterministic. As we will see, the core relationship is staged in conversation with a Catholic priest's vocationally parallel crisis of faith in order to synthesize a Christian appropriation of these Platonic themes. On top of this task, Malick's highly medium-conscious film implicates the role of cinema as a means to communicate and function as an analogous mode of memory. Malick's film thus enacts the specifically Augustinian strategy of theologizing art in light of a Christian phenomenology of memory and desire for God.

Augustine on Silence and "Words from the Soul"

Coming down from *la merveille*, language falters. This is a familiar phenomenon in Malick. The trajectory of *Thin Red Line* (1998) to *Hidden Life* (2019) charts a decrease in dialogue in favor of visual argument.[14] As with Maurice Merleau-Ponty, Malick privileges the aesthetic experience of the eye.[15] In *Wonder*, the most notable manifestation of an adjective-generating "Malickean" visual style is the ballet-like choreography of Olga Kurylenko. As an expression of Augustine's "silent words," *Wonder*'s balletic form invokes traditions of cosmic dance or the Psalmist's commission to "praise his name with dancing" (Psalm 149:3). It is also highly self-conscious of the medium in which it is presented. Across the couple's relocation from syzygy tides in France to the crop fields of Oklahoma, Marina's dance is always conducted with deference to camera position. As in the "eye" of memory, Malick's subjects are mindful of the viewer. In this dance, Marina frequently crosses the camera's line of sight on Neil, invoking a Bergmanian overlap of lovers. Here, however, Malick is concerned rather with the phenomenological and sacramental constitution of two lovers as one body.[16] Accordingly, at the end of their visit to *la Merveille*, Marina says in voiceover, "Love makes us one. Two. One." Marina's "words from the soul" (that is, the voiceover's frequent function in the film),[17] alongside her balletic enactment of this relationality, suggests an Aristophanic model of love, a model divinely inflected in the context of the priest Quintana's intermezzo sermons on the one body of Christ (see Mark 10:8 and Rom. 12:5).[18]

Following this symposiac formulation, Marina's desire for her lover turns to desire for the divine.[19] In a moment of reflection, Marina discovers her love is ordered differently than it was at the abbey. After the ecstatic Merveille prelude and a long period of diegetic silence, we find Marina's daughter (of her former marriage) suddenly interrogating her mother over her unhappiness. If the film's pacing has confused some critics, this rhythmic jar is a prime suspect. And there is indeed a temptation to interpret the transition from the joy of Mont-Saint-Michel to this sudden suggestion of unhappiness as a kind of bathos. As later encounters with Quintana suggest, however, Marina's paradoxical nadir springs from an unanticipated desire for the divine in the midst of her experience of erotic love: the realized both-two-and-oneness in her relationship with Neil divulges a sense of insufficiency in a mere binitarian construal of their relationship. Marina's memory of an "unspoken word" alongside her sense of lack within the supposed fulfillment of erotic desire points her towards a third term. As in Paweł Pawlikowski's 2013 film *Ida* (another affair framed, in a sense, by a monastery), there is an eschatological question imbedded in the romance: "What's next?"

Returning to Neil's native Oklahoma, the household replaces the monastery as the principal arena for *Wonder*'s interrogation of this desire. Here, Malick (more than any director besides Bergman or Cassavetes) attends to the experiential exactitudes of marriage. *Wonder* in particular draws attention to an iceberglike reality of relationships generally: that, however much dialogue transpires between two persons, an overwhelming fraction of domestic relationships occur in the private arena of the mind. Further, Malick follows Bergman in demonstrating that these internal schemata require points of contact to remain correspondingly oriented; otherwise, two distinct and rival conceptions of the relationship can develop in tandem. This is the danger for Neil and Marina, who are almost never seen speaking to each other. The middle of *Wonder* explores the experience of this interpersonal unknowing in the light of their faith (or lack thereof) in the memory of their love's certainty in France—an increasingly disparate memory for each.

As ever significant to his argument, *To the Wonder*'s theological dialectic is staged by Malick laconically. Amongst the director's thin-scripted corpus, *Wonder* has the most to do with silence. Lead Olga Kurylenko even notes to interviewers that her audition for the role was conducted in silence.[20] When Roger Ebert writes that "essentially this could be a silent film," he is not far off.[21] Although Ebert's "silent film" remark is posed neutrally, the critic's consideration of silence elsewhere in the review—particularly with respect to Neil—suggests deficiency. "As the film opened," Ebert writes, "I wondered if I was missing something."[22]

Against this line, I argue that the film's several detractors are misguided in treating all Malick's silences equally. Importing two kinds of silence suggested in *Confessions*, we may posit with Augustine's help that Ebert's "something missing" is a filmic grammar of silence.[23] The saint's first silence, described *ex negativo* at the outset of *Book X*, is an utter silence, a kind of doubt where epistemological mires about the knowability of the self inhibit even the effort of speech. As with Plato, Augustine views this silence unfavorably, accepting no excuse for eschewing the pursuit of self-knowledge and its origins. Versus this inertially silent, memory-doubting state, Augustine names a "hope" in scriptural self-revelation (1 Cor. 13:12; Eph. 5:27) as well as the "desire" to "do the truth" that motives his literary effort: "that is why I speak."[24]

So, we have one silence-speech dyad where silence is something unfavorable. Against this disordered silence of the spirit, though, Augustine differentiates a holy silence, one that ostends only physically. On the model of this silence, the saint's confessions proceed not "by [auditory] words or sounds, but by words from my soul and a cry from my mind."[25] Since the two relationships in the film—Marina and Neil; Father Quintana and his parish—make sparse use of speech, Malick employs other cinematic tools to convey presence or lack, to convey Augustine's "words from the soul" beneath the physical silence of the players.[26] If, as for Ebert, "something" is still "missing" in interactions between characters, this is precisely the point: the lack mirrors and refabricates the human experience of mental inscrutability. For Marina and Neil, as well as for the audience in relation to them, the leap to supply a "something" to their silence requires an act of faith. Referring always back to the image of *la merveille*, Neil and Marina's marital happiness hinges on the reality or ephemerality of love remembered.

Forgetting the Wonder: Ephemeral Memory

Notwithstanding occasional glimpses and moments of recollection of their memory of wonder, *Wonder*'s Neil-Marina arc is from this point framed as a failure; it proceeds on the tragic, disintegrative register of precursor films like Bergman's *The Passion of Anna* (1969). Despite Marina's desire to trace her memory to its *telos*, a desire vocationally actioned in efforts to annul, remarry, and start a family, Neil remains doubly silent, doubting his memory of Marina's love the moment he encounters a former lover.[27] If Kurylenko's character appears to obey gravity by courtesy, Affleck's Neil is comparatively stolid. Critics have not been entirely kind to this latter role; Affleck himself acknowledged a challenge in committing to the part on the level of his co-lead.[28] David Denby writes, "Perversely, Malick has drained Affleck of vitality. He comes alive only in sex scenes."[29] Against this take, this chapter's thesis suggests that Neil's pursuit of pleasure and tenuous grasp of identity is precisely appropriate to his memory-doubting character. For, according to Augustine, those who "hear about themselves" from God "could not say 'the Lord is lying.'"[30] Though Neil and Marina have heard this voice of God in France, Malick makes clear the theological stakes of phenomenological approaches to the memory of that speech: either the memory of God's voice at Merveille is experienced as a thing eternal, an indelible part of oneself in one's relation to it; or else one tricks oneself into the solipsistic conception of memory of the lesser man in the *Phaedrus*.[31] Even if Neil heard, per Augustine, his "true self" at Mont-Saint-Michel, his spiritual future falters on attitudes towards the residual phenomenon of that voice. His relationship fails as many do: in doubting memory as a kind of oblivion, in doubting whether one has loved at all.

As a perverse consequence of the intersubjective "I in you, you in me" coherence of their marital union, Neil's silent denial of memory comes to infect his partner. Although

Marina usually embodies a position of faith, her lapses turn on doubts of the eternal grounds of memory and, correspondingly, of art. This dynamic of doubt unfolds midway through the film as Marina digests her husband's as-yet unrealized proclivity for infidelity. Watching Neil watch another woman at a swimming pool, her voiceover murmurs, "I write on water . . . what I dare not say." The paired shot of Marina tracing fingers through water is intertextually laden. We have, on one hand, classical connotations of futility invoked in Keats' epitaph or Aquinas' apocryphal dismissal of the *Summa*; on the other, the image of Christ writing on sand. This cryptic comment, however, is best understood through the Platonic-Augustinian vein on art and memory established from the film's inception. Looking to the *Phaedrus*, Socrates speaks against words *en ýdati grápsei* (ἐν ὕδατι γράψει), or "written in water."[32] In Plato's example, these denote deliberately transient words which sum to "pleasure" and "amusement," hoarded "pastimes" or "memorials," an inferior kind of memory shored up "against . . . the forgetfulness of old age."[33] This image is reiterated through Epicurean traditions instantiated in works like Byron's *Don Juan*, where poetry is written "upon the stream, / To swim or sink."[34]

The middle of *Wonder* in this way demonstrates the damage of Neil's unfaithfulness to the whole body of marriage. Neil's attitude towards memory is reminiscent of both Plato's lesser man and his heir in *Don Juan*. Like Plato's ephemeral "defenses" against old age, Neil accumulates extra-marital gratification to Don Juan's anti-eschatological end of making "some hour less dreary."[35] Seeing this, Marina's otherwise unwavering trust in her memory of *la merveille* warps in tandem. Absorbed in the possibility of a child in spite of her failing marriage, Marina flees Neil and seeks impregnation from a stranger. Accordingly, all outer signs of Marina's "words of the soul" fall silent in the spirit of her relegation of speech to water. Her dancing ceases; a potential paramour presents a stringed instrument which goes conspicuously unplayed. Malick's medium itself accords with this situation, fixing shots and minimalizing music. The pertinent sequence is one of phenomenological and psychological insight: it presents the world as it seems when love is lost.

Conversely, when Marina's faith finally recovers towards the end of the film, art comes back with it. Her dancing resumes at length; she cuts images out of art history textbooks, literalizing Augustine's mnemonic palace of "the treasures of innumerable images."[36] Her final dance of the film, a visual quotation of Caspar David Friedrich's *Frau vor untergehender Sonne* (1818), references a painting variously interpreted as an image of Christ, death, or a reified philosophical horizon.[37] The eschatological dance is scored, again, with *Parsifal*.[38] (While this reprise most immediately recalls Marina's experience at *la Merveille*, it equally imbeds a musical enactment of difference from her Platonic "newborn" origin: *Wonder* ends in A-flat major, the furthest possible key from the D minor of the film's opening "Awareness.")

Opposite Neil, Marina's spiritual amendment thus follows Augustine on Plato. Socrates, seeking an alternative to pleasure-driven "words written on water," hails the word which is "written on the soul of the hearer together with understanding," which can "distinguish between those it should address and those in whose presence it should be silent."[39] After describing a similarly graven "word" and "silence-as-word," Augustine acknowledges a writerly audience "conjoined with me in mortality" that extends, like memory, both backwards and forwards: he confesses for the ears of "some who have gone before, some who follow after, and some who are my companions in this life."[40] The words of the saint's confession, alongside the Christian faithful preceding him in death, are thought to participate in something beyond a water-writ mortality. Marina's spiritual convalescence—one that, with the film itself, resolves back on the image of Mont-Saint-Michel—follows this Augustinian recovery of the eternal in memory and art. This dialectic of presence and absence finally bears on the film medium itself, pointing at last to the endurance of wonder beyond the experience of the theater.

Father Quintana on Art and the Divine

Although *Wonder* may have conceivably ended here as a vacuumed account of Neil and Marina's love story, the secondary arc of Javier Bardem's Father Quintana introduces a further self-reflective layer to Malick's theological thesis. In terms of plot, Quintana merely doubles the Augustinian problem of the film. If not of Mont-Saint-Michel precisely, Quintana's spiritual crisis plays out in relation to his memory of a robust relationship with God held prior to his Oklahoman pastoral placement. Yet beyond this, Quintana textures the film as locus of metacinematic reflection. His role mediates ekphrases on film in general and, through his sermons, the specific case of Marina and Neil. Quintana's parish janitor, to the first point, iterates an edifying theory of art in a theologically inflected ekphrasis on the spiritually "warming" phenomenon of stained glass. In his sermons, Quintana functions as an analogous window to film history, one which in turn illuminates the situation of Marina and Neil. Quintana's significant contribution in the film is thus the emergent solution he stages: the reorientation of human desire for God through art.

Channeling Augustine, Quintana points us to the divine by way of art. At the most immediate level, Quintana is himself a literary/cinematic mnemonic for the grace-grappling priest. Quintana's precedents are patent, according almost exactly with Richard Rosengarten's category of literary Catholic priests who "prove transformative in spite of themselves."[41] Rosengarten enumerates Graham Greene's "whiskey priest," as well as "Ignazio Silone, J. F. Powers, Flannery O'Connor, Walker Percy, and Shūsaku Endō."[42] Malick's cinematic inheritance adds to the list Bergman's Tomas Ericsson, Maurice Pialat's controversial prophet of *Sous le soleil de Satan* (1987), and, most prominently, the country curate of Robert Bresson's *Diary of a Country Priest* (1951)— these last two reiterations from the novels of George Bernanos.

Quintana's unambiguous typification of this *tout est grâce* priest of film history is itself a kind of staging of film as memory.[43] Just as Marina's conversion turns on a recognition of the eternal conservation of *la merveille*, Quintana's empathetic participation in his predecessors' conversions demonstrates that art, as memory, can function as a nexus of desire for the divine. Marina remembers *la merveille*; Quintana "remembers" Bresson. Both memories point to the God that grounds them. It is in this way appropriate that Quintana's arc ends with a *tout est grâce* metanoia enacted through a prayer-poem—St. Patrick's Breastplate—which litanizes Christ's grounding of all relationality: "Christ beneath me, Christ above me."[44] Through a faithful, kenotic recitation, Quintana invokes and accords with his quotational catalogue of artistic predecessors. Incredibly, whereas Malick's filmic forebears from Soviet cinema (*Kino-Pravda*, Tarkovsky's *Nostalghia* [1983]) and *La Nouvelle Vague* traditions (Godard, Alain Resnais' "memory" trilogy, etc.) tend to privilege the destabilization of memory, *Wonder* repurposes French-Soviet editorial techniques to accomplish the opposite.[45] Jump cuts, ellipses, and autonomous camera movements from Quintana to prisoners and sick parishioners function together as a phenomenological protreptic, habituating the viewer to a charitable expansion of a world's horizon.

In his sermons, Quintana meanwhile confirms that the kenotic sacrifices of lovers and priests can be frustratingly undesirable for a fallen humanity.[46] "You shall love," Quintana tells the heedless couple, "whether you like it or not." Quintana's "like it or not" again implicates Augustine on desire for God. Augustine asks God, "When I love you, what do I love?"—questions *Tree of Life* and *To the Wonder* pose almost verbatim. *Wonder* points to the very answer Augustine proceeds to supply: it is not "limbs welcoming the embraces of the flesh," but a dutiful "bond of union that no satiety can part."[47] In this dialectic of memory and pleasure, Malick transitions from a quest of self-knowledge to a knowledge of oneself only in God. Tellingly, Malick's theatrical trailer ends with a quotation from Father Quintana's sermon on erotic desire in relation to the love of God: "Know each other," he says, "in that love that never changes." Quintana's Trinitarian qualification to the Platonic dictum is thus identical to Augustine's. "There is something of the human person," writes the saint, that, without God, "is unknown even to the 'spirit of man which is in him.'"[48]

Moving from the theatrical trailer to the film itself, the viewer may be surprised to find Quintana's resounding commission to "know each other" relegated to the background of *To the Wonder*'s soundscape. In general, in fact, Father Quintana's sermons are barely audible. And yet, this is no accident; like C. S. Lewis in *The Screwtape Letters*, Malick is attuned to the phenomenological peculiarities of homily. There is good theology to be had on Sundays—but, like the children of Auden's "Musée des Beaux Arts," neither Neil nor Quintana particularly want to put their ears in the way of it just yet. As with Neil and Marina, Quintana's spiritual inertia turns on his attitude to experience, memory, and intentionality: "Everywhere you're present. And still I can't see you. You're within me. Around me. And I have no experience of you. Not as I once did."[49] Following Augustine, it is only through a cognate faith in memory—trusting one's love of God "as [one] once" had—that Quintana is able to grasp the very claim he qualifies: "Everywhere you're present."

Conclusion: A Phenomenological Context

In this chapter, we have seen how Platonic images of memory and desire in *To the Wonder* are Christianized in an explicitly Augustinian fashion. I conclude by briefly applying this thesis to some contextually relevant film theory. Commenting on Malick's Heideggerian background[50] alongside the phenomenological accomplishment of *Days of Heaven* (1978), Stanley Cavell argues that, through Heidegger, Malick has discovered how to acknowledge ... a fundamental fact of film's photographic basis: that objects participate in the photographic presence of themselves; they participate in the re-creation of themselves on film; they are essential in the making of their appearances. Objects projected on a screen are inherently reflexive, they occur as self-referential, reflecting upon their physical origins.[51]

For Cavell, this phenomenological "solution" to an epistemological, Hamletian art-life problem comes at a price. Relative to film objects "capable of such self-manifestation," Cavell is wary that "human beings" may be "reduced in significance," or otherwise "crushed by the fact of beauty left vacant."[52] Through this posited "self-manifestation" and the consequent "aestheticizing" force of cinema, Cavell thus functionally echoes a Thomistic objection to the idea that objects are "conserved in being" by God. That is, many objects appear to be grounded by their own being and thus "by their very nature cannot not-be."[53] As in Thomas' objection, Cavell's fear of "human reduction" comes from the functional divinization of art: that art (or, analogously, memory) may seem to autonomously sustain that which it re-presents. As Cavell demonstrates, this is a dangerous claim for both the philosopher and the saint.

While a plurality of critics interprets Malick with authoritative deference to Heidegger or Kierkegaard or Merleau-Ponty, I argue that we should equally privilege Malick's œuvre as something which does form-specific phenomenological work itself.[54] Such treatment of Malick in an irreducibly hyphenated capacity as filmmaker-theologian brings to light theological solutions embedded in Malick's own Heideggerian staging. For, as we have seen, the view of art pervasive in *To the Wonder* follows Thomas and Augustine: art's "potentiality to not-being" falls not to things created, but to divine conservation.[55] As Quintana makes repeatedly clear, if Neil and Marina's memories of wonder are to accord and persist in rightly order love, it is only on the basis of a shared conservation in God. Malick's approach to memory in *Wonder* thus approximates F. R. Leavis' "necessary faith" in art as "something in which minds can meet," but grounds this faith in God rather than in Cavell's re-creation or Leavis' "re-creative response of individual minds."[56] For Malick, insofar as Marina's memory of *la merveille* "reflects upon its physical origins," it necessarily reflects on the divine conservation of those phenomena. Insofar as the film itself reflects on its human origins, it implicates human subjects and the "making of their appearances" on the highest order.

Built upon these theological theses, *To the Wonder* is preoccupied with a filmic description of what it is like to love and yet doubt the memory of that love's basis. Ultimately, Neil fails to trust memory or its divine implications; Marina and Quintana meanwhile take experiences of memory and art as nexuses of desire for God. Neil's love fails precisely because he makes the phenomenological mistake of the *Philebus*: denying the phenomenal integrity of memory, he subordinates it to pleasure. Marina and Quintana, on the other hand, awaken a desire for God through memory—and this despite its temporarily unpleasurable consequences. Malick's aesthetic concern in *Wonder*, then, is not merely a question of the relationality of memory, art, and desire to life, but, in true Augustinian fashion, of the relationality of memory, art, and desire to God.

Notes

1. This paper acknowledges three debts. The principal commitment is to the recent strides of Paige Hochschild, Kevin Grove, and other scholars working on memory in Augustine. The second is to feedback from Colton Williamson and participants in Notre Dame's "Art, Desire, and God: Phenomenological Perspectives" conference. The third is a small corner of film scholars committed to reading Malick in an irreducibly hyphenated capacity as filmmaker-theologian. In this latter camp, Augustine is frequently footnoted but rarely centralized. Putting critical engagements with film in conversation with scholars of Augustine, I hope to show that, beyond mere resonance, Augustine is a principal influence in Malick's later works.
2. David Calhoun, "Entranced by the Spectacle of Truth: Wonder and Ascent in Plato and Terrence Malick's *Knight of Cups* and *To the Wonder*," in *Plato and the Moving Image*, ed. Shai Biderman and Michael Weinman (Leiden: Brill Rodopi, 2019), 194–209.
3. Julie Hamilton, "'What Is This Love That Loves Us?': Terrence Malick's *To the Wonder* as a Phenomenology of Love." *Religions* 7, no. 6 (2016): 1–15. For a specifically Catholic take on love in *Wonder*, see also Kathleen Urda's helpful "Eros and Contemplation: The Catholic Vision of Terrence Malick's *To the Wonder*," *Logos* 19, no. 1 (2016): 130–47.
4. Roger Ebert, "A few characters in search of an author," *RogerEbert.com*, April 6, 2013. https://www.rogerebert.com/reviews/to-the-wonder-2013. Accessed January 2, 2021.
5. See Plato, *Philebus*, trans. Robin Waterfield (London: Penguin, 1982). See also the "flame" image that bookends Malick's *The Tree of Life*.
6. For this observation and other insights on music in Malick, I am wholly indebted to personal guidance of composer Stephane Crayton, especially in the form of our conversations in November 2020.
7. Richard Brody's review in *The New Yorker* points out that although cast lists give "Neil" and "Marina," the couple remains unnamed in the movie. For Brody, this gestures to "*the*" love story in the fashion of F. W. Murnau's *Sunrise* (1927). Richard Brody, "The Cinematic Miracle of 'To the Wonder.'" *New Yorker*, April 10, 2013. https://www.newyorker.com/culture/richard-brody/the-cinematic-miracle-of-to-the-wonder. Accessed January 2, 2021.
8. Jim Hemphill and Emmanuel Lubeski, "Lyrical Images," *The ASC—American Cinematographer*, April 2013. https://theasc.com/ac_magazine/April2013/TotheWonder/page1.html. Accessed January 2, 2021.
9. Bilge Ebiri. "Radiant Zigzag Becoming: How Terrence Malick and His Team Constructed *To the Wonder*," *Vulture*, April 18, 2013. https://www.vulture.com/2013/04/how-terrence-malick-wrote-filmed-edited-to-the-wonder.html. Accessed January 2, 2021.
10. The similar images of water-like land as a symbol of human fallenness suggests possible influence from the Lewis novel. See the opening chapters of C. S. Lewis, *Perelandra: A Novel.* (London: Bodley Head, 1951).
11. Plato, *Philebus*, trans. Robin Waterfield (Harmondsworth: Penguin, 1982), 93.
12. Marina condemns Neil for ascribing a sense of immortality to pleasure: "You thought we had forever. That time didn't exist."
13. For a robust exposition on *Philebus*, memory, and pleasure in relation to Augustine, see Paige E. Hochschild's *Memory in Augustine's Theological Anthropology* (Oxford: Oxford University Press, 2012), 25 ff.

14 For the most comprehensive collection of theology in Malick's work to date, see Christopher Barnett, and Clark J. Elliston, eds., *Theology and the Films of Terrence Malick* (New York: Routledge, 2017).
15 The suggestion here that Malick favors a visual mode of communication for spiritual storytelling is largely uncontroversial. Such a claim is the basis of most studies of Malick's formal decisions. Stefanie Knauss, for example, distilling and applying Francisca Cho's position, argues that Malick's films "privilege images over plot and evoke the mystery of non-being through the contemplation of reality (Cho 2017: 106)." See Stefanie Knauss, "Religion and Film: Representation, Experience, Meaning," *Brill Research Perspectives in Theology* 4, no. 1 (2020): 80, citing Francisca Cho, *Seeing Like the Buddha* (Albany: State University of New York Press, 2017), 106.
16 Although this sort of line of argument is usually offered to feed into the biographical mythos of philosophers-turned-filmmakers, it also speaks to an unpretentious eye for charity. Malick's latest *A Hidden Life* (2019) is concerned with visually communicating good works through Franz Jägerstätter's hands—which, given the limits of his setting, usually amounts to humble *A Man Escaped*-style bread breaking. Here, *To the Wonder* is similarly interested in the silent "speech" imbued in the gravity of small gestures within the micro-lifeworld of the household. Burnt dinner drives Neil out of the house in Bergmanian fashion; a fight draws out the distance of a Hitchcockean staircase between the lovers.
17 For a complication of this position, see Gabriella Blasi, "The Cinema of Entanglement: How Not to Contemplate Terrence Malick's *To the Wonder*, *Voyage of Time*, and *Knight of Cups*," *New Review of Film and Television Studies* 17, no. 1 (2019): 20–37.
18 See Aristophanes' account in Plato, *Symposium*, trans. Robin Waterfield (Oxford: Oxford University Press, 1994).
19 Of the various art forms Marina engages in the film, the Cluny museum's unicorn tapestries most conspicuously distill Malick's themes of vision and desire. What I would have to say here about these has already been said (and in more insightful fashion) by Julie Hamilton in her "What Is This Love That Loves Us?": "In the Cluny, Marina's shadow lingers above the 'sight' tapestry from the Lady and the Unicorn tapestry series, one of six concerning the five allegories of the senses. The unicorn sees itself in the mirror held by the lady, paralleling Marina's own introspection. The final tapestry, *mon seul desire* [sic] (my sole desire), symbolizes love rightly ordering the senses and desires." Hamilton, "What Is This Love That Loves Us?," 8.
20 "To the Wonder: Making Of," *To the Wonder*, directed by Terrence Malick (2012; Hollywood, California: Brothers K Productions), DVD.
21 Ebert, "A few characters in search of an author."
22 Ebert, "A few characters in search of an author."
23 Malick's "opening up" to the explicit influence of the *Confessions* approaches Harold Bloom's concept of *Apophrades*—a concept which explains, in turn, Malick's proliferated output post-*Tree of Life*. The influence of *Confessions* on Malick is well defended, though mostly in relation to *The Tree of Life*. See, for example, a survey of Peter Candler, Paul Camacho, and others in section 3.1 of Paul Cerero, "Standing at God's Threshold: Film Viewing as Dwelling in Terrence Malick's *The Tree of Life*," *Church, Communication and Culture* 4 (2019): 152–71.
24 Augustine, *Confessions*, trans. Henry Chadwick (Oxford: Oxford University Press, 2008), 179. See also Augustine on the Psalms' "conjunction of voices with redemptive consequences" in Kevin Grove's "'The Word spoke in our words that we might speak in his': Augustine, the Psalms and the poetry of the incarnate Word," in *Poetic Revelations:*

Word Made Flesh Made Word, ed. Mark S. Burrows, Jean Ward, and Malgorzata Grzegorzewska (New York/London: Routledge, 2017): 29–42.
25 Augustine, *Confessions*, 179.
26 This brings to mind also Kevin Grove's Augustinian take on Dante's image of "a word so hard to hear it needs sight to make it understood." So Father Quintana, struggling to muster words for prayer, supplicates: "Teach us to see you." See Kevin Grove, "Becoming True in the *Purgatorio*: Dante on Forgetting, Remembering, and Learning to Speak," in *Dante, Mercy, and the Beauty of the Human Person*, ed. Leonard J. DeLorenzo and Vittorio Montemaggi (Eugene, OR: Wipf & Stock, 2017): 30–47.
27 Neil's two relationships turn on speech: although Neil makes small talk with his former lover, we do not hear him speak directly to Marina once over course of the film. The affair with Jane (played by Rachel McAdams) eventually falls silent as well as she is made "into nothing. Pleasure. Lust."
28 David Denby, "Commitments: 'To the Wonder' and 'The Company You Keep.'" *New Yorker*, April 8, 2013. https://www.newyorker.com/magazine/2013/04/15/commitments. Accessed January 2, 2021.
29 David Denby, "Commitments: 'To the Wonder' and 'The Company You Keep.'"
30 Augustine, *Confessions*, 180.
31 Plato, *Phaedrus*, in *Platonis Opera*, ed. John Burnet (Oxford: Oxford University Press, 1903).
32 Plato, *Phaedrus*, sec. 276c, 472.
33 Plato, *Phaedrus*, trans. Walter Hamilton (London: Penguin, 1995), 78. See Plotinus' *First Ennead*, Book 5.8.
34 See Canto XIV.11 in George Gordon Lord Byron, *Don Juan*, ed. T. G. Steffan, E. Steffan, and W. W. Pratt (London/New York: Penguin Books, 1986), 473. Approaching despair, Father Quintana considers the spiritual consequences of such a position: "What is it like to be a stream that has dried up?" See 1 Kings 17:7–24, where the solution is likewise grace.
35 Curiously, a number of young filmmakers citing Malick as their principal influence have appropriated his techniques to advance this very epicurean position. Michał Marczak's *All These Sleepless Nights* (2016), which is unapologetically Malickean in style, explores memory and oblivion in Warsaw's party scene: "I'm collecting all these experiences . . . and I'm afraid I'll drown in the present." See also the treatments of memory in Malick-influenced films like David Gordon Green's *All the Real Girls* (2003), Andrea Arnold's *Wuthering Heights* (2011), Alejandro G. Iñárritu's *Birdman* (2014), and Shane Carruth's *Upstream Color* (2016).
36 Augustine, *Confessions*, 185. Julie Hamilton cites this line in relation to Malick's "visual poetics," which "feed the life of memory, resurrecting what is harbored deep within the consciousness of his characters, reanimating their past within the present." Hamilton, What Is This Love That Loves Us?." Neil represents the (intentional) failure of this poetics. The most on-the-nose metaphor of the film makes a fair deal over the fact that Neil, in contrast to Marina, never unpacks his belongings.
37 See Thomas Noll, "Die Allegorische Landschaft Bei Caspar David Friedrich: Möglichkeiten Und Grenzen Der Interpretation," *Wallraf-Richartz-Jahrbuch* 72 (2011): 281–96.
38 This film's final "dance" sees Marina drinking dew from tree branches. See Job 29:19; 38:28.

39 Plato, *Phaedrus,* 77. See the light-emitting words inscribed on the grail in *Parsifal.*
40 Augustine, *Confessions,* 143–44.
41 Visual quotations of Caspar David Friedrich in the six-film span between *Tree of Life* and *Hidden Life* are catalogued by multiple reviewers. See, for example, Ray Pride's "Daunting Beauty: A Review of A Hidden Life," *Newcity Film,* December 23, 2019. https://www.newcityfilm.com/2019/12/23/daunting-beauty-a-review-of-a-hidden-life/. Accessed January 2, 2021.
42 Richard Rosengarten, "When a Vow Turns Out to be . . . a Vow: 'Fleabag,'" *Sightings,* University of Chicago Divinity School, April 20, 2020. https://divinity.uchicago.edu/sightings/articles/when-vow-turns-out-be-vow-fleabag. Accessed January 2, 2021.
43 Neil and Marina's literary resonances are likewise multiple. Neil reminds us Walker Percy's Binx Bolling pre-conversion; Marina of the joyous "fool" on the order of Wagner's Parsifal or Dostoevsky's Lev Nikolayevich Myshkin (and indeed *The Idiot* was, according to the film's "making of" featurette, "required reading" for the cast.) Even accounting for these resonances, it is Quintana's character who most clearly relates artistic memory to desire for God.
44 See Marina's voiceover on her arrival to Oklahoma: "What is this love that loves us? That comes from nowhere. From all around. The sky. You, cloud. You love me, too."
45 See Alain Resnais' *Hiroshima mon amour* (1959), *L'Année dernière à Marienbad* (1961) and *Muriel ou le Temps d'un retour* (1963). *Wonder* scholarship on the whole perhaps makes too much of the influence of Godard's jump cut innovations and not enough of Resnais' thematic anxieties. French New Wave quotations have also been overvalued in general in comparison to Malick's many Soviet influences.
46 On Malick's use of light, see Daniel Garrett, "Beautiful Light, Vibrant Things, Speaking Minds: Terrence Malick's *To the Wonder,*" *Offscreen* 19, no. 7 (July 2015). https://offscreen.com/view/terrence-malick-to-the-wonder. Accessed January 2, 2021.
47 Augustine, *Confessions,* 183.
48 Augustine, *Confessions,* 182.
49 Husserl argues that "memory" (an act in the present) and "what is remembered" (which is past) "appear as *not* simultaneous." Malick's theological investigation looks at God as the object of memory, exploring the consequences of the recognition (or lack thereof) of God's eternal "simultaneity" in (and, indeed, grounding of) experience. Quintana's "error" follows the Augustinian paradox of relegating God and memory to the past. See John Brough, "Husserl on Memory," *The Monist* 59, no. 1 (January 1975): 41.
50 Malick studied Heidegger at Oxford under Gilbert Ryle and published an English translation of *Vom Wesen des Grundes* (Northwestern University Press, 1969).
51 Stanley Cavell, *The World Viewed: Reflections on the Ontology of Film,* enlarged edition (Cambridge, MA: Harvard University Press, 1979), xv–xvi.
52 Cavell, *The World Viewed,* xv–xvi.
53 Thomas Aquinas, *Summa Theologica,* trans. Fathers of the English Dominican Province (London: R & T Washbourne, 1922), I, q. 104, a. 1, obj. 1, 19–20.
54 Such a position is explored generally in the introduction to *Plato and the Moving Image* (2019) and more specifically in Christopher B. Barnett, "Spirit(uality) in the Films of Terrence Malick," *The Journal of Religion and Film* 17, no. 1 (2013): 1–29.
55 Aquinas, *Summa Theologica,* I, q. 104, a. 1, obj. 1, 19–20.
56 F. R. Leavis, *Nor Shall My Sword: Discourses on Pluralism, Compassion and Social Hope* (London: Chatto & Windus, 1972), 62.

Bibliography

Augustine. *Confessions*. Translated by Henry Chadwick. Oxford: Oxford University Press, 2008.
Aquinas, Thomas. *Summa Theologica*. Translated by the Fathers of the English Dominican Province. London: R & T Washbourne, 1922.
Barnett, Christopher B. "Spirit(uality) in the Films of Terrence Malick." *Journal of Religion and Film* 17, no. 1 (2013): 1–29.
Barnett, Christopher and Clark J. Elliston, eds. *Theology and the Films of Terrence Malick*. New York: Routledge, 2017.
Blasi, Gabriella. "The Cinema of Entanglement: How Not to Contemplate Terrence Malick's *To the Wonder*, *Voyage of Time*, and *Knight of Cups*." *New Review of Film and Television Studies* 17, no. 1 (2019): 20–37.
Brody, Richard. "The Cinematic Miracle of 'To the Wonder.'" *New Yorker*, April 10, 2013. https://www.newyorker.com/culture/richard-brody/the-cinematic-miracle-of-to-the-wonder. Accessed January 2, 2021.
Brough, John. "Husserl on Memory." *The Monist* 59, no. 1 (January 1975): 40–62.
Byron, George Gordon Lord. *Don Juan*. Edited by T. G. Steffan, E. Steffan, and W. W. Pratt. London/New York: Penguin Books, 1986.
Calhoun, David. "Entranced by the Spectacle of Truth: Wonder and Ascent in Plato and Terrence Malick's *Knight of Cups* and *To the Wonder*." In *Plato and the Moving Image*, edited by Shai Biderman and Michael Weinman, 194–209. Leiden: Brill Rodopi, 2019.
Cavell, Stanley. *The World Viewed: Reflections on the Ontology of Film*, enlarged edition. Cambridge, MA: Harvard University Press, 1979.
Cerero, Paul. "Standing at God's Threshold: Film Viewing as Dwelling in Terrence Malick's *The Tree of Life*." *Church, Communication and Culture* 4 (2019): 152–71.
Cho, Francisca. *Seeing Like the Buddha*. Albany, NY: State University of New York Press, 2017.
Denby, David. "Commitments: 'To the Wonder' and 'The Company You Keep.'" *New Yorker*, April 8, 2013. https://www.newyorker.com/magazine/2013/04/15/commitments. Accessed January 2, 2021.
Ebert, Roger. "A few characters in search of an author." *RogerEbert.com*, April 6, 2013. https://www.rogerebert.com/reviews/to-the-wonder-2013. Accessed January 2, 2021.
Ebiri, Bilge. "Radiant Zigzag Becoming: How Terrence Malick and His Team Constructed *To the Wonder*." *Vulture*, April 18, 2013. https://www.vulture.com/2013/04/how-terrence-malick-wrote-filmed-edited-to-the-wonder.html. Accessed January 2, 2021.
Garrett, Daniel. "Beautiful Light, Vibrant Things, Speaking Minds: Terrence Malick's *To the Wonder*." *Offscreen* 19, no. 7 (July 2015). https://offscreen.com/view/terrence-malick-to-the-wonder. Accessed January 2, 2021.
Grove, Kevin. "Becoming True in the *Purgatorio*: Dante on Forgetting, Remembering, and Learning to Speak." In *Dante, Mercy, and the Beautiy of the Human Person*, edited by Leonard J. DeLorenzo and Vittorio Montemaggi, 30–47. Eugene, OR: Wipf & Stock, 2017.
Grove, Kevin. "'The Word spoke in our words that we might speak in his': Augustine, the Psalms and the poetry of the incarnate Word." In *Poetic Revelations: Word Made Flesh Made Word*, edited by Mark S. Burrows, Jean Ward, and Malgorzata Grzegorzewska, 29–42. New York: Routledge, 2017.
Hamilton, Julie. "'What Is This Love That Loves Us?': Terrence Malick's *To the Wonder* as a Phenomenology of Love." *Religions* 7, no. 6 (2016): 1–15.

Hemphill, Jim and Emmanuel Lubeski. "Lyrical Images." *The ASC—American Cinematographer*, April 2013. https://theasc.com/ac_magazine/April2013/TotheWonder/page1.html. Accessed January 2, 2021.

Hochschild, Paige E. *Memory in Augustine's Theological Anthropology*. Oxford: Oxford University Press, 2012.

Knauss, Stefanie. "Religion and Film: Representation, Experience, Meaning." *Brill Research Perspectives in Theology* 4, no. 1 (2020): 1–103.

Leavis, F. R. *Nor Shall My Sword: Discourses on Pluralism, Compassion, and Social Hope*. London: Chatto & Windus, 1972.

Lewis, C. S. *Perelandra: A Novel*. London: Bodley Head, 1951.

Noll, Thomas. "Die Allegorische Landschaft bei Caspar David Friedrich: Möglichkeiten und Grenzen Der Interpretation." *Wallraf-Richartz-Jahrbuch* 72 (2011): 281–96.

Plato. *Phaedrus*. In *Platonis Opera*. Edited by John Burnet. Oxford: Oxford University Press, 1903.

Plato. *Phaedrus*. Translated by Walter Hamilton. London: Penguin, 1995.

Plato. *Philebus*. Translated by Robin Waterfield. London: Penguin, 1982.

Plato. *Symposium*. Translated by Robin Waterfield. Oxford: Oxford University Press, 1994.

Pride, Ray. "Daunting Beauty: A Review of A Hidden Life." *Newcity Film*, December 23, 2019. https://www.newcityfilm.com/2019/12/23/daunting-beauty-a-review-of-a-hidden-life/. Accessed January 2, 2021.

Rosengarten, Richard. "When a Vow Turns Out to be . . . a Vow: 'Fleabag,'" *Sightings*, University of Chicago Divinity School, April 20, 2020. https://divinity.uchicago.edu/sightings/articles/when-vow-turns-out-be-vow-fleabag. Accessed January 2, 2021.

Urda, Kathleen. "Eros and Contemplation: The Catholic Vision of Terrence Malick's *To the Wonder*." *Logos* 19, no. 1 (2016): 130–47.

6

Life in the Heart of Cinema: Michel Henry's New Phenomenology and Cinematic Form

Joseph G. Kickasola

This chapter marshals Michel Henry's phenomenology in service of a deeper understanding of cinematic form. Contrary to what may be expected, Henry's phenomenological aesthetics reveals how certain aesthetic dimensions of the cinema ought not be treated as secondary to more conceptual or structural elements such as story, character, or representational concerns. Rather than mere ornaments to concept, properly "life-oriented" sensations and feelings (yielded through formal means, such as cinematography, sound design, editing, etc.) point to a more originary, foundational, and generative dynamism that, in Henry's account, founds all phenomena.

Such an application of Henry's thought faces particular challenges, and addressing them will be one of this chapter's primary tasks. Henry rarely mentions film, and his aesthetic principles appear to lean away from some of the hallmark traits of cinema. What follows is not an attempt to understand the whole of cinema in light of Henry's thought, but rather to trace in it what Henry identifies as "a 'more'" in artistic creation that lies beyond representation, and so make a case that the cinema is a viable artform for Henryan consideration.[1] Ultimately, this "more" in cinematic arts may be "More" in the grandest sense. We shall not ignore the explicitly theological character Henry's thought takes towards the end of his career. A full account of the implications of Henry's theology for cinema is beyond the scope of this chapter, but one might consider this a fruitful beginning. The seeds of such a theology are laid throughout what follows, and the conclusion will put forward some suggestions regarding how an Henryan theological aesthetics of cinema might begin to be realized.

We begin by briefly expounding Henry's fundamental concept of life, identifying some of the problems it creates for cinematic aesthetics.[2] We then address Henry's aesthetics, specifically targeting how it may be applied to the sensory and experiential dimensions of cinema. There follows an analysis of the opening scene of Krzysztof Kieślowski's *Blue* (1993) that puts these ideas into concrete application, but also yields suggestive theological possibilities, making way for Henryan theological applications to close.

Life and Art in Henry

Phenomenological life is the distinctive and governing concept in Henry's work, and it is perhaps best approached through the phenomenologist's notion of the duality of appearing. Experience has two aspects. There is on the one hand an ekstatic experience of the phenomenon in "the world," which is associated with visibility, externality, objectivity, and representation. Classic phenomenology, he argues, missteps by focusing solely on this exterior world, framing intentionality as consciousness "of" something and thereby placing consciousness in a constant outward, ekstatic posture unable to consider the life that makes phenomenality possible. Trapped in ekstasis, we are cut off from the source of phenomena, isolated from the life that binds us to others and to the world. This unwittingly reinforces a larger, worrying cultural trend: a kind of "barbaric" objective scientism that programmatically disconnects us from the deep subjectivity of life and destroys culture.[3] On the other hand, there is the domain of life. Presented as pure manifestation, preceding and enabling all other manifestations as their ground, life stands as an immanent totality within which and by which all other manifestations occur. It is invisible, immanent, and immediately grasped.[4] Here, life is not limited to an experience of animation or sensation, but refers to manifestation proper, that which makes the appearance of sense possible. Because it is radically immanent, it reveals and affects nothing else but itself (i.e., it is "auto-affective"). Life for Henry is self-revelation as such, phenomenality itself; it is power or force, endlessly sustaining and generating.[5] Thus Henry rethinks intentionality as already characterized by the prior auto-affection of life that, in this way, serves as the ground for all intentional subjectivity.

Ultimately, Henry will identify this phenomenological life with the God of Christianity in whom the Apostle Paul says "we live, move, and are."[6] Thus in *I am the Truth* the phenomenologist writes that "[e]verywhere that something like a self-revelation is produced there is Life. Everywhere there is Life, this self-revelation is produced.... God is Life—he is the essence of Life, or if one prefers, the essence of Life is God."[7] Regardless of whether one follows Henry this far, what is most important here is that Henry does not dismiss the external world as insignificant in developing his notion of life, but enfolds it within a radically immanent ontology in which aesthetics orients us toward a fundamental reckoning with the invisible power that is life. In order to respond to what he describes as a kind of barbarism, he encourages a turn to art as one site for the revelation of life. Through Henry's aesthetics and his theological articulation of his phenomenology of life, we will glimpse how art might lead us to salvific heights. Henry's focus on Christianity walks us to this theological threshold. At its maximal strength, we will see that the cinema may amplify and clarify the notion of the divine Life abiding amid the evanescent world of appearances and material decay.

"Elusive" as phenomenality is, Henry argues that any artistic form that generates a sense of life necessarily gestures beyond itself, beyond the world's continually decaying, self-emptying realm of appearances.[8] Henry gives clues as to what specifically counts as such a gesture in art in his book *Seeing the Invisible: On Kandinsky* and in an interview published as "Art et Phénoménologie de la Vie."[9] An exposition of his aesthetics will enable us to see how cinema might have tremendous life-expressing potential.

Drawing on the painter Wassily Kandinsky's ideas, Henry describes the aforementioned duality of experience in the Kandinskian terms of the "external" and the "internal."[10] The external refers to the appearing of phenomena in all its visible properties. The "internal" refers to the phenomenon's invisible manifestation in feeling. This manifestation is directly associated with the revelation of life. As Henry writes,

> In what way, then, can the Internal be revealed, if it is not in or as a world? It is revealed in the way of life. Life feels and experiences itself immediately such that it coincides with itself at each point of its being. Wholly immersed in itself and drawn from this feeling of itself, it is carried out as pathos. Prior to and independently from every regard, affectivity is the 'way' in which the Internal is revealed to itself, in which life lives itself, in which the impression immediately imprints itself and in which feeling affects itself.[11]

Art deals in the experience of the internal for Henry. In this way art is invested with a revelatory task that is missed when we relate to artworks simply in their visible or external appearances. Instead, what is present in art serves to signal the immanent pathos of its own construction. Art here serves as an opening for life's expression, an invitation that does not take us elsewhere, but draws us deeper into immanence, into the original experience of living.[12] In this experience we rediscover ourselves and the significance of heightened feeling and sense as stemming from life and not merely oriented *toward* something in the world. Through sensory experience, art brings us closer to life by opening us to our own lived experience as affectively constituted in auto-affection.

Given the elemental powers of art and its ability to serve as an affective passage to life, it becomes clear why Henry prized non-representational visual art, such as that of the abstract expressionist Kandinsky. Representational art, as the height of visibility and reference, tempts us toward an ekstatic focus on phenomena-as-objects. Abstract forms, by contrast, are more "internally" driven in that they are not directly signaling external referents but rather point to experience, or the auto-affection of life in the depths of subjectivity. Although every phenomenon has a visible and invisible aspect, abstract images shift the weight of the phenomenon towards the internal, pathetic realm of feeling through their short-circuiting of representation. Their visible forms gesture away from external visibility and towards the internal invisibility of life. "Because art accomplishes the revelation of the invisible reality in us with an absolute certainty," he writes in *Seeing the Invisible*, with an allusion to the certainty one feels in the experience of love, "it is a salvation."[13] Indeed, in the later theological trilogy he will describe this salvation as the subject's re-birth in Life.[14] Though obviously "external" in the sense of "visible," visible forms function as a material grace, unattached to any particular worldly object, leading us into art's fundamental, generative, affective domain of life. In this manner, at least some "visible" objects have a way of weighting our experiences toward the internal, a principle that will prove essential for cinema.

Saving a Seat for Henry at the Cinema: Story and Struggle

Marked by representation and reference, yet also intense sensory experience, suffering, joy, and imagination, the alignments and challenges of cinema end up turning the Henryan aesthetic ideal "inside out." That is, in the hands of an aesthetically sensitive filmmaker, cinematic arts can be shaped to express life even within a generally representational frame. We must, however, first address reservations that Henry had regarding at least some moving images. Television (and "the media") receives scornful—though passing—treatment in Henry's discussions of the malaise of "barbaric" contemporary society.[15] It seems that Henry's concerns stem from a certain naturally *ek-static* quality of engagement the medium ostensibly promotes. For example:

> It just so happens that people today are no longer popular, spontaneous, instructive, real or alive. A mediation has separated people from themselves. The media has replaced the free play of life and its sensibility with the substitute of an unreal, artificial, stereotypical, consumer world where life can only flee instead of realize itself.[16]

Indeed, for Henry, isolation (from others and the self) is a central evil of contemporary existence, and television or "media, these images that are anti-art," foster a perverse "kind of fascination with regard to the world of radical alienation."[17] This appears to be, fundamentally, a teleological problem: despite all its powers for sensation and emotion, television allegedly fosters a movement from life toward the world according to an alienating objectivism and materialism. The suggestion is that "media" deploys the dynamics and power of life against itself, resulting in an alternate, "unreal" world that falls quite short of the "creative" worldmaking that Henry heralds in his aesthetics.

Henry's focus is clearly on a larger root problem, of which isolated television viewing is presented as a symptom: a reductive scientific ideology eliminating all forms of knowledge except the radically ekstatic, measured, and verifiable knowledge of "the world." Through media that stem from this "barbarism," one trades "growing" subjectivity (where the world and others are progressively bound together in life) with dull, vacant images that fill empty time and absorb the subject in isolation. "The media world," Henry writes, "thus does not offer a self-realization of life; it offers escape."[18] Space does not permit a full critique or engagement with Henry's contestable account of television, and its typical placement within the relatively cloistered home may make it fundamentally different in its reception and "practice" from the cinematic arts,[19] but the teleological dimension is the central warning to which we must attend. That is, to the degree that any moving image distracts us from authentic, inward living toward life (as opposed to simply the observation of others living) and toward isolated and empty substitution and "escape," moving images are, indeed, anti-life.

Yet, provided that a proper teleology is maintained, isolation and distraction avoided, and "barbaric" ideology rejected, then cinema may yet be a force for life in Henry's account. Avoiding these dangers depends not on the particulars of the medium itself so much as how in the cinematic arts moving images are used and aesthetically shaped. Indeed, it is through examination of the particulars of the cinema that we see the aesthetic potential for a life-oriented cinema to emerge.

Let us return to the duality of appearing discussed earlier. Though far more accepting of representation, classical film theory has also considered a duality that bears some alignment with that of Henry, that between formalism and realism. Many early "formalists" argued that film's formal qualities are precisely what distinguish it from a mere recording of "reality," making it a candidate for "art."[20] The notion that film might "represent the real" in the sense of ekstatic reality presents numerous theoretical and philosophical problems that film scholars have worked through for decades, with most agreeing that the "inherently realist" characterization of cinema is reductive at best.[21] On first look, Henry's dismissal of representation and his failure to address the significance of story seems to be a glaring weakness for any Henryan cinematic aesthetics. However, Henry was also a published novelist, so he obviously understood and appreciated story and the fictional imagination.[22] Indeed, Henry speaks highly of the imagination in *Seeing the Invisible* and describes its capacity to operate at the immediate level of life, such that we may say that any act of imagination finds resonance in the internal dimension of life.[23]

Of course, some works harness and direct these powers more effectively than others. It is difficult to discern, from Henry's writings, which fictions would qualify as truly life-affirming and which would inevitably end in isolating and barbaric dead ends, but certain emphases throughout *Seeing the Invisible* yield clues to the puzzle. For example, Henry argues that a painting of the sea of Venice is an experience of the "immensity" of that sea more than it is an experience of the material particulars of the painting itself or significations towards the real world itself.[24] Art is successful to the degree that it makes us feel more of the "immensity" there than of the referential particulars of a given body of water in the external world. It may be more accurate to say that we experience life when we see the external "sea" more purely expressing the power that has always founded its manifestation, life. Though material signs have a slight role to play in Henry's aesthetics, they remain effective only insofar as they direct us toward the animating power of life undergirding their appearance, as Henry admits they do (abstractly rendered, yet clearly representational as they are) in reference to the three riders of *Romantic Landscape* (1911).[25] Even identifiable figurations, such as Kandinsky's riders, may overcome the hindances of representation and grasp the immediacy of life if they are sufficiently steered from representational ends. Perhaps this is why, Henry admits, Kandinsky himself appreciated the work of Henri Rousseau, who considered himself a "realist" of some sort.[26] While Rousseau's "Poultry Yard" painting is fully representational, Kandinsky argues he has already separated the object from its "practical meaning" and revealed its "interior sounds" through an emphasis on simple geometry, elementary shading, central open space, line, etc.[27] For example, the eponymous yard of the painting dominates the lower half of the frame as a large trapezoid, dwarfing most everything else, while sky rules the top half the painting. Through simplicity, the formal is clearly more prominent and powerful than any representational functions the yard, chickens, or surrounding buildings might have. So, Henry's measure is not simply a continuum of lesser or greater abstraction,[28] but the degree to which something "more" emerges and truly creative imagination is generated, for "to imagine is to posit life."[29] It is clear that representational art is not completely "off the table," so to speak, providing that representational functions are dethroned in favor of life-oriented sensations.

Any representational cinema worthy of true acclaim from Henry, then, must prioritize aesthetic feeling and counter the tendency toward "habitual facticity,"[30] a phrase that represents a human *ek-static* habit of seeing things for their practical use-value, amputated from the immanence of life. In this light, we may say at this stage that something of the traditional cinema's central powers may be retained if the proper emphasis is applied to the *power* of story rather than to the power of *story*—that is, if the emphasis is upon the "suffering" or affective experience of a film's story rather than on its linear storytelling alone.

Elemental Forms: Sight and Sound

Since abstract form is the royal road to life for Henry, we must seek out the abstract even within the representational.[31] For example, when Henry discusses the common artistic subject of the Adoration of the Magi, he focuses upon the artist's decision to use a particular shade of yellow on Balthazar's robe as expressive of an affective, inner, invisible, and powerful reality, rather than an attempt to depict the actual robe worn by the man.[32] The robe yields the experience of yellow, which gestures towards the auto-affective inner "tone" of yellow that yields particularly intense and signature feelings. Whatever the power or inner "tone" of a color (or a line, or a point) may be,[33] cinematographers and cinematic art directors make many of the same sorts of choices Quattrocentro painters once made. Manipulation of color, shading, illumination, directionality, saturation, and visual shape all lie within their artistic range, and they are employed not simply for their external signification, but for their abstract aesthetic qualities.

We must also must account for the auditory dimensions of cinematic experience. Henry himself (*à la* Schopenhauer) argues that music is powerful to the degree of its affective expressivity in life.[34] Henry seems more inclined to look past or through temporality in music to see the atemporal affectivity at its root. In the same way that visual forms can steer us away from representation, temporal presentations like music and sound design (and some dimensions of editing) may be manipulated to steer us toward affective force and away from rigid, objective ekstatic chronology.

The Intensification of Life: Time, Movement, Bodies

Henry recognizes the possibility of aggregating aesthetic powers through synthetic art forms, or what Kandinsky called "monumental art."[35] When the visual and musical components of cinema are combined and viewed abstractly, we see that cinematic experience is multimodal and even multisensory (what cinematic sound theorist Michel Chion calls "audio-vision").[36] This understanding of cinema may align us with the goals that Henry himself expressed regarding painting: "the profusion of life . . . its intensification and exaltation."[37] "Intensity" is most often a dynamic felt in our bodies, and that dynamic is central for aesthetics. For instance, Henry seems to champion abstract dance styles that more directly drive the viewer to the "manifestation of Force at its proper site."[38] Cinema can abstract a body and its movement away from practical application and external *telos* towards its internal nature as a "bundle of powers" immediately associated with life as the source of the body's powers itself.[39] Expression, body, and self all find a unity in life. Time and movement must be reimagined within the unity of expression, body, and self in life. Henry calls this "a pathos-filled temporality" in which there is no separation from self, "a temporality without intentionality, a simple *affective becoming*."[40] It is thus is more accurate to say that Henry values art forms that work *through* their temporalities, movements, and formal powers to draw attention to the atemporal, invisible source of life.

Michel, Meet Krzysztof: Kieślowski's *Blue* in Light of Henryan Aesthetics

It remains to put a cinematic Henryan aesthetics into practice; that is, to understand, specifically, how a film might carry us into life. Many of our observations above have hinged upon an orientation to life that can be difficult to discern without concrete analysis. This *telos* will be largely discerned through the relationship of form to "content" or story, and the manner by which the power of story is amplified and the ekstatic and "practical" concerns of exposition, cause, and effect, character establishment, specific locales and times, etc. are de-emphasized. There are many films that might be deemed "Henryan" in small or large ways, but what is most needful is to find a filmmaker who makes accomplished stylistic use of principles Henry has described within a more standard cinematic narrative. To that end, the opening scene to Krzysztof Kieślowski's *Blue* (1991) stands as a potent example.

This film begins in the realm of pure, unidentified sensation. The screen is black, a blank "canvas" accompanied by a disquieting, rumbling, but indistinct soundtrack. The visuals eventually yield to pulsing, slowly emerging gray/black vertical lines. We eventually come to see "we" are beholding a massive, dominant car tire moving on a highway, the camera in the unlikely position of riding beneath a car. So, while the scene eventually arrives at representational status, it begins wholly in the unexpected, unmeasured, and fully sensuous, a strategy that, in many respects, calls attention to the energic, phenomenal foundations of all that we will see. In Henryan fashion, the aesthetic approach has positioned us, initially, not within the realm of easy representation but directly into power, a realm of force and feeling, before we know what worldly "form" the power is taking. This will prove to be an aesthetic pattern throughout the film.[41] Even as part of the identifiable phenomenal world, such a view is very unlike the "habitual facticity" of a pedestrian perspective. It imaginatively foreshadows a crisis to come and does so in dynamic rather than verbal terms.

No music plays, but the sounds we hear beat in a steady, relentless musical rhythm. This may be a fate rhythm, but is also a clear, aesthetically derived unity of sense with the visuals, which all "beat" in aestheticized synchrony: the pulsating whir of the tires in this first shot, followed by other rhythmic images: a rush of lamp posts passing by, the pulses of wind through a candy wrapper (held by a child's hand outside the moving car), the whoosh of air as lights pass over the windshield. When the car pulls to the shoulder of the road the ominous drip of fluid from a faulty brake line maintains the rhythm. Indeed, all these sounds form a continuous aural procession through the sequence and ultimately match the pace of a hitchhiking boy's game of stick and wooden ball. At the very moment he wins his game, the family loses and the rhythm is suddenly broken: the car passes him and smashes into a tree. This rhythm, at once relentlessly chronological and otherworldly, sets us up for an experience of sudden, shocking atemporality, befitting an entrée to eternity.

Many engaging abstract visuals accompany this aestheticized soundscape. The candy wrapper in the wind creates a visual dance of blue and silver color, and Anna's hand (in monumental closeup, isolated from her body, before we know there is an "Anna" or even a girl) takes on an abstract formal quality by its pronounced dominance in the frame. The hand is always also the line and the potential for power, Henry says. Because life is immanent and art intensifies it, the image of a moving hand is a voyage deeper *into* the experience of living amid life as it is expressed in the hand. It at once represents, to use Henry's words, a "hand" ekstatically, while also demonstrating and guiding us through the truth of its "metaphysical condition," its "infinite capacity to produce movement," its nature as "power as such."[42]

When Anna's face finally appears, she stares directly at us, a knowing icon through glass, while reflected abstract flares and shapes regularly glide over her visage. Wondrous, mysterious distortions of light also overlay her view of the road while in the tunnel. The world is saturated in moving, abstract visual form, to the point where the world of representation, of "habitual facticity," is overtaken by the sensuous. In the subsequent shots of the dripping brake fluid (dominant in the foreground) the abstraction of Anna walking back to the car in the background is striking. She remains dramatically out of focus, as Kieslowski doggedly refuses a conventional "rack focus" from the harbinger of the brake fluid to the girl. Her amorphous form never solidifies. She appears to be slipping from the concrete world, at once, a foreshadowing of her "external" death, and a marker of a life ultimately enfolded within Life.

A hazy blue-gray miasmic frame follows. Two yellow dots emerge, coming into being as the remarkably colorful headlamps of the car in fog, passing the hitchhiking boy, Antoine, on the side of the road. Most importantly, we *do not see* the most obvious external event, the wrenching crash; we only hear its mechanical agony as we read Antoine's bewildered, then alarmed, expression. This climactic moment is held in the realm of the imagination, while our only visible connection to the tragedy is through the gaze and expression of another human being. This invisibility, paired with an auditory paroxysm, leaves us floating in an unregulated, atemporal time. We see the boy look to his right, and only then see the aftermath. A panicked dog dashes from the frame, and, after a moment, sheets of paper leap from the mangled, smoking car, seemingly launched by an unseen power. After another disoriented moment, a lonely beach ball makes its tragic departure from its owner, lightly rolling, yet determined to continue on. Antoine runs to the scene, and Kieślowski cuts to an enormous wide shot: one solitary tree standing (still growing, still abiding), amid a vast plain. And yet the tree, and Antoine's tiny running form is belittled in the bottom of the frame, the frigid blue/grey heavens weighing down from above, while the little colorful ball continues skipping, a splash of swirling color bounding across a cold, blue landscape.

By withholding nearly all dialogue or contextual narrative information and throwing experiential weight to the formal elements, Kieślowski has begun this film in Henryan fashion, emphasizing the *power* of story over the power of *story*. In doing so, he sets the stage for drama on both the temporal and spiritual planes. The many images that lean toward abstraction exude an elemental, primary aura, unfolding in forceful, aesthetic terms, strongly suggesting the receiver think and process beyond the named and categorized world of "habitual facticity." And, yet, on a corporeal level, we find our experience also in a kind of tragic sympathy with the forces at play in the scene, most pointedly at the moment when the car crashes into the tree (which, again, we imagine and hear, but do not see). These forces point to high irony (why does the crash occur exactly when Antoine wins the game?), a primary characteristic of the human existential struggle for meaning and higher order. In Henryan terms, this serves as an experiential exemplar of the "suffering" inherent in our experience as lived bodies and the struggle between what we can or wish to do and what we cannot; power and powerlessness.

We have discerned all this in our bodies. As several film theorists have all argued from cultural, phenomenological, and cognitive camps, film is a corporeal, multi-sensory event that should not be seen solely in audio-visual terms.[43] Throughout this sequence the senses have been engaged: the visual and aural, the proprioceptive (the sense of one's body in space, under the car), the haptic (entailed in shot of the hand), the vestibular (balance, as the camera moves or doesn't). In this short example we see many forces in concert with each other, and the scene is immensely rich in the life-oriented aesthetics that Henry advocates. Throughout, the numerous "energies" and forces in this scene amount to an aggregate intensification of life in our experience. Likewise, it presents an aestheticized temporality that *also* reveals a timeless power that precedes and outlasts it.

It may seem odd that "life" could be found in a scene so obviously tragic. However, this scene initiates a film that will ultimately suggests, at every sensual level, life has not been vanquished. As Julie grieves, she attempts to abandon her identity, her very self, and to utterly forget the "self" who was her daughter. Yet, within an Henryan framework, this is impossible, as "the living *ego* [*moi*] is indeed a sort of auto-movement, an auto-transformation, like a ball that rolls and never parts from itself."[44] Throughout the rest of the film Julie struggles with loss, and life, which continues to make demands of her: that she open herself anew to love, cease from self-isolation and anonymous living, to "grow," not only re-embracing herself, but reconstituting herself within auto-affectivity, a life that grounds.

The greatest emblem of this insistent "call" of life is a regular appearance of the color blue, found throughout the film in numerous places and objects, aesthetically emphasized. However, the zenith of chromatic force is achieved through unexpected, periodic and overpowering moments where the visual field is entirely overtaken by blue, accompanied by thunderous choral music;[45] these are truly "monumental" artistic moments, disrupting temporality with the *parousia* of life, beyond time and without limit.

As an agnostic, it is unlikely that Kieślowski would subscribe to Henry's theological language. Yet, he spoke several times about his intuition that there is something beyond the material: "The world is not only bright lights, this hectic pace, the Coca-Cola with a straw, the new car.... Another truth exists...a hereafter? Yes, surely. Good or bad, I don't know, but ... something else."[46] His aesthetics only reinforce this intuition.

The same techniques that suggest something aesthetically and ontologically "more" haunts Julie throughout the story culminate gloriously in the final images of the film. Having found a capacity to love again, Julie is suddenly able to cry (an explosion of both suffering and joy, pure pathos), her face overlaid by reflected, abstract visuals (just as her daughter's was, in the film's beginning); an image of pathos, between visible and invisible worlds, free from a cold, unfeeling, barbaric realm of anxiety, denial, self-destruction, and isolation.[47] The abstract images, paired with a magnificent soundtrack (a choir extolling the virtues of love in a musical rendering of 1 Corinthians 13), make this "resurrection" of Life clear and potent.

Conclusion: Henryan Aesthetics, the Cinema, and the Theological Gesture

By appropriating Henry for cinema studies, we can better see how cinematic form, like life, refuses to be determined by external imposition. It opens onto excess by turning us toward our irreducibility. It helps us to understand that "resurrection," whether experiential or theological, is not about going elsewhere, but signals a return to who we are and who we hope to be. While the application of an Henryan aesthetics to cinema is limited and does not speak to the full range of cinema's powers or functions, it does highlight how the force of cinematic form can point to forces beyond those of plot, narrative context, or character psychology, and emulates the "suffering" dynamic of power and powerlessness that characterizes our phenomenal lives.

At a minimum, this suggests an important "prophetic" role for cinema. This may be a means to apply Henryan aesthetics to a range of films, even those less obviously "Henryan." As mentioned, Henry's concerns about contemporary media seem to boil down to a *telos* that leans toward an isolating, idolatrous materialism that reduces human beings to "something that feels nothing, that does not feel himself ... to waves of particles, chains of acid."[48] Any film that seeks a different *telos* may also, quite naturally, immanently, find resources for the task. For instance, even if we believe the cinema should adopt a more "naturalist" aesthetic, in the sense of not being obviously formally adventurous, the degree to which brute materialism is rejected and the *plentitude* of phenomenality that *already constitutes* "ordinary" life is highlighted through aesthetic strategy (e.g., documentaries, "slow" cinema, etc.), that may be the degree to which the call of pure phenomenality, life itself, is amplified.

However, in a Henryan aesthetic, cinema at its fullest will plunge us into the primordial dance of life itself. As we have seen, our experience of cinema is one of power and multiplicity, not entirely contingent on representation, while not abandoning the world either. Cinema invites more than mere observation, more than "the practical" affordances it offers; it implicates us in life insofar as it presents moving images that "move" us toward joy and suffering. Cinema transforms because it requires us to be moved by movement, and so more closely to examine the drama of beholding anything, or anyone at all. Through a foregrounding of aesthetic experience, Kieślowski's *Blue* suggests the world is *for* something beyond it; a teleology that lurks through flashes of color, startling and glorious sounds, impassioned moving forms in dynamic tension with each other. We are constantly negotiating with the age-old question, as articulated by Leibniz: "Why is there something rather than nothing?"[49] The sheer plentitude of aesthetic energies in this film suggests that many "somethings" are happening at multiple levels. Indeed, the relative lack of contextual information (plot, character, etc.) suggests we experience these "happenings" in a much larger, more open manner, beyond chronology or plot, or even a Euclidean frame.

Henry argues the "more" of art is truly more of ultimate reality, and so begins his theological step, from "life" to "Life." The cinema described and analyzed above doesn't merely "tell a story" or "convey information" about certain people and what they did. Rather, it perceptually engages us in a dance, at once amid and beyond the sway of time, about the timeless truth of living. This chapter has argued that cinema is not only accommodated within an Henryan framework, but may serve to fill an essential role in the "intensification of life," and, on a theological level, serve as conduit for the salvific process of being "reborn" into Life. With a proper Henryan understanding of cinema established, we may assert that, for Henry, cinema can prove just as salvific as he claims art is in other contexts. Throughout his theological trilogy Henry identifies Life as the ground of all being, namely the Christian God, and insists we find ourselves in this Life. In Life we share a certain ontological identity with Life itself through the Son of God ("the First Living"[50]), Jesus Christ. This means that, within an Henryan soteriology, any rebirth in life is in some sense a rebirth in the divine Life, which equals a kind of resurrection. For Henry, art—within which we must include cinema—is a particularly important vehicle for this spiritual transformation: "Art is the resurrection of eternal life."[51] To live and move and be might seem commonplace, but to recall, in the deepest parts of ourselves, the Source and Power that enables and grounds us might be the greatest work the cinema can perform.

Notes

1 Michel Henry, *Seeing the Invisible: On Kandinsky*, trans. Scott Davidson (London: Continuum, 2009), 105.
2 I will capitalize "life" only when speaking of the divine Life in order to preserve the distinction that Henry makes in his theological trilogy.
3 Michel Henry, *Barbarism*, trans. Scott Davidson (London: Continuum, 2012).
4 Michel Henry, *I Am the Truth: Toward a Philosophy of Christianity*, trans. Susan Emanuel (Stanford: Stanford University Press, 2003), 29.
5 For example: "It is true that 2 + 3 = 5. Except that what is true in this way … must first show itself to me. It … presupposes an original truth, a first, and pure manifestation— an unveiling power without which no unveiling would be produced, and without which, consequently, nothing true in the second sense, nothing unveiled, would be

possible." Michel Henry, *Incarnation: A Philosophy of Flesh*, trans. Karl Hefty (Evanston, IL: Northwestern University Press, 2015, 24).
6 Acts 17:28, trans. David Bentley Hart, *The New Testament: A Translation* (New Haven, CT: Yale University Press, 2017).
7 Henry, *I Am the Truth*, 27–28.
8 Henry, *I Am the Truth*, 13.
9 See Michel Henry, "Art et Phénoménologie de la Vie," in *Phénoménologie de la Vie*, vol. 3, *De l'Art du Politique* (Paris: Presses Universitaires de France, 2003), 283–308. This interview originally appeared under the same title in *Prétentaine*, 6, Esthétiques (1996): 27–43. All translations original.
10 Henry, *Seeing the Invisible*, 6–7.
11 Henry, *Seeing the Invisible*, 7.
12 My thanks to J. Aaron Simmons for this insight.
13 Henry, *Seeing the Invisible*, 20.
14 See Henry, *I am the Truth*; idem, *Incarnation*; and idem, *Words of Christ*, trans. Christina M. Gschwandtner (Grand Rapids, MI: Wm. B. Eerdmans, 2012).
15 Henry describes television as "the truth of technology ... the practice of barbarism, *par excellence*." Henry, *Barbarism*, 129.
16 Henry, *Seeing the Invisible*, 73.
17 Henry, "Art et Phénoménologie de la Vie," 301.
18 Henry, *Barbarism*, 141.
19 See Julian Hanich, *The Audience Effect: On the Collective Cinema Experience* (Edinburgh: Edinburgh University Press, 2018).
20 E.g., Rudolf Arnheim, *Film as Art* (Berkeley: University of California Press, 1969), and Sergei Eisenstein, *Film Form: Essays in Film Theory*, trans. Jay Leyda (New York: Harcourt, 1969).
21 The bibliography on this issue is enormous, but Dudley Andrew helpfully summarizes the classic debate in *The Major Film Theories* (Oxford: Oxford University Press, 1976).
22 Henry published four novels: *Le Jeune Officier* (Paris: Gallimard, 1954), *L'Amour les Yeux Fermés* (Paris: Gallimard, 1977), *Le Fils du Roi* (Paris: Gallimard, 1981), and *Le Cadavre Indiscret* (Paris: Albin-Michel, 1996).
23 "The imagination is immanent, because life experiences itself in an immediacy that is never broken and never separates from itself; it is a pathos and the plenitude of an overflowing experience lacking nothing.... The imagination brings into being what has not yet taken place in being: hitherto inexperienced tones, impressions, emotions, feelings and forces.... The movement of the imagination is thus nothing other than the movement of life, its internal becoming, the tireless process of its coming into itself, an arrival in which it is felt in ever more vast, differentiated and intense experiences." Henry, *Seeing the Invisible*, 107–08.
24 See Henry, "Art et Phénoménologie de la Vie," 302 f.
25 Henry, *Seeing the Invisible*, 43.
26 See Henry, *Seeing the Invisible*, 93 f.
27 Wassily Kandinsky, "On the Question of Form," in *The Blue Reiter Almanac*, ed. Wassily Kandinsky and Franz Marc, trans. Henning Falkenstein (Boston, MA: MFA Publications, 1974), 160–69.
28 He even dismisses some abstract painters who are driven solely, in his view, by merely reducing representation and so remain in the *ek-static* tradition. Henry, *Seeing the Invisible*, 14–15.

29 Henry, *Seeing the Invisible,* 107.
30 Henry, "Art et Phénoménologie de la Vie," 283.
31 Pure, abstract visual formalism in film is not representative of cinema as a whole, but can be readily found in avant-garde and experimental films. For example, something like a Kandinskian aesthetic operates in many films by Stan Brakhage.
32 Henry, "Art et Phénoménologie de la Vie," 291.
33 The ascription of particular feelings to specific colors (e.g., Henry, *Seeing the Invisible*, 82) is contestable, but the general principle stands: that feelings immediately engendered by colors transcend their representational functions.
34 Henry, *Seeing the Invisible,* 113.
35 Henry, *Seeing the Invisible,* 102–05. Henry is clear that mere "addition" or aggregation is not sufficient. While Richard Wagner's idea of *Gesamkunstwerk* is a conceptual predecessor, here both Henry and Kandinsky distance themselves from Wagner's allegedly ekstatic operatic ideal. Monumental arts must be directed toward life inwardly, teleologically; art that aims at external meaning "teaches us nothing" and can only be creative if "the source of its tones is the tones of the movements themselves—the abstract movements—that lack any objective meaning and are reduced to their pure subjectivity." Ibid., 104.
36 Michel Chion, *Audio-Vision: Sound on Screen* (New York: Columbia University Press, 1994).
37 *Seeing the Invisible*, 16.
38 Henry, *Seeing the Invisible,* 44.
39 Henry, "Art et Phénoménologie de la Vie," 293.
40 Henry, "Art et Phénoménologie de la Vie," 307.
41 Indeed, this aesthetic strategy is a hallmark of Kieślowski's *oeuvre*. See Joseph G. Kickasola, *The Films of Krzysztof Kieślowski: The Liminal Image* (New York: Continuum, 2004), chapter 2.
42 Henry, *Seeing the Invisible,* 44. The context here is hand movement in modern dance.
43 To name a few, see Vivian Sobchack, *Carnal Thoughts: Embodiment and Moving Image Culture* (Berkeley: University of California Press, 2004), Laura U. Marks, *The Skin of the Film: Intercultural Cinema, Embodiment, and the Senses* (Durham, NC: Duke University Press, 2000), and Luis Rocha-Antunes, *The Multisensory Film Experience: A Cognitive Model of Experiential Film Aesthetics* (London: Intellect, 2016).
44 Henry, "Art et Phénoménologie de la Vie," 295.
45 Much later in the film, this music is revealed as Julie's, written with her late husband. One can interpret this in symbolic terms, but only belatedly. Again, Kieślowski insists on the force of the "otherworldly" power in the moment, with deliberate obfuscation of any initial diegetic or narrative "explanation" or interpretation.
46 Quoted in Annette Insdorf, *Double Lives, Second Chances: The Cinema of Krzysztof Kieślowski* (New York: Hyperion, 1999), xv, from an interview with *Télérama* (Paris: September 1993).
47 The very symptoms of an "ordinary existence where the pathetic force of life remains unspent" is "killing our world," according to Henry. Henry, *Seeing the Invisible*, 123.
48 Henry, *I am the Truth*, 269.
49 Gottfried Leibniz, *The Monadology: An Edition for Students*, trans. Nicholas Rescher (University of Pittsburgh Press, 1714/1991), 135.
50 Henry, *I am the Truth*, 57.
51 Henry, *Seeing the Invisible*, 162.

Bibliography

Andrew, Dudley. *The Major Film Theories*. Oxford: Oxford University Press, 1976.
Arnheim, Rudolf. *Film as Art*. Berkeley: University of California Press, 1969.
Chion, Michel. *Audio-Vision: Sound on Screen*. New York: Columbia University Press, 1994.
Eisenstein, Sergei. *Film Form: Essays in Film Theory*. Translated by Jay Leyda. New York: Harcourt, 1969.
Hanich, Julian. *The Audience Effect: On the Collective Cinema Experience*. Edinburgh: Edinburgh University Press, 2018.
Hart, David Bentley. *The New Testament: A Translation*. New Haven, CT: Yale University Press, 2017.
Henry, Michel. "Art et Phénoménologie de la Vie." In *Phénoménologie de la Vie*, vol. 3, *De l'Art et du Politique*, 283–308. Paris: Presses Universitaires de France, 2003.
Henry, Michel. *Barbarism*. Translated by Scott. Davidson. London: Continuum, 2012.
Henry, Michel. *I Am the Truth: Toward a Philosophy of Christianity*. Translated by Susan Emanuel. Stanford, CA: Stanford University Press, 2003.
Henry, Michel. *Incarnation: A Philosophy of Flesh*. Translated by Karl Hefty. Evanston, IL: Northwestern University Press, 2015.
Henry, Michel. *Seeing the Invisible: On Kandinsky*. Translated by Scott Davidson. London: Continuum, 2009.
Henry, Michel. *Words of Christ*. Translated by Christina M. Gschwandtner. Grand Rapids, MI: Wm. B. Eerdmans, 2012.
Insdord, Annette. *Double Lives, Second Chances: The Cinema of Krzysztof Kieślowski*. New York: Hyperion, 1999.
Kandinsky, Wassily. "On the Question of Form." In *The Blue Reiter Almanac*, edited by Wassily Kandinsky and Franz Marc, translated by Henning Falkenstein, 160–69. Boston, MA: MFA Publications, 1974.
Kickasola, Joseph G. *The Films of Krzysztof Kieślowski: The Liminal Image*. New York: Continuum, 2004.
Leibniz, Gottfried. *The Monadology: An Edition for Students*. Translated by Nicholas Rescher. University of Pittsburgh Press, 1991.
Marks, Laura U. *The Skin of the Film: Intercultural Cinema, Embodiment, and the Senses*. Durham, NC: Duke University Press, 2000.
Rocha-Antunes, Luis. *The Multisensory Film Experience: A Cognitive Model of Experiential Film Aesthetics*. London: Intellect, 2016.
Sobchack, Vivian. *Carnal Thoughts: Embodiment and Moving Image Culture*. Berkeley: University of California Press, 2004.

Part Two

Carnal Encounter

7

Scandal in the Cornaro Chapel: Desire for God and *The Ecstasy of St. Teresa*

Martha Reineke

The Ecstasy of St. Teresa, Gian Lorenzo Bernini's greatest sculptural achievement, was received by his contemporaries as a compelling testimony to faith (Plate 3). Yet, in the following centuries, art historians and critics, from Burkhardt to Lacan, have been confounded by the sculpture's evocation of the erotic.[1] I attribute the acute discomfort of the work's commentators to features of modernity that create seemingly impassable disjunctions between the erotic and the religious, as these are reflected in tensions between popular and institutional religion and replicated by art historians. Situating *The Ecstasy of St. Teresa* within its cultural context, I turn to Mieke Bal, Gilles Deleuze, and Maurice Merleau-Ponty to sketch a less fraught encounter. Although they are children of modernity, their work suggests a fresh approach to *The Ecstasy of St. Teresa*. Illuminating the holy desire that infused Bernini and that drew the faithful to the Cornaro Chapel, their insights invite us to consider all features of humanity—our bodies, our passions, and our minds—when characterizing divine love and the human longing for God.

Scandal and Modernity: Retrieving the Erotic within the Religious

Although baroque art has been described as a scandal to the force of dispassionate reason in modernity, René Girard reminds us that "scandal" does not reference easily avoided obstacles or readily resolvable tensions. Arguing that the Greek *scandalon* is best translated as "stumbling block," Girard maintains that scandal causes us to stumble again and again, caught between aversion and desire. Across the centuries, why have we tripped repeatedly over Bernini's carved block of marble, both repelled and fascinated by its stunning beauty and sensuality? Can we experience the sculpture in ways more evocative of Bernini and the faithful of his day than of their successors? If so, drawing once again on rich resources for the creative imagination that emerged during the Renaissance and reached new heights in the Baroque, we can attest anew to the positive role of the body and sexuality in Christian life and thought.

With this aim in view, I contrast my argument with Hans Urs von Balthasar's theological aesthetics of the baroque. Both von Balthasar and I link the spirit of the baroque, visible in its art and sculpture, to an era in which women's mystic spirituality predominated, and we identify the erotic as a feature of that spirituality.[2] Yet, when von Balthasar extricates the erotic from sexual desire, consigning the erotic to the spiritual, he implicates it in a mind/body dualism. Rather than upholding the affirmation of embodiment in baroque spirituality, as I hope to do, he remains scandalized.

Initially, von Balthasar is fascinated by female mystics' "metaphysical sublimity"; yet, his attraction is matched by his aversion. The mystics' sensibilities sometimes "deviate," and the sublime "slips down to the level of the private and erotic."[3] He strives to avoid scandal entirely when discussing Angela da Foligno, stating that she "issues harsh warnings" such that "every kind of particular eros" is transcended.[4] With Catherine of Siena, he upholds the "elucidation of what is contained in every genuinely evangelical vision,"[5] conforming to a "passionate indifference."[6] Finally, von Balthasar's discovers in Ignatius an insurmountable barrier to physical passion tainting the human desire for God.

Ignatius becomes for von Balthasar the simulacrum of a scandal-free baroque. "Representing ... a fragment of eternal knowledge," Ignatius's contemplation "becomes completely transparent to divine will and demand."[7] Accordingly, he brings about "a new awareness of the manifestation of divine glory in the world."[8] With Ignatian spirituality providing a frame, "worldly beauty" comes to align with the "greater glory of God."[9] Moreover, when the "centre of unity and gravity" in God to which art and architecture point is beset by political machinations that threaten to ascribe to these works lesser forms of glory,[10] von Balthasar suggests, Ignatian spirituality quickly rebalances that center. Obedience "completely purifies all the powers of intellect, will and emotion and stretches them to the limit in order to place them at the disposal of God's eternal, free and loving will."[11] Ignatius solidifies for von Balthasar a permanent separation of the erotic from sexual desire: That which ascends and transcends is carried ever higher and away from that which descends and deviates. In ascribing to eros this telos, von Balthasar commits to the full spiritualization of eros.

When von Balthasar turns his attention to eros in the modern period, he is tripped up by scandal once again. He does criticize "oversimplifications of the modern period" that exchange a "spiritualistic flight from the world" for "piety of the world."[12] Yet, when von Balthasar claims that "pious metaphysical eros" becomes "primarily sexual" in the unfolding of modernity, he delineates matter from spirit in ways that are thoroughly modern in conception and, precisely for that reason, scandalous.[13] After all, as modernity emerged from the Enlightenment, challenging tradition, custom, and law and elevating reason as a guide for human activity, for every demonstrated truth claim stemming from the practice of reason, countervailing claims described a subject in the grip of forces and processes unforeseen and unimagined in the premodern era. As doubts multiplied, key features of the Enlightenment—rationality, identity, and representation—fell into crisis. In a world that purportedly had buried God and taken full possession of reason, modernity both captured rising concerns about the status of that achievement and attested to the impact of unseen forces on humans' imaginative and ethical consciousness.[14] In this new world, mystics were not freed of scandal; rather, in sway to

Plate 1 George Rickey, *Two Open Triangles Up Gyratory*, 1982, stainless steel. Raclin Murphy Museum of Art, University of Notre Dame, Gift of the George Rickey Foundation, 2009.046.001 © 2023 George Rickey Foundation, Inc. / Licensed by Artists Rights Society (ARS), New York.

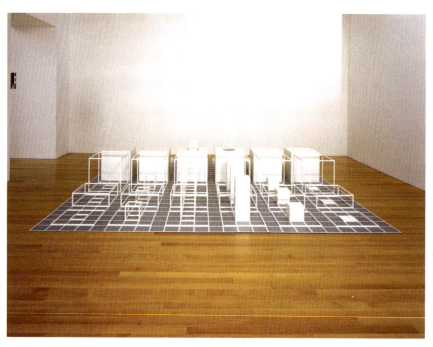

Plate 2 Sol LeWitt, *Serial Project I (ABCD)* (1966), baked enamel on steel units over baked enamel on aluminum, 20 in. × 13 ft. 7 in. × 13 ft. 7 in. The Museum of Modern Art, New York, Gift of Agnes Gund and purchase by exchange, 515.1978.a-ssss. © 2023 The LeWitt Estate / Artists Rights Society (ARS), New York. Digital image, The Museum of Modern Art, New York/Scala, Florence.

Plate 3 Bernini, *Agony and Ecstasy of St. Teresa*, seventeenth-century marble, Getty Images 115623504. Credit: Mondadori Portfolio / Contributor.

Plate 4 Sheila Gallagher, *Plastic Lila* (2013), melted plastic on armature, 81 × 64.5 in. Crystal Bridges Museum of American Art, Bentonville, AR © 2023 Sheila Gallagher.

Plate 5 Sheila Gallagher, *Plastic Glenstal* (2012–2013), melted plastic mounted on armature, 48 × 81 in. © 2023 Sheila Gallagher.

Plate 6 Sheila Gallagher, *Rasa* (2013), single channel video, Courtesy of September Gallery © 2023 Sheila Gallagher.

Plate 7 Sheila Gallagher, *Plastic Paradisus* (2013), melted plastic mounted on armature, 53 × 47 in. © 2023 Sheila Gallagher.

Plate 8 Milton Avery, *China Christ*, 1946, Oil on canvas. Raclin Murphy Museum of Art, University of Notre Dame, Gift of the Milton Avery Trust, 1992.009 © 2023 The Milton Avery Trust / Artists Rights Society (ARS), New York.

new forces that both fascinated and repelled those who looked on, their desires were attributed to hysteria or its sublimation. Because von Balthasar separates the metaphysical from the physical under the constraints of modernity, he is subject to the modern devolution of the mystical. His dispassionate center cannot hold.[15]

While discussing mystics, von Balthasar states that "important people" such as Teresa of Avila "have to remain unmentioned."[16] Confronting the challenge she poses to von Balthasar, from which he turns away, I contend that, in order to comprehend Teresa's faith or Bernini's sculpture, we must consider sexuality as a feature of the human relationship to divine eros. In sway to modernity post-Freud, we may balk. Nevertheless, as Louise Nelstrop observes, when we accept that "physical and spiritual sensation cannot be prised apart," a nuanced interplay between body and soul opens up before us.[17] Bernini is well chosen as our guide, for he is not constrained by celibate longing that glosses over erotic desire in flights of metaphysical fancy or by forces of modernity that assign libidinal urges to mystics which they must sublimate lest they succumb to them. *The Ecstasy of St. Teresa* becomes an invitation to consider anew the sexual love to which Teresa of Avila's mystical theology attests. After all, as Simone Weil so eloquently states, "To reproach mystics with loving God by means of the faculty of sexual love is as though one were to reproach a painter with making pictures by means of colors composed of material substances. We haven't anything else with which to love."[18]

Not Baroque? *The Ecstasy St. Teresa* in Art Historical Perspective

The baroque has been described as "the grit in the oyster of art history," as Helen Hills reminds us in *Rethinking the Baroque*.[19] Even though the baroque "is foundational in the very formation of the discipline of art history," historians sideline it. Hills advocates re-engagement, perceiving in the baroque positive features that have troubled others. Her insights have salience for reflecting on *The Ecstasy of St. Teresa*. Hills emphasizes that the baroque radiates from within culture "a spiritual presence that endows its spaces and fragments with a collective unity," thereby facilitating engagement "with the material without treating materiality too hastily as [an] instantiation of idea."[20] The baroque enfolds us, eliciting from us an embodied grasp, demanding our immediate connection. In this way, as Mieke Bal confirms, baroque epistemology is "anchored in the inseparability of mind and body, form and matter, line and color, image and discourse."[21]

Most suggestive for our exploration of *The Ecstasy of St. Teresa* is Bal's claim concerning the defining feature of baroque: for the first time in Western history, *the human subject is self-reflectively aware of its relationality with an other*.[22] The baroque becomes home to a novel epistemological posture that is fundamentally relational and joined with humans' newly emergent capacity to take a point of view.[23] As Bal explains, the baroque "establishes a relationship between subject and object, and then goes back to the subject again, a subject that is changed by that movement." "Folded into one another," firm distinctions between subject and object are abandoned.[24] As relationality reweaves the social fabric, time and space are reconfigured. Solicited by the other, the subject's dynamic interactions rework the field of memory.[25]

Bal's description of baroque epistemology opens to understanding three aspects of the Cornaro Chapel and its centerpiece, *The Ecstasy of St. Teresa*: the space's theatrical elements, the sculpture's attestation to Teresa's embodied desire for God, and the Eucharistic symbolism which pervades the whole. These features affirm Teresa's relationship with her Beloved and facilitate worshippers' participation in that relationship. As we perceive *The Ecstasy of St. Teresa* in ways similar to Bernini and the faithful of his time, we can commence reimagining Christian spirituality. The erotic is not something to be sublimated, rather, embodied sexual expression is integral to human life. Considering our sexuality as a formative feature of Christian life, we can bring the erotic and the spiritual to fullness, without denying their bodily origin and physical expression.[26]

The Theatre of the Cornaro Chapel: A Cataphatic Theology

Throughout his life, Bernini was active in theatre, staging dramatic productions on behalf of others and offering his own. However, Bernini's contribution to theatre as a visual form has been seen as a liability for his work as a sculptor. Accused of eliciting from worshippers only superficial engagement with the stories that he depicts in his sculptural groups, Bernini's critics throw "baroque theatricality" at him as an epithet. So also do they disparage Bernini's artistic achievement as "stagecraft," especially in regard to the Cornaro Chapel.[27] Yet, those who deem Bernini's theatrically informed perspective ill-suited for religious works distort his singular achievement. Incorporating techniques of drama in his art in an exemplary and original way, Bernini introduces his contemporaries to that definitive feature of the baroque: responsive self-awareness.[28] As Bernini makes relationality intrinsic to the reception by worshippers of figures he cuts from stone, he materializes the theological, bringing together heaven and earth, spirit and body.

In contrast to individuals who respond voyeuristically to *The Ecstasy of St. Teresa*,[29] when we immerse ourselves in the baroque, we are afforded a sensual and intimate connection free of scandal. Bernini's thespian expertise is instrumental in creating this affect. As Genevieve Warwick explains, while Bernini shares with his sculptor peers a commitment to animate life in stone, to make marble speak,[30] unlike them he focuses on how the "the acting body finds the most eloquent gestural language in order to signify its affective meaning."[31] Effective acting crystallizes and intensifies bodily forms, strengthening mimetic ties between the actor and the viewer. When this relational deepening of experience elicits a replicable response, theatrical gestures become ritualized.

Bernini takes inspiration for the Cornaro Chapel from Ignatius's *Spiritual Exercises*. A devout Catholic, he is well-versed in Ignatian spirituality. Placing Ignatius in service to a different end than has von Balthasar, Bernini is able to step free of scandal. Transposing lessons from the *Spiritual Exercises* to the Cornaro Chapel and melding them with theatrical expression, he creates a spiritual language of gesture that facilitates worshippers' ritualized responses. Popular conventions of prayer influenced by the *Exercises* enjoin the faithful to experience Christ's passion mimetically: Their prayers are "structured by the affective memory of bodily experience."[32] The *Exercises* ask that persons in the act of prayer "picture a scene"; Teresa, whose own spiritual expression reflects a Jesuit influence, describes in her writings "making pictures" in her mind as she prays.[33]

Inspired by David Albertson, I suggest that Bernini's theatrical exposition of Teresa's spirituality is "an imaginative cartography of mystical space grounded in a cataphatic theology."[34] Albertson argues that theologians who dismiss cataphatic spirituality for purportedly naïve pictorial thinking mischaracterize its revelatory power, bypassing a fruitful conjunction between popular and institutionalized religious expression. Mystics who embrace cataphatic theology actively participate in "a divine activity of space creation, opening new worlds, shaping new geometries."[35] Exemplary representatives include Bernard of Clairvaux, who mapped scriptures as sacred space rather than sacred history; Hildegard of Bingen, who created in inner geometry of the body that revealed a cosmos of sacred meaning; Ignatius, for whom prayer begins when the "imagination compares an interior landscape for the soul to inhabit"; and Teresa of Avila.[36] In her *Interior Castle*, she traverses liminal spaces which include *moradas* ("mansions" or "dwellings"), imagining a complex architecture of the contemplative soul in relationship with God.[37]

Significantly, Albertson expressly aligns the power of cataphatic imagery with theatre and ritual performance. Pictorial images are limited by semantic content and can devolve into allegories or illustrations. However, when images take on a third dimension and are staged, the resulting animation is no longer predicative but fully liturgical.[38] A dynamic mapping of sacred space, presented theatrically in a sculptural group, transforms ordinary space, resulting in a profound experience of the divine.[39] Viewed in this light, as Warwick suggests, Bernini's sculpture can be "apprehended through the cultural prism of Catholic mysticism's long history of conjoined devotions."[40] Thanks to Bernini's cataphatic mapping of sacred space in the Cornaro Chapel, its eucharistic symbolism realizes its liturgical promise. When Teresa's body is presented as a tabernacle and she is joined in nuptial ecstasy with her Beloved, worshippers engage in bodily mimesis, forging a powerful affective bond with God.[41]

Making Marble Signify: A Body Ablaze with Love

Hills states that baroque art enfolds the viewer, eliciting embodied knowing. That is why worshippers are taken up into the life of God as they stand before *The Ecstasy of St. Teresa*. As Bernini sculpts Teresa's transverberation, marble becomes flesh, and this flesh becomes ours. That Teresa's body, all but hidden under voluminous folds of marble, produces this effect appears counterintuitive; however, as I will demonstrate in what follows, appealing to Deleuze and Merleau-Ponty for insight, we can grasp how Teresa's hidden form not only attests to her fully embodied communion with her Beloved but also supports worshippers' deep connection to God.[42]

An exceptionally skilled artist, Bernini could have sculpted Teresa's body as he did Ludovica Albertoni's. In the *Blessed Ludovica Albertoni*, folds of clothing cling to Ludovica's figure, flow between her legs, and compress under the pressure of her fingers as, touching one breast, she writhes rapturously.[43] Sculpting *The Ecstasy of St. Teresa*, Bernini eschews a similarly intimate display, choosing instead to swathe Teresa's body in capacious draperies. Rippling across the marble surface, their folds conceal Teresa's paroxysm when the angel's arrow enters and withdraws from her body. Writing of this moment, Teresa says:

> When he drew it out . . . he left me completely afire with a great love for God. The pain was so sharp that it made me utter several moans; and so excessive was the sweetness caused me by this intense pain that one can never wish to lose it, nor will the soul be content with anything less than God. It is not bodily pain, but spiritual, though the body has a share in it—indeed, a great share.[44]

Teresa attests to a powerfully embodied encounter with God even though her body is concealed by Bernini's rendering of her form. Why and how does Bernini create this effect?

Warwick suggests that in carving marble to create the impression of billowing fabric, Bernini obscures Teresa's body in order that she not be taken as an object of desire. Notwithstanding that some art historians ascribe to Teresa a languid pose suggestive of death, Bernini does not hide Teresa's *desire*; it remains manifest. Teresa's head is thrown back; her lips are parted in a moan; her eyes are rolled into their sockets behind half-closed lids; the toes of her exposed foot are curled, and she is spasming through her pelvis.[45] The line that the arrow will follow when the angel thrusts it again goes to Teresa's pelvis, not her heart. In all these ways, demonstrating an artist's eye for detail, Bernini affirms the unity of the spiritual and sexual as he ably depicts the physiology of female orgasm (face, feet, and torso). Even as Bernini's chisel against the stone fully exposes Teresa's scandalous desire, the layered folds of marble protect Teresa from objectification and emphasize her *agency*: she is "the agent and mark of her spiritual longing, aflame with love for God."[46] The marble, highly polished and deeply undercut to enhance the reflection of light,[47] doubles over and over on itself, all but leaping upward, spreading like flame, becoming the visual counterpart to Teresa's words: "*toda abrasada*."[48]

Writing on *The Ecstasy of St. Teresa* with reference to Walter Benjamin's essay on translation, Bal explains this remarkable effect. Although she entertains the notion that Bernini is transmitting Teresa's account of her transverberation into a new language of sculpture, Bal ultimately discounts this possibility. After all, when Bernini "sights, cites, and sites" Teresa's transverberation, the result differs profoundly from what typically counts as translation (e.g., a one-for-one exchange of a Spanish for English word). Seventeenth-century engravings that "illustrate" the transverberation more closely resemble that mode of translation.[49] By contrast, Bernini evokes the exact moment Teresa and her Beloved are joined. As Giovanni Careri confirms, Bernini "lovingly and in detail incorporates the *original mode of signification*."[50] By showing Teresa's body in flames, Bal insightfully observes, Bernini removes all distinctions between interior and exterior, subject and object, divine and human. In this way, the blaze signifies ecstasy.[51] In marked contrast to Lacan's crude "translation" of Teresa's transverberation,[52] which imputes to Teresa a desire for more orgasm-producing penetration,[53] Bernini faithfully renders Teresa's words, preserving in stone the moment when divine fire already has spread through and from her body. The angel stands poised to reinsert the arrow; however, Teresa already is one with her Beloved.

Yet, we may ask, how exactly do the voluminous folds and rising flames that Bernini has sculpted show Teresa in that moment of sanctified communion? An answer to our question can be found in Deleuze. For him, as Hills reminds us, folds are the synecdoche of baroque signification: the baroque endlessly produces them, twisting and turning, layering fold upon fold. The folds do not serve a decorative purpose; rather, they bear forth the desire of the body beneath them. Attentive to Deleuze, we can consider that, as Teresa's body burns, these folds are born to infinity. This "going beyond" is profoundly baroque.[54] As Hills affirms, the surging of the baroque is not an excess to be decried; rather, when sculpture and architecture veer into each other, overrunning limits, the soul no longer can be separated from the body or the sacred from the profane.[55]

Merleau-Ponty's notion of the flesh, sketched in posthumous writings published as *The Visible and the Invisible*, helpfully augments Deleuze's suggestive account, facilitating our understanding of how rippling folds of drapery bring directly to the fore Teresa's mystical encounter with God. Merleau-Ponty describes the flesh as folds in being. For him, the fundamental relationality of being is attested to by the coiling over of the visible on the invisible, flesh on flesh. Writes Merleau-Ponty,

> If ... the flesh ... is not the union or compound of two substances but thinkable itself, if there is a relation of the visible with itself that traverses me and constitutes me as seer, this circle which I do not form, which forms me, this coiling over of the visible upon the visible, can traverse, animate other bodies as well as my own.[56]

Merleau-Ponty depicts this relation as a chiasm. A kinship between the sensing and the sensed makes relationality possible. Yet, in these late writings, Merleau-Ponty provides no point of departure for the sentience he celebrates. He assumes a subject already formed and does not explain how "tactility" itself—the condition for touching and being touched—comes into being.

Merleau-Ponty is more forthcoming in his lectures on Malebranche, transcribed by Jean DePrun.[57] As highlighted by Judith Butler, Merleau-Ponty sets forth in these lectures the founding conditions of touch.[58] He observes that Malebranche rejects Descartes' "I think, therefore I am," replacing it with "I feel, therefore I am." Expressly evoking the baroque epistemology to which Bal has called our attention, Malebranche avers "I can feel only that which touches me."[59] But what initiates that possibility? Malebranche responds that nothing is more certain than "sentiment" to furnish the grounds of existence. By "sentiment," he means "that which alone reveals to us a dimension of divine life, this profound life of God [that] is only accessible through grace."[60] Grace, in other words, the moment of "being touched by God," inaugurates our existence as relational beings.

Bernini shares Malebranche's views concerning touch and revelatory experience. Confirming that sculpture captures the essence of the baroque, Bernini cites fundamental differences between illusions created in painting and direct realizations in sculpture of the mysteries of faith and the essence of being.[61] As Margaretha Rossholm Lagerlöf points out, in Bernini's writings the sculptor challenges the notion that sight is central to mystical experience.[62] For him, sculpture elicits from us a tactile desire that brings our vision to life. Definitive to Bernini's notion of *bel composto* is the moment when we become able to "witness to a sacred event" because of "the feeling of a visual touch."[63] The sculpted white marble folds and fire of *The Ecstasy of St. Teresa* are exemplary of this graceful witness.

"If I had not Created Heaven . . . :" The Cornaro Chapel as Eucharistic Event

The eucharistic and nuptial symbolism of the Cornaro Chapel bring to full expression worshippers' communion with God. By convention from medieval times, a chapel is "a church inside a church." Here, songs, chants, prayers, and tableaus of biblical stories and the lives of the saints are woven into and through the liturgy supported by a chapel's architecture and decor.[64] Bernini's Cornaro Chapel magnifies this tradition, mapping coordinates of sacred space that direct worshippers to a center, the *Ecstasy of St. Teresa*. More than a background setting for these sacred enactments, as Lavin attests, the chapel provides for a multi-sensory, all-encompassing existential event.[65]

In a novel instantiation of the baroque, eucharistic symbolism pervades the chapel, centers on the altarpiece, and rises therefrom toward heaven. The barrel vault depicts moments of Teresa's spiritual development, moving worshippers in temporal progression as they draw closer to the altar.[66] The chapel cladding features a variety of marbles and precious stones in an array of colors which, when subjected to Bernini's complex light treatments, produce luminescence, intentionally recalling Teresa's depiction in *The Interior Castle* of rooms in which the soul resides in prayer and inviting the worshipper to conceive the chapels as the soul's home. Complementing this imagery is the altar niche, which suggests the *sancta sanctorum* of prayer.[67] Balconied boxes set in the chapel walls on either side of the altar contain images of the Cornaro family and religious figures. Pointing to faith and reason as alternative routes to salvation, they guide worshippers into proper relationship to the sacrament and prepare them to bear witness to the eucharistic meaning of Teresa's presence at the altar.[68] On the left, they portray an internal path, posing in attitudes of logical reflection, prayer, and reflection; on the right, they attest to an external path that acknowledges revelation, communication and action. Highly animated in their respective roles, they seem "real," generating an empathetic response from the observer. Urging worshippers toward the vanishing point that is the altar, these sculpted images invite worshippers to join them as witnesses to its tableau.[69]

The altar's eucharistic symbolism is introduced by a gilt bronze, lapis lazuli relief of the Last Supper on the altar front.[70] The altar niche, with an interior higher and wider than its opening, enshrines the sculpture group in a tabernacle.[71] Heightening the effect is a sunburst display of metal, which was lit at one time by reflecting mirrors and two thousand hidden lamps. Associated with *Quarant'ore* devotions, the sunburst contextualizes a cycle of prayer and a ritual avowing the saving power of the Eucharist and Christ's resurrection in anticipation of his second coming.[72] Teresa's own writings have offered prayer as a metaphor for eucharistic communion. Now, further fusion of her body with Christ's, attested to in the transverberation, aligns her wounds of love with those of the crucified Christ.

In bodily mimesis with Christ's suffering, Teresa also replicates his death. That Teresa's death is a culmination of her union with her Beloved is demonstrated in a miracle: although she was seventy when she died, at the moment of her passing her features became young and beautiful. Bernini's altarpiece, capturing the moment when the "wound of love" becomes a mortal wound, affords theological and biographical evidence of a young and beautiful Teresa dying in Christ. In this way, as Lavin eloquently suggests, Teresa does not die *for* her faith but *of* her faith.[73] Similarly to the mimetic powers of prayer, the conformity of Teresa's body to her Beloved creates affective links between sacrifice and resurrection that can be replicated by the faithful: "Through physical empathy with his [Christ's] sacrifice the faithful might approach an understanding of God's love."[74]

Placing out of view underlying stonework that supports *The Ecstasy of St. Teresa* and adding multiple sources of illumination from above, Bernini creates the illusion that Teresa is rising through the clouds into the glory of divine light. Levitation is more than a sign of sanctity in this tableau. Bernini depicts theophany, a prevailing theological motif in the early modern period.[75] At a time when levitation was common among saints,[76] Teresa's stood out because she levitated during the eucharistic offering. As a consequence, her levitations were comprehended as a direct effect of her union with Christ and a contemporaneous confirmation of the doctrine of transubstantiation (affirmed at the Council of Trent in 1551): having partaken of Christ's body, she could share in his resurrection.[77] As Bernini captures the moment when Teresa ascends in response to the call of her Beloved, he joins eucharistic and nuptial symbolism.

Nuptial symbolism throughout the Cornaro Chapel includes angels performing music, flowers strewn loosely among the altar surrounds, a bride's floral crown above the chapel entrance and, most expressly, a stunning declaration of love made to Teresa by her Beloved, which is inscribed above the chapel entrance on a banderole: "If I had not created heaven I would create it for you alone." These words, recorded by Teresa's confessor in her biography and quoted in testimony during her canonization by her niece, connect individual elements of worshippers' experience.[78] Worshippers observe eucharistic devotions as they make their way to the altar. Standing before it at last, they witness Teresa's response to her Beloved in all its ecstatic realization. In this way, Bernini draws together three moments of Teresa's life that elicit participation by the faithful: her mystical marriage, her eucharistic unity with the crucified Christ, and her rising to heaven with Christ at the moment of her death. Embodied love in the fullness of sensual expression, sacrifice, and the promise of resurrection and salvation create a unified experience.[79]

Conclusion

Attending to the defining feature of the baroque—the realization of *the human subject as self-reflectively aware of its relationality with an other*—I have offered an interpretation of *The Ecstasy of St. Teresa* that accounts phenomenologically for Bernini's portrayal of

Teresa's embodied love for God and our responsiveness to it. Analyzing the Cornaro Chapel as theatre, describing its eucharistic symbolism, and homing in on the most powerful feature of the sculpture—the draperies that fold in and around Teresa, becoming flame—I have illuminated the spiritual significance of this sculpture. In these ways, I have suggested that Bernini offers a mystical theology that remains a compelling alternative to competing understandings of the human: the divided Cartesian self and the narcissistic modern personality. Most significantly, I have suggested that Bernini can inspire us today to consider how sexuality is integral to our lives. To the extent that we are able to affirm embodied desire as a formative feature of a faithful life, we can seek, as did Bernini in his day, to bring the erotic and the spiritual to full expression without denying the role human sexuality plays in that effort.

Our efforts to do so have expansive implications beyond supporting an affirmative theological perspective on human embodiment. St. Teresa is the baroque saint *par example*: baroque epistemology not only creates subjects who are reflectively aware of their relationality to an other, it also reconfigures the entire social fabric, transforming how we relate to each other in community. Teresa's desire for God, grounded in impassioned and incarnated experience, not only changed her life with God but also how she lived with others. As Mark McIntosh suggests, Teresa did not perceive that her interior castle belonged solely to an inner self. Caught up in the relationality of all life, she would have disagreed profoundly with that distinctive modern perspective on mysticism.[80] Her stance in the world moved forward from desire for and pleasure in her Beloved to a "blossoming elaboration of the soul and its tantalizing maze of public and private spaces."[81] Teresa's visions were distilled into the joy of loving and living in the world.[82] That is why, attuned to the ultimate relationality of God, she founded religious houses. Her ecstatic experience transformed her soul as an image of God. The proof of her unmediated sharing in the body of Christ—the *corpus mysticum*—was found in works of service to others.

Notes

1 Preserved from Bernini's time is one negative review: Bernini "pulled Teresa to the ground and made this pure virgin into a Venus, not only prostrate, but prostituted." See Irving Lavin, *Bernini and the Unity of the Visual Arts* (New York: Oxford University Press, 1980), 121. The trail of critics came later. In addition to Lacan ("You need but go to Rome and see the statue by Bernini to immediately understand that she's coming. There is no doubt about it"), there is Ruskin ("It is impossible for false taste and base feeling to sink lower"), Burkhardt (Bernini forgets "all questions of style because of the scandalous degradation of the supernatural"), and Stendhal (Stendhal pardons "'the Cavalier Bernini all the evil' he had done to the arts"). See Tom Hayes, "A 'Jouissance' Beyond the Phallus: Juno, Saint Teresa, Bernini, Lacan," *American Imago* 56, no. 4 (1999): 336–37.
2 Hans Urs von Balthasar, *The Glory of the Lord: A Theological Aesthetics*, trans. Oliver Davies et al., vol. 5, *The Realm of Metaphysics in the Modern Age* (Edinburgh, Scotland: T & T Clark International, 1991), 78–79.
3 von Balthasar, *The Glory of the Lord,* 5:80.

4   von Balthasar, *The Glory of the Lord,* 5:84.
5   von Balthasar, *The Glory of the Lord,* 5:91.
6   von Balthasar, *The Glory of the Lord,* 5:92.
7   von Balthasar, *The Glory of the Lord,* 5:107–08.
8   von Balthasar, *The Glory of the Lord,* 5:107.
9   von Balthasar, *The Glory of the Lord,* 5:110.
10 von Balthasar, *The Glory of the Lord,* 5:112.
11 von Balthasar, *The Glory of the Lord,* 5:113.
12 von Balthasar, *The Glory of the Lord,* 5:642.
13 von Balthasar, *The Glory of the Lord,* 5:642.
14 Michael H. Whitworth, ed., *Modernism* (Malden, MA: Wiley-Blackwell, 2007), 7. Anthony J. Cascardi, *The Subject of Modernity* (New York: Cambridge University Press, 1992), 128.
15 The effects of "modernizing" Teresa of Avila's spirituality, most often when her actions are interpreted in a psychological register, point to the pervasiveness of a dualistic mindset. Franco Mormando, whose scholarship has been recognized by the American Catholic Historical Association and whose 2013 book *Bernini: His Life and His Rome* has been translated into several languages, redeems Teresa only because he condemns Bernini: The problem with Bernini's display of a sexually aroused Teresa "is Bernini's own libido." He turns to art in order that his libido be "sublimated in an ecclesiastically sanctioned form." See Franco Mormando, *Bernini: His Life and His Rome* (Chicago: University of Chicago Press, 2013), 99, 105–08, 164–65.
16 von Balthasar, *The Glory of the Lord*, 5:81.
17 Louise Nelstrop, "Erotic and Nuptial Imagery," in *The Oxford Handbook of Mystical Theology* (New York: Oxford University Press, 2020), 338.
18 Simone Weil, *The Notebooks of Simone Weil*, trans. Arthur Wills, vol. 2 (London: Routledge Kegan & Paul, 1976), 472.
19 Helen Hills, ed., *Rethinking the Baroque* (New York: Routledge, 2011), 3.
20 Hills, *Rethinking the Baroque*, 31.
21 Mieke Bal, "Baroque Matters," in *Rethinking the Baroque* (New York: Routledge, 2011), 188.
22 Bal, "Baroque Matters," 189.
23 Bal, "Baroque Matters," 189.
24 Bal, "Baroque Matters," 190.
25 Bal, "Baroque Matters," 191.
26 As Robin Jensen, Patrick O'Brien Professor of Theology at the University of Notre Dame, stated as respondent to the original presentation of this paper, Catholic theologians talk regularly about spiritual and intellectual formation as essential to human growth in the development of a closer relationship with God. They talk less often about how bodily formation, including sexual expression as a positive feature of that formation, should and can be similarly subject to faithful development over the course of our lives.
27 Genevieve Warwick, *Bernini: Art as Theatre* (New Haven, CT: Yale University Press, 2013), 5; Lavin, *Bernini and the Unity of the Visual Arts*, 147–49.
28 Lavin, *Bernini and the Unity of the Visual Arts*, 146–47.
29 Salacious features some male viewers find compelling in the sculpture are illuminated by Bal's notion of "responsive self-awareness" as defining the baroque. For example, Mormando recalls the tired trope that the Cornaro Chapel is "the most astounding peep show in art" and Lacan says of Bernini's statue, you "understand immediately that

she's coming." See Jacques Lacan, *Feminine Sexuality: Jacques Lacan and the École Freudienne*, ed. Juliet Mitchell and Jacqueline Rose (New York: W. W. Norton & Company, 1985), 147, and Mormando, *Bernini*, 161. Their voyeuristic/pornographic gaze," oblivious to Teresa of Avila's spiritual agency to which the sculpture attests, shows an incapacity to respond to an other, especially a female other who draws on her own body and her sexual feelings to express her faith. With "knowing" humor aimed at St. Teresa as an object of their gaze, they preserve their fragile subjectivity at the expense of a responsive knowing that would leave them vulnerable before a woman's erotic power. Lacan protests too much when he ascribes *jouissance*—or the spiritual power of the sexual—to Teresa, but says that she knows nothing of it. Lacan, *Feminine Sexuality*, 147.

30 Warwick, *Bernini*, 12.
31 Warwick, *Bernini*, 10.
32 Warwick, *Bernini*, 66.
33 Warwick, *Bernini*, 72.
34 See David Albertson, "Cataphasis, Visualization, and Mystical Space," in *The Oxford Handbook of Mystical Theology* (New York: Oxford University Press, 2020), 347–68.
35 Albertson, "Cataphasis, Visualization, and Mystical Space," 364.
36 Albertson, "Cataphasis, Visualization, and Mystical Space," 362–63.
37 Teresa of Avila, *Interior Castle*, trans. E. Allison Peers (Mineola, NY: Dover Publications, 2007).
38 Albertson, "Cataphasis, Visualization, and Mystical Space," 350.
39 Albertson, "Cataphasis, Visualization, and Mystical Space," 353.
40 Warwick, *Bernini*, 75.
41 Warwick, *Bernini*, 9–10.
42 Conventional treatments of Teresa's transverberation prior to Bernini's treatment portrayed her standing before the angel ready to receive the angel's arrow, kneeling in prayer while levitating, or reclining in a swoon. Bernini preserves the levitation by creating the illusion that she is floating in air, and also shows Teresa reclining. For a history of previous depictions with images, see Warwick, 64–65; Lavin, *Bernini and the Unity of the Visual Arts*, 113–18.
43 Shelley Perlove, *Bernini and the Idealization of Death: The "Blessed Ludovica Albertoni" and the Altieri Chapel* (University Park, PA: Penn State University Press, 1990), 33.
44 Teresa of Avila, *St. Teresa of Avila Three Book Treasury - Interior Castle, The Way of Perfection, and The Book of Her Life*, trans. E. Allison Peers and the Benedictines of Stanbrook (New York: Chump Change, a Harper Collins imprint, 2019), 313.
45 Opting to describe a death pose is Warwick, *Bernini*, 72; Lavin, *Bernini and the Unity of the Visual Arts*, 109) and Robert T. Petersson, *The Art of Ecstasy: Teresa, Bernini, and Crashaw* (New York: Atheneum Books, 1970), 93–95 exemplify the counter-argument.
46 Warwick, *Bernini*, 69.
47 Warwick, *Bernini*, 67.
48 Lavin, *Bernini and the Unity of the Visual Arts*, 111.
49 Mieke Bal, "Ecstatic Aesthetics: Metaphoring Bernini," in *Compelling Visuality: The Work of Art in and out of History* (Minneapolis, MN: University of Minnesota Press, 2003), 8.
50 Giovanni Careri, *Bernini: Flights of Love, the Art of Devotion*, trans. Linda Lappin (Chicago, IL: University Of Chicago Press, 1995), 78. Emphasis mine.
51 Bal, "Ecstatic Aesthetics: Metaphoring Bernini," 18–20.
52 Lacan, *Feminine Sexuality*, 147.

53 See discussion in Jacqueline Rose, "Introduction II," in *Feminine Sexuality: Jacques Lacan and the École Freudienne* (New York: W. W. Norton & Company, 1985), 52–57.
54 Hills, *Rethinking the Baroque*, 26.
55 Hills, *Rethinking the Baroque*, 30.
56 Maurice Merleau-Ponty, *The Visible and the Invisible*, trans. Alphonso Lingis (Evanston, IL: Northwestern University Press, 1968), 140.
57 Maurice Merleau-Ponty, *The Incarnate Subject: Malebranche, Biran, and Bergson on the Union of Body and Soul*, ed. A. G. Bjelland, Jr., and P. Burke, trans. P. B. Milan (Amherst, NY: Humanity Books, 2001).
58 Judith Butler, "Merleau-Ponty and the Touch of Malebranche," in *The Cambridge Companion to Merleau-Ponty* (Cambridge, UK: Cambridge University Press, 2004), 182.
59 Butler, "Merleau-Ponty and the Touch of Malebranche," 186–87.
60 Butler, "Merleau-Ponty and the Touch of Malebranche," 191.
61 Margaretha Rossholm Lagerlöf, "The Apparition of Faith: Performative Meaning of Gian Lorenzo Bernini's Decoration of the Cornaro Chapel," in *Performativity and Performance in Baroque Rome* (New York: Routledge, 2017), 182.
62 Lagerlöf, "The Apparition of Faith," 180.
63 Lagerlöf, "The Apparition of Faith," 195.
64 Warwick, *Bernini*, 57.
65 Lavin, *Bernini and the Unity of the Visual Arts*, 143.
66 Lavin, *Bernini and the Unity of the Visual Arts*, 131.
67 Warwick, *Bernini*, 157–60.
68 Lavin, *Bernini and the Unity of the Visual Arts*, 97.
69 Lavin, *Bernini and the Unity of the Visual Arts*, 102–03.
70 Lavin, *Bernini and the Unity of the Visual Arts*, 125.
71 Lavin, *Bernini and the Unity of the Visual Arts*, 87.
72 Warwick, *Bernini*, 45.
73 Lavin, *Bernini and the Unity of the Visual Arts*, 114.
74 Warwick, *Bernini*, 67.
75 Warwick, *Bernini*, 77.
76 Carlos M. N. Eire, "The Good, the Bad, and the Airborne: Levitation and the History of the Impossible in Early Modern Europe," in *Ideas and Cultural Margins in Early Modern Germany* (New York: Routledge, 2009), 307–23.
77 Lavin, *Bernini and the Unity of the Visual Arts*, 120.
78 Lavin, *Bernini and the Unity of the Visual Arts*, 139.
79 Lavin, *Bernini and the Unity of the Visual Arts*, 124.
80 Mark A. McIntosh, *Mystical Theology: The Integrity of Spirituality and Theology* (Malden, MA: Wiley-Blackwell, 1998), 69.
81 McIntosh, *Mystical Theology*, 219.
82 Maria Margaroni, "Julia Kristeva's Voyage in the Theresian Continent: The Malady of Love and the Enigma of an Incarnated, Shareable, Smiling Imaginary," *Journal of French and Francophone Philosophy* 21, no. 1 (2013): 83–104.

Bibliography

Albertson, David. "Cataphasis, Visualization, and Mystical Space." In *The Oxford Handbook of Mystical Theology*, 347–68. New York: Oxford University Press, 2020.

Bal, Mieke. "Baroque Matters." In *Rethinking the Baroque*, edited by Helen Hills, 183–201. New York: Routledge, 2011.

Bal, Mieke. "Ecstatic Aesthetics: Metaphoring Bernini." In *Compelling Visuality: The Work of Art in and out of History*, edited by Claire Farago and Robert Zwijnenberg, 1–30. Minneapolis, MN: University of Minnesota Press, 2003.

Balthasar, Hans Urs von. *The Glory of the Lord: A Theological Aesthetics*, vol. 5, *The Realm of Metaphysics in the Modern Age*. Translated by Oliver Davies et al. Edinburgh, Scotland: T & T Clark International, 1991.

Butler, Judith. "Merleau-Ponty and the Touch of Malebranche." In *The Cambridge Companion to Merleau-Ponty*, edited by Taylor Carman, 181–205. Cambridge: Cambridge University Press, 2004.

Careri, Giovanni. *Bernini: Flights of Love, the Art of Devotion*. Translated by Linda Lappin. Chicago: University of Chicago Press, 1995.

Cascardi, Anthony J. *The Subject of Modernity*. New York: Cambridge University Press, 1992.

Hayes, Tom. "A 'Jouissance' Beyond the Phallus: Juno, Saint Teresa, Bernini, Lacan." *American Imago* 56, no. 4 (1999): 331–55.

Eire, Carlos M. N. "The Good, the Bad, and the Airborne: Levitation and the History of the Impossible in Early Modern Europe." In *Ideas and Cultural Margins in Early Modern Germany*, edited by Marjorie Elizabeth Plummer, 307–23. New York: Routledge, 2009.

Hills, Helen, ed. *Rethinking the Baroque*. New York: Routledge, 2011.

Lacan, Jacques. *Feminine Sexuality: Jacques Lacan and the École Freudienne*. Edited by Juliet Mitchell and Jacqueline Rose. New York, W. W. Norton & Company, 1985.

Lagerlöf, Margaretha Rossholm. "The Apparition of Faith: Performative Meaning of Gian Lorenzo Bernini's Decoration of the Cornaro Chapel." In *Performativity and Performance in Baroque Rome*, edited by Peter Gillgren and Mårten Snickare, 179–200. New York: Routledge, 2017.

Lavin, Irving. *Bernini and the Unity of the Visual Arts*. New York: Oxford University Press, 1980.

Merleau-Ponty, Maurice. *The Incarnate Subject: Malebranche, Biran, and Bergson on the Union of Body and Soul*. Edited by A. G. Bjelland, Jr., and P. Burke, translated by P. B. Milan. Amherst, NY: Humanity Books, 2001.

Merleau-Ponty, Maurice. *The Visible and the Invisible*. Translated by Alphonso Lingis. Evanston, IL: Northwestern University Press, 1968.

Mormando, Franco. *Bernini: His Life and His Rome*. Chicago: University of Chicago Press, 2013.

Nelstrop, Louise. "Erotic and Nuptial Imagery." In *The Oxford Handbook of Mystical Theology*. New York: Oxford University Press, 2020.

Perlove, Shelley. *Bernini and the Idealization of Death: The 'Blessed Ludovica Albertoni' and the Altieri Chapel*. University Park, PA: Penn State University Press, 1990.

Petersson, Robert. *The Art of Ecstasy: Teresa, Bernini, and Crashaw*. New York: Atheneum Books, 1970.

Rose, Jacqueline. "Introduction II." In *Feminine Sexuality: Jacques Lacan and the École Freudienne*, 27–57. New York: W. W. Norton & Company, 1985.

Teresa of Avila. *Interior Castle*. Translated by E. Allison Peers. Mineola, NY: Dover Publications, 2007.

Teresa of Avila. *St. Teresa of Avila Three Book Treasury: Interior Castle, The Way of Perfection, and The Book of Her Life*. Translated by E. Allison Peers and the Benedictines of Stanbrook. New York: Chump Change, a Harper Collins imprint, 2019.

Warwick, Genevieve. *Bernini: Art as Theatre*. New Haven, CT: Yale University Press, 2013.
Weil, Simone. *The Notebooks of Simone Weil*, vol. 2. Translated by Arthur Wills. London: Routledge, Kegan & Paul, 1976.
Whitworth, Michael H. *Modernism*. Malden, MA: Wiley-Blackwell, 2007.

8

Art and Desire in the Song of Songs

Richard Kearney

My subject is the Song of Songs, one of the earliest works of Western culture to explore the enigma of sacred desire. The medieval Rabbi Rashi praised the ancient song as the holiest book in the Bible, but its history was not without controversy. From early Talmudic readings, through patristic allegorical interpretations and mystical Christian commentaries, right down to contemporary discussions by phenomenologists and artists, the Song has been a highly debated and contested work.[1] Indeed, one might say that the Song of Songs is as hermeneutically fertile as the multiple flora and fauna that proliferate throughout the poem itself. In what follows I offer a brief note on the phenomenology of art before examining its application to hermeneutic and artistic readings of the text.

I

First, a word about phenomenology and art.

In *Ideas I*, Husserl famously declared: "If anyone loves a paradox, he can readily say, and say with strict truth if he will allow for ambiguity, that the element which makes up the life of phenomenology ... is 'fiction,' that fiction is the source whence the knowledge of eternal truths draws its sustenance."[2] This rather startling statement can mean several things when applied to the phenomenological method. First of all, Husserl claims that fiction—and art generally—enables us to suspend our "natural attitude," namely, the normal lens of prejudices and presuppositions which inform our view of everyday objects. The aim of the phenomenological method is to try and overcome this by an act of imagination which invites us to see things anew, as if it were for the first time. This requires a moment of bracketing or *epoché*, which imagination provides through an act of emancipation: an act which enables us to engage in a second step of awareness—namely, the reduction leading back (*re-ducare*) to the "things themselves," *zu den Sachen selbst*. Then we have the third methodological step, which Husserl calls the free variation of imagination. The claim here is that in order to get to things themselves, to the essences of appearances, we need to multiply the horizons of profiles and perspectives—not just those that are actual, but also those that are *possible*. By freely varying in our imagination all the possible manifestations of a phenomenon—in this case, of the phenomenon of sacred desire—one finally arrives at an intuition of its 'essence' (the fourth step of the method). This is what later phenomenologists like Sartre, Ricoeur, and Bachelard have in mind when they talk about imagination as a laboratory of possibilities, as when Heidegger says that "existence is its possibilities."[3] What these phenomenologists recognized was that intuition always involves *interpretation*—namely a work of hermeneutic imagination which explores and schematizes meaning through a creative process of invention and discovery. This is why phenomenological hermeneutics comes to be defined as an "art of deciphering indirect meaning" (Ricoeur). It approximates art, just as every art form may be said to approximate phenomenology.

II

So, how might we interpret the phenomenon of sacred desire in the Song of Songs, one of the most ancient texts of Western religious literature? Let us begin with a classic verse from the *New King James* version:

> You have ravaged my heart, my sister, my spouse; You have ravished my heart with one look of your eyes, with one link of your necklace. How fair is your love, my sister, my spouse! How much better than wine is your love, and the scent of your perfumes than all spices! Your lips, O my spouse, drip as the honeycomb; honey and milk are under your tongue; and the fragrance of your garments is like the fragrance of Lebanon. A garden enclosed *is* my sister, my spouse, a spring shut up, a fountain sealed. Your plants are an orchard of pomegranates with pleasant fruits, fragrant henna with spikenard, spikenard and saffron, calamus and cinnamon, with all trees of frankincense, myrrh and aloes, with all the chief spices—a fountain of gardens, a well of living waters, and streams from Lebanon."
>
> Song of Solomon 4:9–15, NKJV

The Shulamite replies:

> Awake, O North wind, and come, O South! Blow upon my garden, that its spices may flow out. Let my beloved come to his garden and eat its pleasant fruits.
>
> Ibid., 4:16

In addition to the image of the garden as signifier of eros, a second important motif that bears on our imaginative interpretation of desire is that of the "flame" mentioned in verse 8:6:

> Set me as a seal upon your heart, as a seal upon your arm; for love is as strong as death, jealousy as cruel as the grave; its flames are flames of fire, a most vehement flame.

This verse is the only allusion to God in the entire canticle. Even though the text belongs to early Wisdom literature, the word "God" is never mentioned explicitly. We have the Shulamite woman, the shepherd, Solomon, and an abundant polyphony of plants and animals in this famous garden of love, but the word "God" as such never appears. The closest we get is in the allusive phrase "its flames are flames of fire, a most vehement flame." The Hebrew word for vehement flame is *shalhevetyah*: a unique compound noun known linguistically as a *hapax legomenon* (i.e., a term used once in the text and never again). The last syllable *-yah* has been taken by several rabbinical interpreters to refer to Yahweh, but only by allusion, indirectly and metaphorically.[4] The sole name for divine desire in the entire Song, then, is this strange, unrepeatable word *shalhevetyah*—a fiery, flashing flame, one moment there and gone the next.

This divine devouring flame is one of the central motifs that artist Sheila Gallagher invokes in her work, citing Marguerite Porete, a medieval Christian mystic burned to death because, like the Shulamite, she dared to have a love affair with God. But more on that below. For now let us rehearse a short hermeneutic history of the text as an art of divine desire.

First, there are the great Jewish readings of the Song in rabbinical and Kabbalistic literature from the Talmudists and Rashi to Rosenzweig and Levinas.[5] These comprise well over two millennia of interpretations of the sacred poem. Second, we have the patristic and medieval Christian interpretations from Gregory of Nyssa and Origen (who developed a hermeneutics of multiple levels of interpretation, including the literal, allegorical, and the anagogical) to Christian mystics like Teresa of Avila, John of the Cross, and Bernard of Clairvaux. (The latter, for his part, wrote eighty-six sermons on the Song, composed over eighteen years and delivered to his monks—few of the sermons got beyond the opening line, "let him kiss me with the kisses of his mouth.") These mystics chose the Song for its privileged access to the mysterious paradox of divine desire as at once a lack and a surplus: a desire descending to the flesh and ascending to the spirit in a chiasmic double play—divine love for the human, human love for the divine, a desire beyond desire through desire. This paradox has fascinated contemporary philosophers like Bataille, Kristeva, and Ricoeur, who look to the mystical theo-erotics of Teresa and John to plumb the enigmatic depths of unconscious desire.

Of these philosophical readings I will focus here on that of Paul Ricoeur, entitled 'The Nuptial Metaphor.' Ricoeur argues that the canticle is a work of metaphoricity where human love both is and is not divine, insofar as metaphor carries the tensional double claim that something is and is not something else. Metaphor connotes a sense of likeness, similarity, quasi-identification; this is why metaphor calls for double or multiple association. In the poem's metaphors of sacred eros we have a mix of finite and infinite desire: God is at one moment Solomon, at another the shepherd, and at another the Shulamite woman herself, not to mention the proliferating plurality of spices, fruits, and living creatures that are named again and again throughout the Song.

Ricoeur's use of the term "nuptial" is important. He notes that sacred eros in the Song is celebrated in the ancient Egyptian genre of a marriage poem or epithalamium. The song is nuptial rather than matrimonial because it operates as a promissory note rather than a legal contract. The Shulamite and her lover are not married; in fact, they are convening in a context that is outside of law and social convention while the Shulamite's family and sentinels are trying to prevent them from meeting. There is a sense of transgression in the lovers' desire to enter the *hortus conclusus*. The illicit images of placing the hand in water lilies or of honey overflowing lips, for example, are deeply sexual—alluding to nuptial erotic foreplay rather than to matrimonial procreation. Such metaphorical allusions are part of a permissive congress where the Shulamite and shepherd meet in the form of a nuptial play where the bond between them is a love of loving—a loving that is eschatological rather than literal, embracing yet always still to come. More promissory betrothal than property or possession. The nuptial metaphor evades the confines of a matrimonial contract where social and familial laws enjoin and safeguard matters of maternity, procreation, husbandry, and economy (the laws of the home, *oikos*).[6] Or, to use Kierkegaard's terminology of stages on life's way, the nuptial is "aesthetic" and "religious"—before and beyond the law—in contrast to an "ethical" system of legal commitment and contract. The nuptial connotes a free play of eros between lovers in the first flame of love that, as Ricoeur suggests, serves as the metaphor that the Song of Songs chooses to celebrate the quintessence of human-divine love. The nuptial is a mysterious paradox which names a love for someone who is there—the lovers are embodied in a garden surrounded by spices, flora and fauna, rivers and trees—and yet always still to come. This nuptial metaphor of the "is/is not" chiasm of human and divine desire is what Julia Kristeva calls *the amorous blend* between concrete carnality and a transcendent ideal "yet to come."[7] In the Song of Songs the carnal and the messianic mix in a sigh of nuptiality.

Ricoeur describes the poem accordingly as a surplus of metaphoricity, whereby an eschatological symbolism of love is enmeshed in a charged erotics of the body. This is evinced, he suggests, in the fact that many readers have difficulty identifying the lover and the beloved of the poem. The lovers never clearly identify themselves or go by proper names. Indeed, the term "Shulamite" itself is not a proper name, nor is "shepherd." We are never really certain who exactly is speaking, or to whom. The "he" and the "she" become interchangeable at times. Undecidable. We can even imagine that there are up to three or more characters involved in these voices: a shepherd, a lover, a king, a prophet, Solomon, and (by intimation and association) God. This puts us on constant alert, like the amorous fiancée herself, as we keep vigil for the arrival of the divine lover who, we are told in verse 3:6, is coming up from the desert. But who exactly is coming up from the desert? Who comes when the lover comes? Framed in eschatological terms, we may ask if it is not from the end of the world and the depths of time that love arises? For as Ricoeur notes, it is precisely the primacy of the indeterminate fluid "movements" of love over the specific identities of the lovers that keeps the door of interpretation open. We are kept guessing about the origin of the narrators, the voices, the lovers; and this guarding of the poem as an open text of readings and double entendres—human/divine, finite/infinite, carnal/eschatological—provokes a hermeneutic play of constant de-metaphorizing and re-metaphorizing: a flow of semantic metamorphosis that never permits the song to end. In the final analysis, we do not know if we are listening to the singular voices of human lovers or to "the masterless voice of Wisdom? A hidden God? Or a discreet God who respects the incognito of intimacy, the privacy of one body with another body."[8]

This ultimate not-knowing gives poetic license in a game of "intersecting metaphoricity." For the idea of an intersecting metaphor invites us, as Ricoeur says, "to consider the different and original regions of love, each with its own symbolic play. On the one side, the divine love is invested in the Covenant with Israel and later in the Christic bond, along with its absolutely original nuptial metaphorics; on the other, there is human love interested in the erotic bond and its equally original metaphorics, which transforms the body into something like a landscape."[9] This double "seeing as" of intersecting metaphors coincides with a "saying more" and a "saying otherwise," because it evinces the capacity of love to move along both the ascending and descending spiral of metaphor, "allowing in this way for every level of the emotional investment of love to signify, to intersignify every other level."[10] Indeed, the very intertextuality of the Song signals a radically interreligious hospitality in its invitation to a multiplicity of readings across Jewish and Christian traditions—from the Torah and Talmud to the New Testament and Revelation, from Wisdom and the Prophets to medieval and modern mystical testimonies. "Let us therefore allow these texts to project themselves on one another," concludes Ricoeur, "and let us gather those sparks of meaning that fly up at their points of friction."[11] We are back to metaphors of flame and fire. In view of such rich textual intersignification, we see that "the nuptial is the virtual or real point of intersection where these figures of love all cross." And if this be so, we may confirm the further hermeneutic suggestion that "the nuptial as such is an effect of reading, issuing from the intersecting of texts, only because it is the hidden root, the forgotten root of the great metaphorical interplay that makes all the figures of love refer to one another."[12] The poetics of metaphor expresses a theo-poetics of desire.

If the Song extends the standard range of Western love literature, it also extends the range of religious expression; desire becomes amplified, but so does religion. The amplification of desire takes the form of an emancipation of *eros* from an economy of immanent consumption to a free interplay with transcendence, or rather an interplay between immanence and transcendence, transcendence in and through immanence—where pleasure and deferral, *jouissance* and yearning weave and dance. And the amplification of religion, for its part, takes the form of a re-inscription of theology as both theo-poetics and theo-erotics. The logos of wisdom becomes at once a carnal *eros* and a creative *poiesis*. Theology thus learns to play with tensions and paradoxes in a divine-human comedy of errors and reconciliations, a *coincidentia oppositorum*. In other words, desire introduces a gap into religion—a free space of imaginative and carnal variation (miming the phenomenological method). In the Song, *eros* surpasses itself towards more eros, opening religion to what we might call, following Ricoeur, a *poetics of aporetics*: a language game of enigmas, puzzles, and conundrums. The personas of the Song serve as lovers who promise the coupling, without final consummation, of divine and human desire. The nuptial promissory note par excellence, or as Julia Kristeva puts it in *Tales of Love*, "sensuous and deferred love at once—a concrete kind of passion and an ultimate, transcendent, and deferred ideal."[13]

In sum, what we have in the Song of Songs is a story of transfiguring *eros* as the making possible of the impossible—namely, the impossible love congress between divinity and humanity. This is what sets the biblical *eros* celebrated in the Song apart from other kinds of erotic literature, such as romance, *amour fine*, or libertine fantasy. The poem invites us to participate in a desire beyond desire while remaining desire. It signals a desire that spills beyond the limits of the text itself, sending innumerable ripples through many reiterative readings: rabbinic, kabbalistic, patristic, mystical, and phenomenological. It reverberates right down to the most contemporary voices, not only in philosophy and theology, but also in art and literature. James Joyce himself echoes the Song in the final words of Molly Bloom, who, I would suggest, is the contemporary Shulamite woman par excellence: "and then I asked him with my eyes to ask again yes and then he asked me would I yes to say yes my mountain flower and first I put my arms around him yes and drew him down to me so he could feel my breasts all perfume yes and his heart was going like mad and yes I said yes I will Yes."[14]

III

I turn now to the work of contemporary artist, Sheila Gallagher, whose recent show, *Ravishing Far/Near*, revisits the theo-erotics of the Song in highly creative and challenging ways (Plates 4–7). Gallagher is one of the most important interdisciplinary artists working on religious themes in the twenty-first century. A hybrid practitioner, she explores spiritual and theological questions in many media including video, smoke and plastic trash paintings, live plant installations, and live drawing performances.

For over twenty years, Gallagher has been experimenting with possibilities of representing belief, mystical experience, and the critical relationship between the sacred and the profane. While "spirituality" is considered to be acceptable inspiration and content for certain contemporary visual artists, since the late nineteenth century, "religion" has remained much less so, or at least not explicitly acknowledged. Throughout her career, Sheila Gallagher has been using theological inquiry, meditative practices, and religious imagery in her art exhibitions, public lectures, and projects, including the international interdisciplinary 2019 conference on *Metaphor, Making, and Mysticism* that she organized at Boston College. In a culture where contemporary art practice and religious institutions tend to view each other with suspicion or not at all, Gallagher has been a pioneering bridge builder.[15]

The title of Gallagher's 2013 New York exhibition was *Ravishing Far/Near*, a phrase taken from the Christian mystic Marguerite Porete to describe ultimate desire: a yearning to touch the untouchable. Porete was condemned for imagining that she could become one with God in sacred *eros*—a meeting of the most absolute transcendence with the most intimate immanence. The collision of far and near triggered a ravishing combustion of divine rapture that Porete described as an explosion of fire, "an opening as swift as a lightning flash."[16] Her words are an apt translation of *shalhevetyah* in verse six of the Song of Songs. Porete's only crime was to have written a love poem about a woman who desired God passionately and was desired by God in turn. She played with fire and was burned at the stake in 1310.

Gallagher's artistic passage through flames and gardens in her 2013 exhibition charts a journey of the mystical heart. We, visitor-viewers, are invited to wander through a series of icons and installations which serve as quasi-divine traces—"quasi" because we are not stepping here through an actual chapel, mosque, or synagogue but through a chamber of art images. Entering the gallery space we traverse a playroom of *as if*, where love stories of three wisdom traditions convene and combust: Judeo-

Christian (the Shulamite and shepherd), Hindu (Krishna and Radha), and Muslim (the Islamic tale of Adam and Eve). These different stories collide in alarming and daring ways in an odyssey of interreligious imagination. Gallagher juxtaposes motifs of sacred *eros* in the Song of Songs with those of the Hindu *Gita Govinda* and Hafiz's Sufi love poetry. She re-sacramentalizes the motifs of garden and flame through the transformation of quotidian objects. After disenchantment, characteristic of secular modernity, come hints of re-enchantment. After theistic and atheistic dogmas come ana-theistic epiphanies of eros ("ana-," meaning back, up, again in time and space).[17] Gallagher revisits primal scenes of mystical desire in the most contemporary of idioms.

Let us take some examples. In *Plastic Glenstal*, Gallagher deploys bits of discarded plastic detritus, melted down and recomposed, to form an eco-scape of the various flora cited in the Song of Songs. She reinscribes the ancient canticle in an Irish monastic garden in County Limerick, Ireland in the twenty-first century. The plastic painting is made from everyday scraps of rubbish—bottle caps, detergent bottles, hypodermic needles and credit cards—which are torched, melted, and recombined to mime a holy herbarium. In 2012, Gallagher was a guest at Glenstal Abbey where for decades the Benedictine monks have been cultivating the plants mentioned in the canticle within an enclosed garden. In the Song of Songs, as noted, the female lover self-identifies as a walled garden, a *hortus conclusus*, where passionate love is celebrated and protected at once. In an act of sacred-profane alchemy, Gallagher reconfigures the ancient garden with images of feminine flowers and spices—lilies, roses of Sharon, frankincense, cinnamon, and saffron (all cited in the biblical canticle). The tableau blazes with bliss as nature ignites into multicolored flora made from pieces of throwaway trash. The plastic garden becomes a site of theo-erotic encounter.

In her sound video piece 'Tired of Speaking Sweetly,' Gallagher engages playfully with the Islamic theo-poetics of Hafiz, a renowned Sufi mystic of the fourteenth century. In the poetic world of Hafiz, God plays the role of both host and guest and invites us to do likewise. If God has invited many different people to celebrate in his garden, Hafiz says, we must receive them, no matter how strange their games. We may not even know at times who is the divine lover and who is the human—who is the friend and who is the trickster, who the wooed and who the wooer. There is always a risk in the game of love, and God desires us, it seems, just as much as we desire God. Hafiz's deity is a voyaging stranger who comes and goes, calling and courting his creatures: "God has made love with you," he writes, "and the whole universe is germinating inside your belly." And the *Ravishing Far/Near* catalogue adds this further note: "In Hafiz's universe if God invited many different people to celebrate in his house, we must respect them no matter how strange their games ... God consummates his desire in the love between humans, as they mutually exchange roles of host and stranger, giver and receiver"[18] In Hafiz's world of mystical erotics, the sacred and profane go hand-in-glove.

I conclude with a commentary of what is arguably Gallagher's most daring interactive sound video in the *Ravishing Far/Near* exhibition—*Rasa*. Here the artist engages with the Hindu Garden as a ludic counterpart to the Judeo-Christian-Islamic garden of the Song of Songs. "Rasa" is a Sanskrit word meaning essence, juice, desire, or spiritual rapture. It is also used to refer in Hindu aesthetics to the emotional response of a viewer to an art work. There are no figures present in the video's carefully constructed interior of the Raja Ramanna Hindu Temple. Watching Gallagher's film, we witness the temple garden scene sitting on cushions and surrounded by sugar flowers while smoking hookah. Material flowers and fruits are laid before us tangibly in the viewing space of the gallery, as well as virtually in the viewed space of the video, footage which features an audio score of contemporary movie love scenes (*Heartbreak, Betty Blue, Basic Instinct,* and *Mulholland Drive* to name but a few). The sound score of amorous lust, mixed with love scenes from an ancient Sanskrit poem—the *Gita Govinda*—invites a powerful crossing of the carnal and the intangible: the present and the absent, the visible and invisible, what is here and what is still to come. Gallagher's 'Rasa' presents a scenario of vision and blindness in which we enter the sacred temple with its flowers and icons of mystical erotics before witnessing it ultimately explode in flames. (An explosion recalling both the *shalhevetyah* of the Song of Songs and the incendiary fire which consumed the mystic Porete at the stake). There is a flame now there, now gone, divine desire beyond desire that remains desire.

As in Gallagher's other imagined gardens in the show—*Plastic Lila, Plastic Paradisus, Plastic Glenstal*—there are no lovers visible. There are no human figures depicted as such. There is no sign of the theo-erotic couple, Krishna and Radha. We have a love scene without lovers, or more accurately, we have the love of the lovers intimated but not observed.

So, what do we actually *see* in *Rasa*? As we lie on our cushions with hookah in hand we watch video footage of a model of the nineteenth-century miniature Kangra painting, "Revelry by Night"—a scene which originally portrayed secular lovers reenacting the passions of Krishna and Radha. The space occupied by the couple in the original painting is recognizable as a love bar, but Gallagher's video surprises us. While it opens with a billowing canopy from the Radha Ramana temple in Vrindvan—which the artist visited in January 2013—the three-dimensional environment of the original Kangra painting is now subordinated to the aesthetic priorities of a two-dimensional composition. This conceit of a geometrically tortured stage set is slowly laid bare as the model is engulfed in fire to the soundtrack sampling of sex scenes from Western movies. Krishna and Radha's love play is alluded to rather than exposed (like the background movie lovers who are heard but not seen). Relating the consuming flame of *Rasa* back to the Song of Songs, we recall a desire that, in both works, is announced but still to come. A surplus of desire that never exhausts the theo-erotic play, always inviting *more* readings and viewings—an endless horizon of multiple reinterpretations extending beyond the artwork itself to a whole tradition of hermeneutic readings and rehearsals (in art, religion, philosophy, and theology). Less a *deus absconditus* than a *deus adventurus*. In *Rasa*, Krishna and Radha, like the Shulamite and shepherd, are eternal lovers because they refuse to be fixed or focused. This is a vision song of endless desire between gods and mortals.

Ravishing: Far/Near is an art show that invites us to join in a game where lover and beloved court each other without consummating their desire, across three religious traditions. Work after work, we find ourselves transformed from passive voyeurs into co-creators of an "effect" (another meaning of 'rasa') that plays between deity and devotee, far and near. In doing so, the exhibition lets viewers experience the gap which accompanies the bliss of encounter. Hence Gallagher's repeated insistence on distance and deferral, on frustrated fulfillment, as when the filmed scene goes up in smoke and a black hand brings it to an end. No matter how enticing the flames, the scenes, the sex cries may be, the black hand intervenes. We find ourselves back in a burnt-out bomb shelter, as in the movie scene from Neil Jordan's *After the Affair*, whose erotic sound effects echo in *Rasa*. We are back in gardens where the lovers are gone, and only plastic flowers remain, a love bower of hints and guesses. No matter how near the deities come, they never arrive. The lovers move in a nuptial play between now and the yet to come.

Traces, ashes, ciphers, intimations. This is what we are ultimately left with in Gallagher's show: reminders and remainders of divine desire hovering in the antichamber of *as if*, inviting us to suspend both belief and disbelief. The artwork opens a *topos* where we can enjoy a moment of what John Keats called "negative capability"—namely, the aesthetic capacity to dwell in the midst of "mystery, uncertainty, and doubt, without the irritable reaching after fact, and reason."[19] What we have here is a suitable definition for poetic faith as the capacity to see the world for the first time, peeling back "the film of familiarity" so that we can—as phenomenology puts it—glimpse the essences of things.

In sum, Gallagher's art of desire may be said to rejoin the main moves of phenomenological poetics: free variation of possibilities, suspension of belief/disbelief and a return to the "thing itself" (sacred *eros*) which intuits desire as an imaginative play of interpretations: a play ranging through numerous visual icons, idioms, and genres. Be it the video of Hafiz's poem, 'Barroom View of Love,' the interactive multimedia recital of Sanskrit theoerotics in 'Rasa', the erotic flowers of *Plastic Paradisus* and *Plastic Glenstal*, or the gold leaf mandala of Margaret Porete's flaming heart in *pneuma hostis*—throughout all these works, Gallagher cleaves tight to the eternally recurring mystery of sacred eros.

But, like phenomenology, Gallagher's art never abandons the play of imagination. *Ravishing Far/Near* is an affair of fiction, ultimately, not a profession of faith as such. No matter how much art and religion may flirt, dance, and converse in her exhibition, they do not become one. Imagination and faith are not the same. Gallagher's work is a play *between* religion and art not a conflation of the two. It stages a *liaison dangereuse* between human and divine desire which reveals theo-erotics as theo-poetics rather than theo-dogmatics. Like phenomenological interpretation, the polyvalence of her artistic vision reveals the quintessence of sacred passion without end—desire beyond desire that remains desire.

Notes

1   For key examples of modern philosophical commentaries of the Song, see Paul Ricoeur, "The Nuptial Metaphor," in *Thinking Biblically: Exegetical and Hermeneutical Studies*, ed. André LaCocque and Paul Ricoeur, trans. David Pellauer (Chicago: The University of Chicago Press, 1998), 265–303; Georges Bataille, *Eroticism: Death and Sensuality*, trans. Mary Dalwood (San Francisco: City Lights Books, 1986); and Julia Kristeva, *Tales of Love*, trans. Leon S. Roudiez (New York: Columbia University Press,

1987). I offer a reading of these and other commentaries of the Song by Jewish and Christian mystics in Richard Kearney, "The Shulammite's Song: Eros Ascending and Descending," in *Toward a Theology of Eros: Transfiguring Passion at the Limits of Discipline*, ed Virginia Burrus and Catherine Keller (New York: Fordham University Press, 2006), 306–40.

2 Edmund Husserl, *Ideas: General Introduction to Pure Phenomenology*, trans. William Ralph Boyce Gibson (London: Collier Books, 1962), 200–01.

3 See Jean-Paul Sartre, *The Imaginary: A Phenomenological Psychology of the Imagination* (London: Routledge, 2010); Paul Ricoeur, *Time and Narrative*, vol. 1, trans. Kathleen McLaughlin and David Pellauer (Chicago: University of Chicago Press, 1984); Gaston Bachelard, *The Poetics of Space*, trans. Maria Jolas (New York: Penguin Classics, 2014); and Martin Heidegger, *Being and Time*, trans. John Macquarrie and Edward S. Robinson (London: Blackwells, 2008).

4 See my reading of a number of such Jewish sources in Kearney, "The Shulammite's Song," 312–17.

5 See Richard Kearney, "The Shulammite's Song," 323–40.

6 On the distinction between the nuptial and the matrimonial, see Ricoeur, "The Nuptial Metaphor," 274–77, 294, 298–300.

7 See Julia Kristeva, "A Holy Madness: She and He," in *Tales of Love*, 94–95. See also my hermeneutic analysis of Kristeva's reading of the Song in the chapter "Desiring God" in Richard Kearney, *The God Who May Be* (Bloomington: Indiana University Press, 2001), 58–60.

8 Ricoeur, "The Nuptial Metaphor," 300.

9 Ibid., 300–01.

10 Ibid., 301–02.

11 Ibid., 303.

12 Ibid., 303.

13 Kristeva, *Tales of Love*, 94. See also Lacan's psychoanalytic reading of mystical desire as an unconscious form of *jouir-plus* in his reading of "La Jouissance de la Femme," Jacques Lacan, *Encore, vol. 20,* in *Le séminaire de Jacques Lacan: Texte Établi par Jacques-Alain Miller* (Paris: Éditions du Seuil, 1975).

14 See the concluding lines of Molly's soliloquy in James Joyce, *Ulysses* (London, Penguin Classics, 2022), 933.

15 Sheila Gallagher's work has been exhibited and performed at galleries, museums and performance sites internationally, including such venues as the Museum of Fine Arts, Boston; The Crystal Bridges Museum of American Art, Arkansas; The Smithsonian; The Mint Museum, NC; Moving Image Festival, London; The Hunter Museum of American Art, Tennessee; The Abbey Theatre, Dublin; The Art in Embassies Program; and the ICA, Boston. She is represented by September Gallery and is an Associate Professor of Art at Boston College, where she teaches classes in drawing, mixed media, and contemporary arts practice. In addition to her 2013 show, *Ravishing Far/Near* discussed below, several other one-person gallery or museum shows have explicitly engaged with theological and religious content which is sourced in both the Judeo-Christian tradition as well as Buddhist practices. These include *Unknown Source*, based on the fourteenth century mystical work *The Cloud of Unknowing*, and *Flourish*, an exhibition/installation comprised of paintings, photographs, projected video, sculptural objects, and a live flower installation. Inspired by a Spanish Baroque painter's image of Saint Casilda, a fourteenth century Spanish convert, *Flourish* used the legend of Casilda's miracle to explore ocular metaphors for understanding.

16 Cited by Richard Kearney and Sheila Gallagher, *Ravishing Far/Near* (New York: Dodge Gallery, 2013), 5.
17 See Sheila Gallagher, "Paradise Gardens and the Anatheism of Art" in *The Art of Anatheism,* ed. Matthew Clemente and Richard Kearney (London and New York: Rowman & Littlefield, 2017), 85–100.
18 See Richard Kearney and Sheila Gallagher, *Ravishing Far/Near,* 19. This passage is commented upon in Richard Kearney, *Anatheism: Returning to God after God* (New York: Columbia University Press, 2012), 36.
19 Cited and discussed in Kearney, *Anatheism*, 11.

Bibliography

Bachelard, Gaston. *The Poetics of Space*. Translated by Maria Jolas. New York: Penguin Classics, 2014.
Bataille, Georges. *Eroticism: Death and Sensuality*. Translated by Mary Dalwood. San Francisco: City Lights Books, 1986.
Gallagher, Sheila. "Paradise Gardens and the Anatheism of Art." In *The Art of Anatheism*, edited by Matthew Clemente and Richard Kearney, 85–100. London and New York: Rowman & Littlefield, 2017.
Heidegger, Martin. *Being and Time*. Translated by John Macquarrie and Edward S. Robinson. London: Blackwell, 2008.
Husserl, Edmund. *Ideas: General Introduction to Pure Phenomenology*. Translated by William Ralph Boyce Gibson. London: Collier Books, 1962.
Joyce, James. *Ulysses*. London: Penguin Classics, 2022.
Kearney, Richard. *Anatheism: Returning to God after God*. New York: Columbia University Press, 2012.
Kearney, Richard. *The God Who May Be*. Bloomington: Indiana University Press, 2001.
Kearney, Richard. "The Shulammite's Song: Eros Ascending and Descending." In *Toward a Theology of Eros: Transfiguring Passion at the Limits of Discipline*, edited by Virginia Burrus and Catherine Keller, 306–40. New York: Fordham University Press, 2006.
Kearney, Richard, and Sheila Gallagher. *Ravishing Far/Near*. New York: Dodge Gallery, 2013.
Kristeva, Julia. *Tales of Love*. Translated by Leon S. Roudiez. New York: Columbia University Press, 1987.
Lacan, Jacques. *Jacques Lacan: Encore, vol. 20, Le Séminaire de Jacques Lacan: Texte Établi par Jacques-Alain Miller*. Paris: Éditions du Seuil, 1975.
Ricoeur, Paul. "The Nuptial Metaphor." In *Thinking Biblically: Exegetical and Hermeneutical Studies*, edited by André LaCocque and Paul Ricoeur, translated by David Pellauer, 265–303. Chicago: University of Chicago Press, 1998.
Ricoeur, Paul. *Time and Narrative*, vol. 1. Translated by Kathleen McLaughlin and David Pellauer. Chicago: University of Chicago Press, 1984.
Sartre, Jean-Paul. *The Imaginary: A Phenomenological Psychology of the Imagination*. London: Routledge, 2010.

9

The Touch of God: Woundedness and Desire in James Baldwin and Jean-Louis Chrétien

Thomas Breedlove

What is the relation, in Chrétien's thought, between touch and the wound? To be able to touch, he writes in the last essay of *The Call and the Response*, is to be able to be touched—or, better, to always already have been touched and to be touching in return. Touch, which is inseparable from life, is also the basis of our precarity in the world. "A soft and tender flesh," Chrétien writes, "is one that is easily reached, damaged, penetrated, wounded."[1]

The possibility of being wounded is inherent, it seems, to the capacity of touch. Yet in Chrétien's many returns to wounding and woundedness, there emerges a sense in which the wound is not just one of touch's possibilities. Rather the wound precedes touch and lends to touch its own originary power. Because the wound does not belong to touch but touch to the wound, the wound is what touch unveils: our touching is possible only because of our woundedness. For Chrétien this paradoxical reversal reveals the wound's importance as an image of the ruptured character of finite nature.[2] The wound, like finitude itself, *is* only in its relation to the infinite—to the call that is "the vocation to be."[3] Moreover, this is only one aspect of the wound. In addition to describing finitude's openness, the wound also describes the encounter that reveals finite nature. "Revelation," Chrétien writes in *Lueur du secret*, "must break something in us in order to be heard. It reaches us only in wounding us, an intimate wound that causes hate or love."[4] Similarly, *The Ark of Speech* describes prayer as a wounded word: "It always has its origin in the wound of joy or distress, it is always a tearing that brings it about that the lips open."[5] As the paradigmatic phenomenon of the infinite, prayer, then, is a wound. Or, is it *like* a wound? Here, the very phenomenological status of the wound—whether real or metaphorical—opens the questions to which this essay is addressed. Does Chrétien, in returning to this lexicon of woundedness, speak of physical wounds? Of the rupture and suffering of flesh? What is the relation between wounded being and being wounded, between the phenomena of woundedness and the reality of violence?

Provoked by these questions, this essay has two aims. First, it raises and addresses a question present throughout Chrétien's thought: Are there phenomena of the infinite, distinct in some way from all worldly appearing? This question concerns the very center of Chrétien's project, namely, the possibility of his effort to account phenomenologically for what cannot appear as a phenomenon. It concerns the possibility, in other words, for appearance to reveal the invisible and infinite conditions of its own possibility, conditions which by definition cannot appear.[6] I argue that, despite certain suggestions to the contrary, the fact that Chrétien's infinite call is heard only in the finite response reveals that his project is not an expansion of phenomenology's field but a redescription of worldly phenomena themselves. Thus, to understand the wound in Chrétien's thought we must consider the reality of wounded flesh. Here, my first aim opens onto my second. The latter half of this chapter draws upon two texts by James Baldwin to show that—although often conducted in poetic and abstruse language—the phenomenological motifs of touch, wounding, and desire have unavoidably political dimensions inasmuch as they are always embodied. In short: an analysis of Chrétien's thought reveals that the phenomena of woundedness and desire are manifest only in the world; in bringing Chrétien into conversation with Baldwin, we discover the complexities that attend this worldly appearing.

Phenomena of the Infinite?

While Chrétien's thought never departs from the phenomena of embodied life, he also insists that finitude can be truly understood only in relation to the infinite which lies, nevertheless, beyond finitude's grasp.[7] In Janicaud's familiar critique, this invisible excess undermines Chrétien's project, which wishes, but (we are to understand) fails, "to be phenomenological."[8] Janicaud finds Chrétien, like Marion and Henry, to betray phenomenology in turning to revelation which—as they themselves insist—cannot actually appear within either Husserlian or Heideggerian frameworks. The nominally phenomenal serves, in these projects' turns to theology, only to reintroduce "a metaphysics of the secret divine and the transcendent call."[9] Yet, as François Courtine responds, Janicaud's strictures—however faithful they might be to Husserl—might falsely circumscribe phenomenology. This is the very challenge raised by these philosophers of the "theological turn": *Are there* phenomena of the infinite, as Courtine asks, that could "put into question or crisis" the Husserlian correlation of appearing and what appears?[10]

Yet, if there are such phenomena, must they not still appear in the world itself? Is the difference between revelation and manifestation given by different sets of phenomena or, instead, is it given by different modes of appearing—revelation being distinct from the power of intentionality, belonging to givenness rather than the ego's constitution? For one such as Henry, the revelation of the Infinite—of Life, as he comes to express it—necessarily occurs only in another realm, in the invisibility of self-affectivity.[11] Chrétien, in contrast, refuses absolute delineations between the finite and the infinite. He declines to locate revelation beyond worldly appearances. All the same, he reverts to the necessity of distinguishing the infinite call from the horizon in which it is heard. While "any radical thought of the call implies that the call is heard only in the response," the call itself remains absolutely other than the response.[12] The call appears only as the invisible depth that impoverishes the response,[13] pervading every finite horizon even while it "conserves forever," Chrétien writes, "its radical difference from our own calls."[14] Only in its absolute transcendence and inaccessibility to every intentionality is the phenomenon of the infinite call, for Chrétien, the phenomenon of the *infinite* call. It is different in this way from every worldly appearance, appearing as it does like Marion's saturated phenomenon, that is, "without the limits of horizon or reduction to an ego."[15] In the order of being, the call is before all responses—but transcendently before, wholly beyond the temporal horizon. The call is never heard other than in the responses, but the responses can only bear witness to the call in not being it: their only resource, as Chrétien writes, is their nothingness.[16]

Does this not resolutely consign the call, for its reception, to worldly phenomena? There remains the finite self to whom revelation is given, the dative of manifestation in phenomenology's common grammatical formula. A similar syntax characterizes apophatic theology, which insists that divine revelation never exceeds the finitude of its recipients. Tracing this aspect of Chrétien's thought, Joshua Davis provocatively argues that the phenomenological framework of revealability means that there cannot be separate sets of phenomena, but only different judgments concerning the same experiences.[17] Davis re-describes the contested turn from phenomenology to theology as a turn from theology to phenomenology, an investigation of phenomenal appearance within theological metaphysics of grace, creation, and election.

Whatever the merit of Davis' reversal from theology to phenomenology, he is correct to emphasize how Chrétien himself, while insisting upon the radical difference of the infinite call, nevertheless locates that call only in the phenomena of embodied life. The paradox which so animates Chrétien's thought, then, is nothing other than the relation between revelation and manifestation, the capacity of worldly appearances to be ruptured, opened by what exceeds them. The third chapter of *The Call and the Response* turns to these questions explicitly, insisting both that the call of the infinite is direct and that it is only ever mediated by voices of the world. "God speaks," Chrétien writes, "by giving speech, by making men speak, not by imposing silence."[18] Later in the text, Chrétien extends these reflections to touch. Touch is the phenomenon *par excellence* that reveals our givenness to the world. Does this mean that touch simply *is* the encounter with the infinite—a sacral extension of Merleau-Ponty and, ultimately, a visible and material parallel to Henry's phenomenology of absolute life? Chrétien's answer to this question begins in a determined denial. "Quite obviously," he writes, unmistakably echoing Pseudo-Dionysius, "when passing from the finite to the infinite, all continuity explodes." He continues, "Contact with the infinite must necessarily involve a whole other order beyond contact with the finite."[19] Yet, for all this, Chrétien not only retains a relationship of analogy between the two but goes further in suggesting that touch, precisely because it is essential to our being, might still open us to the wounding encounter with the infinite. "Touch," he writes,

> in its finitude and based on it, is already open precisely to a presence without image or representation, to an intimate proximity that never turns into possession, to a naked exposure to the ungraspable. The excess over me of what I touch and of what touches me is endlessly attested in the caress.[20]

In opening the creature to an ungraspable excess, touch opens the creature to the infinite beyond touch itself, for it is the very reality of the infinite that gives touch this possibility.[21]

Thus, for Chrétien, the infinite call does not express simply one possible interpretation of worldly appearance. Rather it describes the excess that is essential to these phenomena themselves. There is a surfeit to touch, desire, and speaking; in their appearances the horizons of autonomy are ruptured, opening the self to the infinite touch of God that founds our being in the world. This describes not only phenomena "out in the world," for this unknowable excess is also for Chrétien the deepest reality of selfhood: "The innermost point that is my soul is not something that I can call mine, as though I could take a hold of it and appropriate it to myself."[22] As the conclusion to *The Call and the Response* articulates, this reality is given in the phenomenon of touch itself: "When the entire body radiates and burns through this divine touch, it becomes song and word. Yet that which it sings with its entire being, collected whole and gathered up by the Other, is what it cannot say, what infinitely exceeds it—excess to which touch as such is destined, and which in the humblest sensation and least contact here below was already forever unsealed to us."[23] In this passage, the turn to theology is given in the phenomena themselves.[24]

Baldwin and the Politics of Desire

Here we find ourselves in a realm not wholly unfamiliar to Christian theology. The power of touch to unseal the infinitude of divine desire describes a sacramental possibility. Worldly phenomena communicate depths and transcendence which they cannot fully express. Perhaps we hear echoes of theological accounts of the nuptial mystery which attempt to express how the phenomena of desire and touch, of vulnerability and intimacy, can open the creature's encounter with her Creator. There are resonances here, but also determinate differences, such as Chrétien's disinterest in privileging certain normative parameters of touch and locating divine encounter within these strictures. For Chrétien, the humblest touch unveils these dimensions of the infinite call; touch *as such* wounds and ruptures, unveiling the graced nature of existence. Yet if Chrétien illuminates this revelatory power of embodiment and desire, it is here, I want to suggest in turning to Baldwin, that his returns to the body are themselves opened by the complexities of embodied experience.

Two depictions of desire in Baldwin's *If Beale Street Could Talk* reveal that the phenomena of touch and desire must be considered not just in their capacity to unveil the infinite but also in their capacity to deny and occlude encounters with grace. These two depictions belong to two couples in the novel. One is found in the relationship between Tish and her fiancé Fonny. Tish, who is nineteen, narrates the novel, which begins with her announcement to Fonny that she is pregnant. Fonny receives this news while imprisoned on false accusations of rape. He remains imprisoned for the duration of the story, which tells of the fruitless efforts to secure his release. The struggle to free Fonny is the struggle of a black family against a faceless and racist injustice, even while it receives its avatars in police officers and prison guards. The bleak narrative is characteristic of the denial of black life that Baldwin often identifies as constitutive of American identity. In Fonny and Tish's relationship, this denial is answered less by its critical exposure than by the affirmation of life that characterizes their desire for one another. Yet, alongside Fonny and Tish is another depiction of desire, one which portrays the power of violence and racialized Christianity to occlude rather than unveil the grace of touch itself. This depiction is found in the relationship of Fonny's parents, Frank and Mrs. Hunt, to whom Tish never gives a first name.

The contest between these two depictions of desire emerges most forcefully in a single scene, when Tish and her family share the news of her pregnancy with Fonny's family. Mrs. Hunt, who sees Tish as her son's downfall and his imprisonment as a divine reckoning, responds to this announcement by choosing a false sanctity against the vulnerability of their love. She curses the unborn child and prays for it to shrivel in Tish's womb. The scene devolves into violence. Frank strikes his wife, a brutal act both fully his and more than his, for it expresses the violence constitutive of Mrs. Hunt's own Christian identity and the wider racist world in which the characters are caught. Mrs. Hunt—despite, or perhaps because of, the flatness of her depiction—embodies the church into which Baldwin was converted and which he left in his youth. That church, Baldwin reflects in his essays, offered him a necessary "gimmick," a shield against his own fear of his body and its desires. Yet it answered these fears not by bestowing dignity, but by linking the perversity of an oppressive world to the perversity of his body, indexing his precarity as a young black man to a racist lexicon of the flesh's impurity and transgressiveness. In his account of his conversion on "the threshing floor," Baldwin describes the pain that drove him to the church. What he realized on that floor, he remembers, is that "the universe, which is not merely the stars and the moon and the planets, flowers, grass, and trees, but *other people*, has evolved no terms for your existence, has made no room for you ... God's love alone is left. But God," he writes, "and I felt this even then, so long ago, on that tremendous floor, unwillingly—is white."[25] The church, as Baldwin came to believe, was a pedagogue of self-hatred and enslavement—in Clarence Hardy's terms, a symbolic world equating "the black with the ugly."[26] In the lexicon of salvation, white supremacy and the fear of sexuality and desire reached their mutual apotheosis, a denial of black flesh as transgressive which validated the politics of injustice within the horizon of sin and damnation.[27]

All this history is embodied in Mrs. Hunt. When Frank strikes his wife, he answers Christianity's racist condemnation with violence. His abuse recalls a brutal scene from earlier in the novel when Fonny tells Tish about his parents' violent love-making on Sundays when Mrs. Hunt would return from church. He tells her it "was like the game you hear two alley cats playing in the alley. Shit. She going to whelp and *mee-e-ow* till times get better."[28] He remembers how his mother would cry "Jesus! Help me, Lord!" and Frank would respond that he was the Lord, call her "bitch," ask where she wanted the Lord's blessing. "He'd slap her," Fonny tells Tish, "hard, loud. And she'd say, Oh, Lord, help me to bear my burden."[29] Touch, as Baldwin depicts it in this relationship, is capable of foreclosing rather than opening. Frank and Mrs. Hunt's desire is pervaded by racist and theological denial; it bears witness to a certain paradigm of Christian transcendence, but it is a transcendence upon whose altar one must sacrifice the flesh itself.[30] In the story, Frank's violence, while he is never exonerated by this fact, is Mrs.

Hunt's encounter with the only God her racialized faith can imagine. To be touched by the other in such a world is indeed to be wounded but never to be given life. Vulnerability is only another weapon of control, offering a false and solipsistic sanctimony. In refusing to separate Frank's brutality from the self-hatred of Christianity, Baldwin reveals the masochistic and sadistic dimensions of touch. Salvation in the novel demands self-hatred; it inculcates a desire to be punished that spills over into a hatred of others, a hatred of the body, a hatred of sexuality, and a hatred of life.

Yet, in Tish's narration of these scenes, Baldwin contrasts the violent potential of touch with its deepest power to unveil grace. As she relates Mrs. Hunt's condemnation and Frank's abuse, Tish remembers the first night she and Fonny had sex. Tish critiques the violence of Frank and Mrs. Hunt through an affirmation of desire.[31] This affirmation—its excess and vulnerability, the experience of Fonny and Tish in which they receive themselves in responding to one another—marks the phenomenological dimensions of Baldwin's novel. Tish remembers her and Fonny's desire as a confusion of agency, a losing track of subjectivity and autonomy, of the difference between her body and his. "My life," Tish recounts, "was claiming me. I heard, I felt his breath, as for the first time: but it was as though his breath were rising up out of me. He opened my legs, or I opened them."[32] To breathe, Baldwin understands, is already to have life by sharing and receiving it, to have it maximally in a giving and receiving born of desire. This image of the physiological phenomenon of breath is dear to Chrétien; it is one he returns to repeatedly in Claudel, finding there the understanding that every breath repeats our reception of life. "Claudel," Chrétien writes, "never contrasts the act of inhaling God with the act of inhaling the world."[33] The living power of the flesh is also its weakness and need, its dependence upon receiving its life from without. The dilation of breathing "is a self-affirmation that attests to alterity: I am possible only through another, from another, and by taking that other into myself."[34] For Baldwin, the power of intimacy and desire is inseparable from this surrender, from the other-than-oneself that becomes oneself. Fonny and Tish's desire for one another reveals the gift of life itself. "His breath," Tish returns again to the same image in a later passage, "was in my nostrils, I was breathing with his breath and moving with his body."[35] To breathe another's breath marks nothing more or less than the nature of breath itself: the shared reception of life that precedes all initiative.[36] To share breath reveals the excessive grace of life itself, just as to deny another breath is to refuse this grace entirely.[37]

In this sense, desire in Baldwin's novel makes manifests the resources of dependence, that it is our emptiness that allows us to receive and our reception that allows us to give. Their desire for one another, a desire which is always to touch and to be touched, reveals what for Chrétien is constitutive of the phenomenon of touch itself in the final study in *The Call and the Response*: "In man's very flesh, what saves and what endangers increase together proportionally."[38] There is in Baldwin's novel a continual bringing into light of the inseparability of dispossession and reception. The weakness of the flesh is its only resource.[39] There is something in Fonny and Tish's desire for one another that founds their being, that gives dignity not through the autonomy of sanctity but through a giving and receiving that transcends self-sufficiency and self-determination. They discover that the breath with which they have to call one another's names, the hands with which they touch one another, are the breath and hands of the other. To be is *to be given*, to be ruptured by this very givenness. This is an insight Tish expresses in her marveling that in loving Fonny she has discovered not only him but herself. "It's astounding," she writes, "the first time you realize that a stranger has a body—the realization that he has a body makes him a stranger. It means that you have a body, too. You will live with this forever, and it will spell out the language of your life."[40]

To Reveal the Wound

How, then, do these two pictures of desire speak to Chrétien's thought? That revelation is only ever mediated in Chrétien's thought—that the dative of its manifestation remains wholly finite—reveals the importance of the body (of touch, of desire). For Chrétien, the wound describes our givenness to (and from) what exceeds us, a givenness unveiled in the flesh, in the physiological phenomena of breathing and touching. This wound is an image, but it receives its power only because that which it describes is, in fact, life in the flesh.[41] Yet if the phenomenological power of Chrétien's thought of the wound draws always upon the flesh, it is also opened thereby to the wounds of the flesh—to violent ruptures that open to pain rather than grace, to false infinites rather than the infinite itself. The image of the wound opens his thought to the complexities of embodiment and touch that press the horizons of phenomenology into politics and history, to a writer such as Baldwin. There we discover that the surfeit of touch—its capacity to unveil the call that wounds—is never given simply by the phenomenon itself. The relationship of Frank and Mrs. Hunt reveals that the capacity of touch to wound must always include the physical wounds of white-supremacist theology, of denial and hatred. The power given to touch by the infinite can be distorted to occlude the very thing Chrétien celebrates in it.

These wounds, characterized by the politics of violence that deny the flesh are never obscured in *If Beale Street Could Talk*. A lasting image of them appears in the prison glass that separates Tish from Fonny throughout the novel. In the first pages, Tish laments, "I couldn't touch him. I wanted so to touch him."[42] And at the novel's end, the glass still intervenes. "He is with me," she thinks to herself, "but he is very far away. And now he always will be."[43] For Baldwin, all too often, theology serves our temptation to escape finitude, to secure a false autonomy through the imposition of violence—a temptation to make certain others, as he writes, "the receptacle of and the vehicle of, all the pain, disaster, sorrow" which we want to escape.[44]

In these ways the novel only illustrates Chrétien's phenomenological account of finitude insofar as it ruptures the pretense to conclusion which phenomenology, at least since Merleau-Ponty, has wanted to refuse. In the context of Chrétien's interest in the phenomenon of touch itself, the two depictions of desire in the novel are not *available* to philosophy as divergent examples of touch; instead, they are together the complex, uncertain, and irreducible reality that Chrétien's philosophy describes. But this discovery in the novel reveals that the flesh's phenomenological power is complex and historical; it is inseparable from the modalities of its experience. These modalities are not examples that a phenomenology received from Chrétien may or may not choose to consider. Instead, they announce the very stakes of this phenomenology itself in their difficulty and complexity: the fact that phenomenology can be true to itself only in surrendering to that which in the phenomena of touch and woundedness defies description itself. The power of the image of the wound is a haunting power. Chrétien summons it to describe the irreducible, that which defies objectification, appearance, description—that which exceeds the constituting power of the *ego* in Husserl's phenomenology and the ontic determinations of *Dasein* in Heidegger's—and its power as image comes from the fact that wounds themselves defy description, refuse incorporation into stable taxonomies of meaning, resist resolution even in theologies of grace.

There is a risk, a cost, in listening to the flesh and woundedness. This risk recalls another of Baldwin's stories, "Sonny's Blues." The story begins with the narrator learning from the newspaper that Sonny, his younger brother, has been picked up in a police raid, arrested for using and selling heroin. "I couldn't believe it," he thinks, "but what I mean by that is that I couldn't find any room for it anywhere inside me."[45] To believe something, to receive it, is to bring it within, to incarnate it. This, the narrator tells us in the opening paragraphs, is what it means to believe. The rest of the story tells the cost of coming to believe, but also what is received in accepting this cost.

In the story's long final scene, the narrator speaks of accompanying Sonny, now released from jail, to a jazz bar where he hears Sonny play the piano for the first time. Against the story's depiction of the seeming impossibility of escaping the pain of black life in Harlem, this scene sets a different sort of victory over suffering—a victory born of the power of music to take up the realities of black life wounded by oppression, refusing either to shy away from or to accept the denial toward which violence reaches. The narrator realizes that to play an instrument, in an image akin to creation in Genesis 2, is to breathe oneself into it. The musician fills it "with the breath of his life, his own."[46] But to make music is also to tame, "to put in order," with one's one breath a deeper chaos, "the roar rising from the void."[47]

Listening to his brother play, the narrator does not escape his suffering but receives it again, receives it transformed, through the labors of making and listening to music, into that which exceeds suffering itself.

> Sonny's fingers filled the air with life, his life.... Then he began to make it his. It was very beautiful because it wasn't hurried and it was no longer a lament. I seemed to hear with what burning he had made it his, with what burning we had yet to make it ours, how we could cease lamenting. Freedom lurked around us and I understood, at last, that he could help us to be free if we would listen, that he would never be free until we did.[48]

He had made it—the roar, the void, the wound—his, not by conquering it but by being present it to it and making it present. Sonny's music holds the wound up to be seen, revealing the power of the flesh that is wounded over the wound itself.

There is no false redemption in this music. The characters' wounds do not suddenly become avenues of grace. As the narrator intimates in the final paragraphs, the need for music—and for art more generally—is perpetual. It is as constant and ubiquitous as their suffering. "I was yet aware," he thinks, "that this was only a moment, that the world waited outside, as hungry as a tiger, and that trouble stretched above us, longer than the sky."[49] The image of being both wounded and liberated by listening is itself a wound that the story refuses to resolve. Baldwin reminds us that a phenomenology that takes seriously the grace of the flesh can only do so by taking seriously its oppression. The fact that our relationships and religion, even our world itself, can deny the very excess it ought to affirm reveals the capacity of Chrétien's phenomena to do likewise. Here we find, perhaps, the deepest meaning of the convergence of phenomenology and theology: that their power is also their danger, and that their capacity to unveil never escapes the limitations of finitude itself.

The limits of phenomenology, received from Baldwin, are not then phenomenology's conclusion, but its beginning. It is a beginning that presses Chrétien's thought from the phenomenological mode of description into the more difficult task of listening, of listening to music. This task, the narrator understands, is one few ever really accomplish.[50]

Notes

1 Chrétien, *The Call and the Response*, trans. Anne Davenport (New York: Fordham University Press, 2004), 101.
2 Bruce Ellis Benson recognizes this when he writes that, "One might argue that something like this structure of 'wounding' is at the heart not just of Chrétien's own 'theological turn' but also of the theological turn in phenomenology in general." Bruce Ellis Benson, "Chrétien on the Call That Wounds," in *Words of Life: New Theological Turns in French Phenomenology*, ed. Bruce Ellis Benson and Norman Wirzba (New York: Fordham University Press, 2012), 209. As I establish below, it is the wound's anteriority to any *act* of wounding that characterizes this centrality.
3 Chrétien, *The Call and the Response*, 18.
4 Chrétien, *Lueur du secret* (Paris: L'Herne, 1985), 38. "Il faut que la revelation brise quelque chose de nousmêmes pour qu'elle soit entendue. Elle ne nous atteint qu'en nous blessant, d'une intime blessure qui fait haïr ou aimer."
5 Chrétien, "The Wounded Word: A Phenomenology of Prayer," trans. Jeffrey Kosky and Thomas Carlson, in *Phenomenology and the "Theological Turn": The French Debate* (New York: Fordham University Press, 2000), 174.
6 "The concern for respecting the character of the originary, its position prior to anything, requires that these authors do not identify this originary, or more exactly, that they identify it as the unidentifiable, as that which irreducibly surpasses the act by which *I* give it to myself." François-David Sebbah, "French Phenomenology," trans. Robert J. Hudson, in *A Companion to Phenomenology and Existentialism* (Oxford: Blackwell Publishing, 2006), 56.
7 The infinite, Chrétien writes, is the "other Word that wounds body and soul, and which ... if it wounds completely, could never be completely understood—not even in eternity." Chrétien, *The Unforgettable and the Unhoped For*, trans. Jeffrey Bloechl (New York: Fordham University Press, 2002), 125.
8 Dominique Janicaud, "The Theological Turn in French Phenomenology," trans. Bernard Prusak, in *Phenomenology and the "Theological Turn": The French Debate* (New York: Fordham University Press, 2000), 66.
9 Janicaud, "The Theological Turn in French Phenomenology," 68.

10 Jean-François Courtine, "Introduction: Phenomenology and Hermeneutics of Religion," trans. Jeffrey Kosky and Thomas Carlson, in *Phenomenology and the "Theological Turn*," 123. As Courtine elaborates, an affirmative answer to this question obviates the very critique that one such as Janicaud advances. If there is "an 'object' whose modes of being given and appearing would disturb the classic phenomenological procedure . . . [then] the 'phenomenology of religion' might not be simply an ontic, regional science toward which one would be free to 'turn' or not. Rather, it would affect the central aim of phenomenology itself, considered in terms of its own task and style." Ibid.

11 The difficulty posed by the absolute otherness of revelation is answered in Henry's project by a turn to a secret and nocturnal identity. "*Life*," Henry writes, "*has the same meaning for God, for Christ, and for man.* This is so because there is but a single and selfsame essence of Life, and, more radically, a single and selfsame Life." Michel Henry, *I am the Truth: Toward a Philosophy of Christianity*, trans. Susan Emanuel (Stanford, CA: Stanford University Press, 2003), 101. Henry articulates this identification in his many returns to Eckhart: "'God engenders himself as myself,' and because 'God engenders me as himself,' then, truly, because it is his life that has become my own, my life is nothing other than his own: I am deified, according to the Christian concept of salvation." Henry, *Incarnation: A Philosophy of Flesh*, trans. Karl Hefty (Evanston, IL: Northwestern University Press, 2015), 160. As Joseph Rivera aptly suggests, this reversal of phenomenology evacuates the content of the problematic (or possibility) of revelation itself: "All language of 'creaturehood' or 'finitude' or 'human nature' in Henry is no longer justified since human nature is already divine in its essence." Joseph Rivera, *The Contemplative Self after Michel Henry: A Phenomenological Theology* (Notre Dame, IN: University of Notre Dame Press, 2015), 125.

12 Chrétien, *The Call and the Response*, 30.

13 "Nothingness is alone what answers the call because it cannot answer it," Chrétien writes. "To be stripped of any possibility of answering by our own means is the first answer given to the call, the answer that has no beginning, the answer in which the call is heard." Chrétien, *The Call and the Response*, 22–23.

14 Chrétien, *The Call and the Response*, 22.

15 Jean-Luc Marion, *Étant donné* (Paris: Presses de Universitaires de France, 1997), 305, as cited in Anne Davenport, translator's preface to *The Call and the Response*, xxiv. As Anne Davenport rightly notes, this is precisely what differentiates revelation from manifestation: "Revelation defies objectification not only relatively speaking, but absolutely. It cannot be constituted by the ego as its object in *any* horizon and transcends *all* horizons." Ibid., xxvi.

16 "The human voice becomes a place where the world returns to God. It gives what it does not have—which does not mean that it gives nothing—and it can give itself only because it is not in possession of itself, the voice being what does not belong in all speech." Chrétien, "The Wounded Word," 174.

17 Thus, as Joshua Davis argues, there remains in Chrétien's thought the Heideggerian priority of *offenbarkeit*, or revealability, over *offenbarung*, or revelation. There seems to be no getting past the fact that revelation, in order to be phenomenological, must still appear in the world. For Chrétien, as for Marion, if the transcendence of the phenomenon is identified by the mode of its givenness, it still remains the case that "manifestation is itself constrained by what can be legitimately asserted on the basis of the sheer bestowal of the phenomena as such." Joshua Davis, "The Call of Grace: Henri

de Lubac, Jean-Louis Chrétien, and the Theological Conditions of Christian Radical Phenomenology," in *Words of Life: New Theological Turns in French Phenomenology*, ed. Bruce Ellis Benson and Norman Wirzba (New York: Fordham University Press, 2010), 184.
18. Chrétien, *The Call and the Response*, 69. Chrétien critiques the notion that an inner voice might give direct access to the divine call. Our calls and this divine call cannot be two distinct phenomena, he insists: "The call is direct, since it reaches me as a self without substitute, yet is not immediate, since it reaches me always through and by means of the world, by means of the events that unfold and the voice of other human beings." Ibid. The voice of the Word who creates comes not, as it does in Henry, in the nocturnal invisibility of self-affection, but in the speech of others.
19. Chrétien, *The Call and the Response*, 129.
20. Chrétien, *The Call and the Response*, 129.
21. "Only a thought of love . . . gives the flesh its full bearing of intellect and leads touch to its highest possibility." Chrétien, *The Call and the Response*, 129.
22. Jean-Louis Chrétien, *Spacious Joy: An Essay in Phenomenology and Literature*, trans. Anne Davenport (New York: Rowman & Littlefield, 2019), 82. In this passage, Chrétien interprets a line from Saint Teresa of Avila, but the conclusion (a striking image of both the convergence and divergence of Chrétien's infinite call and Henry's auto-passivity of Life) is an apposite description of his own understanding of the woundedness of finite being.
23. Chrétien, *The Call and the Response*, 131.
24. In this way, Chrétien's thought can be described as a turn to theology, but not to (Christian) theological conclusions. This, in my reading, is where Joshua Davis' insightful critique errs. In his judgment, Chrétien missteps in confusing theological categories of revelation with the structure of appearance itself (see especially Davis, "The Call of Grace," 188–90). But this is accurate only insofar as it names the often ambiguous separation in Chrétien's thought (even more than in Marion) between strict phenomenology and a theological interpretation of phenomenology's descriptions. For Chrétien, the structure of appearing does not yield God's act of Creation (an article of faith), but appearing does yield its own impossibility, a givenness or woundedness that points to the irreducible and unobjectifiable which precedes all appearing. In this I perceive a primary parallel between the phenomenological dimensions of Chrétien's project and those of Marion, for whom, Thomas Carlson writes, "the phenomenological critique aims to articulate what (historically) comes 'after' the active, spontaneous subject of modern metaphysics by thinking that which (logically) 'precedes' such subjectivity: namely, the radically passive, nascent self, the *me* that precedes the *I*, which, 'before' being a subject in the mode of consciousness or language, is *called* to be by the unconditional givenness of phenomenality." Thomas Carlson, translator's introduction to Jean-Luc Marion, *The Idol and Distance* (New York: Fordham University Press, 2001), xxi.
25. James Baldwin, "Down at the Cross," in *Baldwin: Collected Essays* (New York: The Library of America, 1998), 304. Baldwin echoed this judgment decades later in "To Crush a Serpent": "Jesus Christ and his father are white, and the kingdom of heaven is no place for black people to start trying on their shoes." Baldwin, *The Cross of Redemption: Uncollected Writings* (New York: Vintage International, 2010), 196.
26. Clarence Hardy, *James Baldwin's God* (Knoxville, TN: University of Tennessee Press, 2003), 30.

27 "What it means to be a Negro in this country is that you represent, you are the receptacle of and the vehicle of, all the pain, disaster, sorrow which white Americans think they can escape. This is what is really meant by keeping the Negro in his place." Baldwin, *The Cross of Redemption*, 96.
28 Baldwin, *If Beale Street Could Talk* (New York: Dell Publishing, 1974), 17.
29 Baldwin, *If Beale Street Could Talk*, 18.
30 "There is a sense in which it can be said that my black flesh is the flesh that St. Paul wanted to have mortified." Baldwin, "White Racism or World Community," in *Baldwin: Collected Essays*, 755. Race, in Baldwin's judgment, had been invented to justify and to explain theologically the oppressive political arrangements of the world, and once so invented, blackness accrued a theological content. In his essay on the relationship between homophobia and racism in Baldwin's thought, Sean Larsen writes that this development invented "the 'Negro' as a theological character. Constructed by early Americans as social enemy and social victim, the non-humanity that diverts attention from inhumanity, the figure is a scapegoat, by which white Americans 'safeguard their purity.'" Sean Larsen, "James Baldwin, Christian Ethics, and the Recovery of Tradition," *Modern Theology* 36, no. 3 (2020): 5.
31 In this way my reading is consonant with much of Vincent Lloyd's reading of Baldwin in *Religion of the Field Negro: On Black Secularism and Black Theology* (New York: Fordham University Press, 2019). Lloyd is correct to distinguish Baldwin from the American transcendentalist tradition with which he is often associated, and his description of Baldwin's prophetic critique of whiteness in American Christianity as a sort of iconoclastic negative theology is apt. That said, Lloyd believes Baldwin to fail in offering in response only a "vague, postracial concept of love," a concept incapable of specifying norms for judging and discerning the justice necessary to love. Ibid., 40. Here my own reading diverges slightly, for I see Baldwin less interested in articulating a rival ethical or theological system and more invested in naming and celebrating what any such system must include: the beauty of a desire that refuses to set holiness or rectitude in competition with the affirmation of life.
32 Baldwin, *If Beale Street Could Talk*, 84.
33 Chrétien, *Spacious Joy*, 182. For Claudel, Chrétien writes, "the root phenomenon is the phenomenon of respiration." Ibid., 168.
34 Chrétien, *Spacious Joy*, 170.
35 Baldwin, *If Beale Street Could Talk*, 85.
36 "This very first consent to being, a consent before all initiative." Chrétien, *The Call and the Response*, 117.
37 The affirmation of breath that characterizes desire and dignity in Baldwin's novel —along with breath's excessive and ungraspable power, for it can be received but never held forever, or even for very long; it can be given but also stolen—links it inescapably to reflections on breath voiced today against racial injustice. Achille Mbembe, writing in 2020 on breathing in the time of a pandemic, perceives that to be a living person is to be a breather: it is *to be* in a way that "eludes all calculation," for it transcendently links the human body forever to the world. But like Baldwin, Mbembe does not separate this miracle of breath from the threat of its suffocation—to be capable of transcendence by our breathing is to be capable of being suffocated and of strangling, both one another and the world itself. "Before this virus, humanity was already threatened with suffocation. If war there must be, it cannot so much be against a specific virus as against everything that condemns the majority of humankind to a premature cessation of breathing, everything that fundamentally attacks the

respiratory tract, everything that, in the long reign of capitalism, has constrained entire segments of the world population, entire races, to a difficult, panting breath and life of oppression. To come through this constriction would mean that we conceive of breathing beyond its purely biological aspect, and instead as that which we hold in-common, that which, by definition, eludes all calculation. By which I mean, the universal right to breath." Achille Mbembe, "The Universal Right to Breathe," *Critical Inquiry*, https://critinq.wordpress.com/2020/04/13/the-universal-right-to-breathe/. Accessed September 10, 2020. The gift of breath is our givenness to the world; it is a givenness that manifests precariousness and grace in equal measure.

38 Chrétien, *The Call and the Response*, 102.
39 "Weakness has a certain force because it turns itself into a resource. One can only defend oneself better by exposing oneself more thoroughly. This is the sense of human nakedness," Chrétien, *The Call and the Response*, 101. As in Anne Davenport's reading of Chrétien, "our very presence to the world and to ourselves dispossesses us of ourselves." Davenport, translator's preface to *The Call and the Response*, xxvii.
40 Baldwin, *If Beale Street Could Talk*, 57.
41 Here Chrétien's reflections in another text interpret his own appeals to the wound. See Jean-Louis Chrétien, "From the Limbs of the Heart to the Soul's Organs," in *Carnal Hermeneutics*, ed. Richard Kearney and Brian Treanor, 92–114 (New York: Fordham University Press, 2015). Investigating traditions of describing the soul or heart with bodily language, Chrétien writes, "The body allows us to *construct* figures and images of what otherwise would remain for the most part unimaginable. The *schema* of the body, moreover, is a dynamic one, a source of ever new figures, but also of new questions and possibilities. More often than not, what comes to appear thanks to this language is given to us with clarity and precision only because of it. This explains why such a language cannot be fixed in a final lexicon, even though a number of stable expressions have emerged historically. The language is supple, labile. It never ceases to renew itself because the body itself contains latently an inexhaustible power of figuration and of figure-ability." Ibid., 107–08.
42 Baldwin, *If Beale Street Could Talk*, 4–5.
43 Baldwin, *If Beale Street Could Talk*, 209.
44 Baldwin, *The Cross of Redemption*, 96.
45 Baldwin, "Sonny's Blues," in *The Jazz Fiction Anthology*, ed. Sascha Feinstein and David Rife (Bloomington, IN: Indiana University Press, 2009), 17.
46 Baldwin, "Sonny's Blues," 46.
47 Baldwin, "Sonny's Blues," 45.
48 Baldwin, "Sonny's Blues," 47.
49 Baldwin, "Sonny's Blues," 48.
50 "All I know about music is that not many people ever really hear it. And even then, on the rare occasions when something opens within, and music enters, what we mainly hear, or hear corroborated, are personal, private, vanishing evocations." Baldwin, "Sonny's Blues," 45.

Bibliography

Baldwin, James. *Collected Essays : Notes of a Native Son / Nobody Knows My Name / The Fire Next Time / No Name in the Street / The Devil Finds Work / Other Essays*. Edited by Toni Morrison. New York: Library of America, 1998.

Baldwin, James. *If Beale Street Could Talk*. New York: Dell, 1988.
Baldwin, James. "Sonny's Blues." In *The Jazz Fiction Anthology*, edited by Sascha Feinstein and David Rife, 17–48. Bloomington: Indiana University Press, 2009.
Baldwin, James. *The Cross of Redemption: Uncollected Writings*. Edited by Randall Kenan. New York: Vintage International, 2010.
Benson, Bruce Ellis. "Chrétien on the Call that Wounds." In *Words of Life : New Theological Turns in French Phenomenology*, edited by Bruce Ellis Benson and Norman Wirzba, 208–21. New York: Fordham University Press, 2010.
Benson, Bruce Ellis, and Norman Wirzba, eds. *Words of Life: New Theological Turns in French Phenomenology.* New York: Fordham University Press, 2010.
Chrétien, Jean-Louis. "From the Limbs of the Heart to the Soul's Organs," *Carnal Hermeneutics*, edited by Richard Kearney and Brian Treanor, 92–114. New York: Fordham University Press, 2015.
Chrétien, Jean-Louis. *Lueur du secret*. Paris: L'Herne, 1985.
Chrétien, Jean-Louis. *Spacious Joy: An Essay in Phenomenology and Literature*. Translated by Anne Ashley Davenport. London; New York: Rowman & Littlefield, 2019.
Chrétien, Jean-Louis. *The Call and the Response*. Translated by Anne Ashley Davenport. New York: Fordham University Press, 2004.
Chrétien, Jean-Louis. *The Unforgettable and the Unhoped For*. Translated by Jeffrey Bloechl. New York: Fordham University Press, 2002.
Chrétien, Jean-Louis. "The Wounded Word: A Phenomenology of Prayer." Translated by Jeffrey Kosky. In *Phenomenology and the "Theological Turn": The French Debate*, 147–75. New York: Fordham University Press, 2000.
Courtine, Jean-François. "Introduction: Phenomenology and Hermeneutics of Religion." In *Phenomenology and the "Theological Turn": The French Debate*, 121–26. New York: Fordham University Press, 2000.
Davis, Joshua. "The Call of Grace: Henri de Lubac, Jean-Louis Chrétien, and the Theological Conditions of Christian Radical Phenomenology." In *Words of Life: New Theological Turns in French Phenomenology*, edited by Bruce Ellis Benson and Norman Wirzba, 181–95. New York: Fordham University Press, 2010.
Hardy, Clarence E., III. *James Baldwin's God: Sex, Hope, and Crisis in Black Holiness Culture*. Knoxville: University of Tennessee Press, 2003.
Henry, Michel. *I am the Truth: Toward a Philosophy of Christianity*. Translated by Susan Emanuel. Stanford, CA: Stanford University Press, 2003.
Henry, Michel. *Incarnation: A Philosophy of Flesh.* Translated by Karl Hefty. Evanston, IL: Northwestern University Press, 2015.
Janicaud, Dominique. *The Theological Turn in French Phenomenology*. Translated by Bernard Prusak. In *Phenomenology and the "Theological Turn": The French Debate*, 16–103. New York: Fordham University Press, 2000.
Larsen, Sean. "James Baldwin, Christian Ethics, and the Recovery of Tradition." *Modern Theology* 36, no. 3 (2020): 538–60.
Lloyd, Vincent W. *Religion of the Field Negro: on Black Secularism and Black Theology.* New York: Fordham University Press, 2019.
Marion, Jean-Luc. *Étant donné*. Paris: Presses de Universitaires de France, 1997).
Marion, Jean-Luc. *The Idol and Distance.* Translated by Thomas Carlson. New York: Fordham University Press, 2001.
Mbembe, Achille. "The Universal Right to Breathe." *Critical Inquiry*, April 13, 2020. https://critinq.wordpress.com/2020/04/13/the-universal-right-to-breathe/.

Rivera, Joseph. *The Contemplative Self after Michel Henry: A Phenomenological Theology*. Notre Dame, IN: University of Notre Dame Press, 2015.

Sebbah, François-David. "French Phenomenology." Translated by Robert Hudson. In *A Companion to Phenomenology and Existentialism*, edited by Hubert Dreyfus and Mark Wrathall, 48–67. Oxford: Blackwell Publishing, 2006.

Part Three

Incarnate Performance

10

Of God and Trout Fishing:
A Phenomenology of *Reel*igious Life

J. Aaron Simmons

Introduction: Risking Heresy

Let me begin with a passage from Anne Lamott's book, *Almost Everything*, that serves as something of an orientation to my concerns in this chapter: "Hope springs from that which is right in front of us, which surprises us, and seems to work."[1]

I love God and I love trout fishing. In fact, my love of each is implicated in my love of the other. Such a claim might seem strange, perhaps even borderline sacrilegious or heretical, but here I stand . . . and even though I could always do otherwise, I choose not to. The reason I see these two loves as so deeply connected is because I consider them both to occur internal to the category of "the religious," which I take to open onto (maybe even be constitutively defined by) eschatological hope. I understand eschatological hope to be distinguished from two other forms of hope, in particular: existentiell hope and existential hope. The key quality of eschatological hope is that it yields a reevaluation of all historical possibilities as non-ultimate. Namely, rather than hoping for *x* to occur at some point in the future (existentiell hope), or hoping for the future as such (existential hope), eschatological hope invites us into a transformed relation to temporality itself such that we are "already" where we hope to be, and simultaneously "not yet" there—hence the continuation of the hope itself, along with the desire that supports it.

In order to offer a phenomenological account of such hope, I will turn to trout fishing as a fecund site in which I find eschatological hope to be liturgically enacted. Hoping for the fish to bite is not something that is fulfilled in catching the fish, but instead is a structure of the experience of fishing. Engaging in what I will term a phenomenology of "*reel*igious life" can teach us important things about the way that hope is connected to lived faithfulness rather than the successful obtainment of a desired object. Namely, usually when we desire *x*, obtaining *x* leads to the termination of the desire. Yet, when it comes to faithfulness as a way of life, the desire for God is not something that terminates in some sort of religious identity, or conversion experience, or final enlightenment. Instead, continuing to desire God is what it means to be faithful. The "having" takes a back seat to the pressing ever toward that which is already right here and always not yet present. When it comes to religious existence and also to trout fishing, what matters is the risky orientation directed toward that which is enacted in the present moment and yet, as such, continues to call us onward. In other words, in religious life constantly striving to become faithful is the true task. Similarly, in reeligious life, the act of fishing is what matters, not catching the fish.

In order to make the case for this thesis about the relationship of hope, desire, and faithfulness, I will draw on the phenomenological analysis of "the unhoped for" by Jean-Louis Chrétien, as well as Søren Kierkegaard's notion of the knight of faith in *Fear and Trembling*. Chrétien and Kierkegaard offer models of religious life that illustrate the role of faithfully enacting eschatological hope. And before beginning in earnest, let me be clear: it should go without saying that I would much rather be fishing than writing this paper, so my reader will surely be forgiven for putting the essay down now and heading to the mountains.

Hope, Desire, and Limiting Out

I don't know any trout fishers who don't hope to catch a bunch of fish. The specific goal is to "limit out"—or to catch the number of fish that you are legally allowed to keep (assuming that they are big enough—or "keepers"—in the first place). In fact, although now I pretty much only practice "catch and release" fishing, I still narrate my fishing trips in terms of "limiting out" or not. In this sense, it might seem that whether or not one was successful in the fishing trip depends upon whether the hope for catching fish comes to fruition as a successfully achieved object—namely, the fish in your creel. Yet, to view things this way forces an economic logic upon a practice that I think resists such a framework. There is no exchange function in trout fishing such that you put in the time and energy and are rewarded with the catch of the day and go home "successful." Instead, trout fishing is an activity that, in its very enactment, calls us further into such action. Catching fish simply invites a continued desire to keep fishing. Not catching fish invites the hope that the next cast changes your luck. Indeed, no one who has fished very much will find it strange to hear of someone who ended up staying on the river hours past when they planned to leave because they continued to live into the hope that "one more cast" will lead to the trophy. Either way, whether at the end of the day you end up limiting out or going home empty handed, the reality is the same: *right now you are fishing*—your hope to catch fish is part of that present experience, but it is not ultimately what matters most.

Let me try to unpack this idea a bit more. Although I hope to catch fish, every minute spent fishing is already the actualization of the thing I really hope for: to be able to spend time fishing. Yet, precisely in the actualization of this hope, here and now, every minute spent fishing is itself also a moment of anticipation, of expectation, for the catch "yet to come" if I continue to fish. In this way, trout fishing positions me in a rather odd temporal relationship to myself: I am already who I hope to be (viz., a person fishing) and yet who I am is not yet who I hope to become (viz., the person who continues to fish—and who maybe catches some fish). I have already achieved that for which I hope and yet I am still living forward because of the continuation of the hope itself. My desire for the future catch is part of what it means to be fishing, and yet catching the fish furthers my desire to keep fishing. This already/not yet structure is characteristic of what we might term an eschatological logic, which stands opposed to the economic logic by which desire is terminated when the object of desire is obtained.

If I am right that eschatological hope is part of what characterizes the "religious" as a category, then it is hardly surprising that many have viewed the act of fishing (and trout fishing, in particular) as a quasi-religious activity. Additionally, there is more than a passing resemblance between trout fishing and religion. Think about it. There are special vests(ments) worn while engaging in the activity that distinguish you from those unaffiliated with the community, such as waders, boots, nets, creels, etc. Fishing, like religious devotion, takes long hours of ritualistic practice in order to achieve mastery. There are all sorts of sacred objects associated with the practice itself: the trout rod that my father bought me when I was a child, the fly or lure that has been passed down for generations, and the lucky hat that is so worn that it barely stays on your head without the help of duct-tape. Further, there is a hidden wisdom handed over only to the initiated that continues to further one's role in the community: the secret "honey-hole" that only you and a few other people know about, or the fly or lure that works with particular trout on a specific stretch of river. Finally, trout fishing is something that is presented to others as an invitation to join the community if they commit themselves to the right dress, rituals, and wisdom. Indeed, the first time I took my son trout fishing, I presented it to him in very much this quasi-religious way: he was being invited into a liturgy that would connect him with his great-grandfather, his grandfather, his father, and eventually (hopefully!) with his own children.[2]

Now, let me be clear that I do not want to get sidetracked into very important, but peripheral, debates about what counts as "religion" or not. Although there is a significant body of work in that area (and I have contributed to it elsewhere),[3] here I am content simply to note the plausible similarities between those cultural traditions that are historically termed "religions" and the specific practice of trout fishing. To that end, my use of the term "quasi-religious" is meant to be a vague descriptor that highlights trout fishing as an interesting phenomenological case-study, rather than a rigidly precise term indicating something sociologically significant about the "religion" of trout-fishing.

The eschatological structure of hope and desire on display in trout fishing is distinct from the other two modes of hope that tend to characterize our lives and our practices: *existentiell* and *existential* hope. Here I am drawing, on the one hand, on the broader distinction between existentiell and existential developed by Martin Heidegger in relation to the ontic and ontological structures of human existence and, on the other hand, on Claude Romano's discussion of expectation.[4] Romano's account is especially helpful because he suggests that there is an expectation proper to historical desire that is distinct from the expectation proper to historical beings capable of such desires. Since I have attempted to unpack these different forms of hope in more detail elsewhere,[5] here I will only briefly consider these various modes of hope in order to get a better sense of why trout fishing offers a distinctive eschatological alternative that might open spaces for thinking well about faithfulness as a way of life.

Existentiell hope is the contingent temporal hope that we have for a specific possible future outcome. Maybe you hope for a new truck, a new dog, or a new dating relationship, say. Existentiell hope is such that it is object-oriented. Upon obtaining that object, the hope disappears along with the desire for the hoped-for object. Once I get the truck, the dog, or the relationship, I am no longer defined by the hope for those objects because my desire has been satiated/fulfilled in the external obtainment of the object. Existentiell hope is a mirror-phenomenon of fear. I find myself in a state of fear always only in relation to some specific future due to a discrete relationship to a threatening object or outcome: the snake in the grass, the bear in the forest, or the loss of some valued thing. Fear is overcome by existentiell hope insofar as such hope allows us to live toward a future in which the feared object/outcome is defeated by the obtainment of an object/outcome that we desire. Existentiell hope and fear are both characteristics of our being the sort of beings who stand in relation to external states of affairs that are affectively impactful on who we are trying to become.

Existential hope, alternatively, is the sort of hope that simply and necessarily accompanies the existence of finite beings like us. Namely, insofar as we are temporal, hope attends our basic sense of the world and ourselves. We project ourselves into the future because we hope for the future itself. We go to bed hoping for tomorrow, we brush our teeth because we expect that we will be alive for the coming weeks and months in which bad dental hygiene would come back to bite us. In other words, existential hope is not the hope for a *particular* future, but for *the future, as such*. It is the way desire accompanies what it means to be temporally constituted. It is existential hope that allows history to be the context of expectation. In light of where I have been, I now hope to go someplace else. In this way, my present is constructed by the complicated tension of memory and expectation that defines the human condition *as historical*. Accordingly, existential hope is a mirror-phenomenon of anxiety. Unlike fear, anxiety has no direct object, but simply attends our existence due to the vulnerability that defines it. Existential hope is what helps keep anxiety at bay, but it is only because we are beings who are threatened by anxiety that we are beings capable of existential hope. Existential hope and anxiety are phenomena that would be unintelligible to beings who are either atemporal or invulnerable. Yet, we are neither of those things and so our very being (and our becoming) is framed by the interplay between such hope and anxiety.

If existentiell hope is a matter of objective-obtainment, existential hope is a matter of subjective-identity in so far as it structures my relationship to desire as an historical phenomenon. Romano hits on this idea when he describes the sort of expectation attendant to existentiell hope as temporary—it passes into and out of existence as our desires emerge, get disappointed or fulfilled, and then get abandoned as we move on to new desired outcomes and objects. On this model of existentiell hope, we are "turned and directed toward the future, … to which a certain event, if it takes place, would correspond."[6] Alternatively, Romano notes that the sort of expectation that accompanies existential hope is that which is a "permanent" facet of human existence.[7] Importantly, existential hope is not able to stand on its own without existentiell hope. Reminiscent of Husserl's distinction between a fulfilled or unfulfilled intention, existential hope without existentiell hope is too vague to be of much help when it comes to narrating our historical lives. It is a frame without content. The contingent objects of existentiell desire allow the necessity of existential hope to appear as a background condition, and yet the framework of existential hope is what makes any desire for a specific object possible for beings like us. It is this bivalent relation that makes our lives such that, simply because we abandon the desire for *x* (say, because we get it), doesn't mean that we now no longer desire some other *y*—desire for *the future* attends any desire for *a particular* future. Whereas existential hope without the accompanying specificity of existentiell hope is empty, existentiell hope without the framework of existential hope is literally hopeless since there would be no "time" in which we could move into the future where our hopes could be, as Husserl would say, *fulfilled*.

Notice that both of these varieties of hope are matters of human meaning playing out in history—that is, they both function according to the "not yet" directionality of human striving. But, what if history is not ultimate? Or, asked slightly differently, what if we are "already" what we are "not yet"? This is where we transition into the domain of eschatological hope. Eschatological hope is the "hope against hope" about which John Caputo speaks so often.[8] It is the hope that animates Viktor Frankl's account of living through the holocaust in *Man's Search for Meaning*.[9] It is the hope that Kierkegaard discusses when he suggests that we are suspended above 70,000 fathoms and yet there find faith.[10] This hope is neither a hope for some particular outcome, nor it is the hope that attends temporal existence, it is the hope that repositions history in relation to eternity such that the already/not yet comes into a lived tension. In such a relation, as C. S. Lewis says in *The Four Loves*, "all that is not eternal is eternally out of date."[11]

The philosopher that I think has done more to position eschatological hope in the context of embodied religious existence is the new phenomenologist Jean-Louis Chrétien. Although Chrétien uses different terminology than I am proposing here, in his discussion of "the unhoped for" he is quite clearly presenting hope in the register that I have termed "eschatological." "Hope," he notes, "disassociates itself from all calculation."[12] He details that this notion of the unhoped for is marked by its desire for what is ordinarily considered impossible—i.e., it is entirely cut off from the normal despair that attends the frustration of existentiell desire. In this way, the eschatological framework of the unhoped for stands apart from the "ordinary attitude, in which one hopes only for the possible, and in which one hopes greatly for it."[13] Chrétien admits that such a strange form of hope is "wholly other than [what] most people hope" because it ruptures the calculative logic by which we so often understand finite value.

Eschatological hope or the unhoped for is a matter of non-economically relating to the eternal significance of each moment, rather than of an economic evaluation of this moment's instrumental importance to a particular future that we desire. "The *unhoped for*," Chrétien continues, "is what transcends all our expectations, and the inaccessible is that to which no path takes us, whether it is one that is already traced or one that we project in thought."[14] I love the way that Chrétien expresses this point because it gets at the heart of the already/not yet structure I am describing. The unhoped for is not some-thing, but it is the depth dimension at play in relation to a God for whom all things are possible. "Biblical hope," Chrétien explains, "has as its object what can be hoped for only from God, thus what is impossible by any human force, and what we neither could nor would have to hope for from ourselves and by ourselves."[15] There is an old saying that one never stands so tall as when falling on one's knees. This is exactly right. Chrétien's account of prayer as a "wounded word" beautifully captures this idea.[16]

He claims that the phenomenon of prayer humbles us (even in our embodied posture) because it exposes us to what we cannot fully grasp, imagine, or circumscribe. Yet, it also elevates us by (literally) positioning us in relation to the transcendent. God meets us in prayer, Chrétien suggests, because there we also meet ourselves as standing before-God.

It is in such statements that Chrétien strikes me as a trout fisherman. To go trout fishing requires that we embrace humility at the very same instant that we stand out as irreducible to objectivity. Not being humbled by mountains and rivers will lead to devastation. Only by appreciating one's insignificance in comparison with them can one faithfully navigate them with appropriate respect. Yet, doing so occasions an understanding of selfhood as not merely a matter of natural processes and causal relationships. Having tripped many times while wading through a rough patch of whitewater, I have fallen frequently on my knees (and ripped many pairs of waders in the process). In those moments when the immediacy of embodied vulnerability was all too humbling, as is also the case with prayer, I better appreciated the dignity of the human condition. Here we stand as always already flawed, finite, and fallible, and yet we are so much more. It is when the waters threaten to overwhelm me that I get a glimpse of what it means to approach selfhood as a task of constant becoming. To illustrate this point, listen to Chrétien's description of what is involved in hoping for the unhoped for:

> [These] two seemingly inverse movements—humiliation and uplifting, dejection and exaltation—constitute the space in which the unhoped for is received: together they signify that the unhoped for is not and cannot be our work, they recognize and confess its excessive character. And the thought of the unhoped for goes together with the thought of humility.[17]

Eschatological hope maintains our desire (whether religious or quasi-religious) because it refuses finality. Fishing fosters the desire to keep fishing, prayer fosters the desire to keep praying, living fosters the desire to keep living. All three are oriented toward a seemingly impossible goal: to finish what constitutively remains open. Again, though, with God all things are possible. In relation to God, we already are what we are never quite yet able to be. Similarly, here and now I am a fisherman, but only by continuing to desire to go fishing will I continue to become one.

In summary, then, we should note that existentiell hope without eschatological hope risks being defined by achievement, rather than defining what achievements are worth seeking. Alternatively, existential hope without eschatological hope risks being future-oriented without ever having a meaningful vision of the future. Ultimately, eschatological hope allows us to appreciate both existentiell and existential hope as crucial aspects of our embodied existence as faithful. This shift from the economic logic of success to the eschatological logic of faithfulness is the key to appreciating the "religious" dynamics in play in my love of God and in my love of trout fishing. In order to fill in this idea a bit more, let's now look at Kierkegaard's account of the knight of faith as an example of what such faithful living into eschatological hope might involve.

The Failure of Success: Kierkegaard on Faithfulness

Kierkegaard's most sustained consideration of faith, as recounted by the pseudonym Johannes de Silentio in *Fear and Trembling*, is anything but straightforward.[18] *Fear and Trembling* is a text notorious for its layered presentation and lack of hermeneutic clarity.[19] Indeed, what else would we expect from an author whose name indicates that he isn't able to say anything (John of Silence)? Although the interpretive options attending this text are myriad, whatever else it is, it is a text that attempts to define "faith" and then present a lived example of what such faith would look like in practice. The "knight of faith" is an honorific that Silentio applies to Abraham, but also (and perhaps more interestingly) as a way of life or mode of existence that is not an historical relic, but a contemporary possibility. Consider the following account in which Silentio imagines running into the knight of faith on the street:

> The instant I first lay eyes on [the knight of faith], I set him apart at once; I jump back, clap my hands, and say half aloud, "Good Lord, is this the man, is this really the one—he looks just like a tax collector!" But this is indeed the one. I move a little closer to him, watch his slightest movement to see if it reveals a bit of heterogeneous optical telegraphy from the infinite, a glance, a facial expression, a gesture, a sadness, a smile that would betray the infinite in its heterogeneity with the finite. No! I examine his figure from top to toe to see if there may be a crack through which the infinite would peek. No! He is solid all the way through. His stance? It is vigorous, belongs entirely to finitude: no spruced-up burgher walking out to Fresberg on a Sunday afternoon treads the earth more solidly. He belongs entirely to the world . . . He finds pleasure in everything . . . He attends to his job . . . He goes to church . . . He takes a walk to the woods . . . Toward evening, he goes home, and his gait is as steady as a postman's On the way, he thinks that his wife surely will have a special hot meal for him when he comes home—for example, roast lamb's head with vegetables . . . His wife does not have it—curiously enough, he is just the same.[20]

Here we see a variety of important dynamics in the life of faith. First, faith does not attest to an external transformation. The knight of faith is indistinguishable from the tax collector—that is, he could be anyone. There is nothing about him that allows for external recognition. Faithfulness, Silentio indicates, is not about external status, but about internal orientation. As Silentio notes, "he is solid all the way through." Unlike Moses' encounter with God that left him literally glowing and his transformation visible from a far distance, the knight of faith is able to get lost in the crowd, as it were.

Second, Silentio stresses the surprising fact that the knight of faith "belongs entirely to the world." This is striking because we often think that a life of faithfulness will become fairly detached from earthly concerns in order to set one's gaze on the eternal. For example, in my own Pentecostal tradition, we used to say of people that they were "so heavenly minded that they were of no earthly good." In other words, their "faith" led them to be so "holy" that they were unable to get their hands dirty in the messiness of the human condition. Rather than "finding pleasure in everything," as does the knight of faith, they found everything to be a distraction from what really mattered—but in doing so, they lost sight of the truly meaningful. Religion became their sole focus and faith, for them, named a rejection of worldly living. Importantly, Silentio does not allow faith to slide into such detached resentment. Instead, it is presented more like what one finds in C. S. Lewis' imaginative picture of the eschaton in *The Great Divorce*.[21] Therein, Lewis suggests that far from heaven being a rejection of worldly embodiment, it actually signifies as a glorification and deepening of such embodiment. The grass is greener, the sky is bluer, the water is wetter, the mountains are higher, the eschatological experience is more—rather than less—embodied. In this way, Lewis invites us to entertain the possibility that Christian redemption is not about an escape from the human condition, and creation more generally, but instead is about a decisive plunge into what it means for that condition to be seen "as good" by God (see Genesis 1:10, 12, 18, 21, 25, and 31).

In Silentio's account of lived faith, we are presented with a nondescript, unremarkable, and decidedly worldly individual. And yet, he is entirely different from the others. Faith changes everything. The knight of faith is somehow able to avoid giving in to the overwhelming temptation to hopelessness (due to the mundane reality of his job, his church, and the day in, day out routine of his life) and is somehow unaffected when his desire (for roast lamb) is thwarted by the cold reality of leftovers. This inner transformation that leads him to embrace his existence as an occasion of joy (rather than refusing it in escapist rejection or in nihilistic denial) highlights the dynamics of eschatological hope. Simply put, the knight of faith's identity is not defined by success, but by faithfulness.[22] Faithfulness is not about having or obtaining or being something, but is about continually becoming what already critically defines your identity as directed beyond itself. For example, I can be a successful swimmer by winning a swim meet, or a successful entrepreneur by founding a company and expanding it until a very lucrative exit, but I cannot be a successful father or husband in the same way because what it means to be invested in my son or wife is to be continually directed toward becoming ever more faithful to them.[23] Faithfulness is about continuing in a direction that matters. Success is about reaching the end of the road in order then to change direction.

As Silentio notes, the knight of faith "is continually making the movement of infinity, but he does it with such precision and assurance that he continually gets finitude out of it."[24] As such, he is able to "express the sublime in the pedestrian."[25] Silentio shows that faith is not about a specific outcome such that faithfulness is a matter of existentiell hope. Moreover, he demonstrates that faith does not maintain temporality as an ultimate horizon such that faithfulness would be a matter of existential hope. Instead, Kierkegaard, via the perspective offered by Silentio, invites us to be transformed by the example of the knight of faith as we learn that faith is a revision of how history itself signifies as non-ultimate. Temporality is ruptured by eternality in order that the eternal signifies as temporally significant, and does so *at every moment*. This is why the knight of faith can attend to his job, go to church, take walks in the woods, and navigate the commonplace realities of social life while still somehow finding "pleasure in everything." Faithfulness is a matter of eschatological hope insofar as it is a "task for a whole lifetime."[26] It reminds us that we have more work to do and that such work is worth doing. However, faithfulness also lets us see that if we think that we could eventually be done with the world, then we would never have begun appropriately living in it in the first place.

Drawing on Silentio's discussion of the knight of faith allows us to see how thinking about faithfulness as the lived outcome of eschatological hope allows us to understand how the knight of faith can be "just the same" even though his specific desires for external achievements might not come to pass as he (existentielly) hoped they would. It is important that Silentio qualifies this description with the words, "curiously enough." In doing so, he acknowledges the way that the knight of faith has existentiell hopes, but is not defined by them. He is "just the same" because he is *already* what he hoped to be: faithful. And yet, he is *not yet* finished with becoming faithful because a task for a lifetime is not something that admits of historical finality.

Conclusion: A God who Goes Fishing

Whenever I feel hopeless, I go trout fishing. I do so because it reminds me where my hope really lies. It connects me to the idea that the eternal is not somewhere else, but is performed in how we inhabit temporality. In this way, trout fishing helps me to see religious life as something that invites joy at every moment (despite the frequent disappointments that attend finitude) instead of something that defers joy as an external object only to be obtained "when this life is o'er," as the old hymn says.[27] Trout fishing signals that the religious goal is not to "fly away," but to cast the fly into just the right spot here and now. Trout fishing helps me live into the fact that God is invested in our lives, and not just concerned about our after-life.

That said, like the knight of faith's relation to the roast lamb, I do desire to limit out on trout, but if I don't catch anything, curiously enough, I am just the same. Well, at least I try to be. The difficulty of faithfulness is not allowing it to be just a matter of expressed commitment, but instead always positioning it as a lived orientation. Similarly, even though I do hope to spend eternity with God—whatever that involves— such that I can sing "Hallelujah, by and by," I think that Levinas was right to say that we would likely only be worthy of the coming Messiah if we were to live as if the Messiah were never going to come.[28] The point is that we must already be who we are trying to become; we can't wait until later to start becoming who we want to be. Accordingly, I go fishing in order to be someone who goes fishing—catching fish is a nice side-benefit, but not the main object. C. S. Lewis says somewhere that joy is found in desiring—this is exactly right when it comes to existentiell hope. Lewis recognizes that when we desire an object, the obtainment of that object often leaves us cold and without a good sense of how to move forward since our prior existence was narrated by the desire that no longer signifies. Yet, in eschatological hope, our desire is never exhausted because it is not about having, but about becoming. And, as Kierkegaard (this time under the guise of Johannes Climacus) reminds us: becoming a self is not something that one finishes, but something that continually structures one's existence.[29]

There are surely other phenomenal activities that invite the structural enactment of eschatological hope, but for me trout fishing is distinctive for two reasons. First, it invites me to become who I already am, and to desire that which is *already* the case and somehow remains *not yet* finished. Second, it anchors me in the idea of *kenosis* as key to lived faithfulness. We already saw in Chrétien how hoping for the unhoped for brings humility and exaltation together. This kenotic logic is profoundly on display in trout fishing. Trout fishing is an essentially humbling activity because no matter how good you are at it, you are keenly aware that many of the aspects that make the activity possible lie decidedly beyond your control: the river flow, the fish behavior, the weather, hatch patterns, and the stream access, etc. To go trout fishing is to abandon the idea of self-sufficiency. It is to embrace the notion that you don't control what awaits you at home for dinner, as it were. But, at the very same time, it calls us to be ourselves because my decision is what facilitates any possible outcome: what fly or lure to use, which weight of line, whether to present the fly from upstream or downstream, etc. Religious life, like trout fishing, is about faithfulness as an investment in what we think matters. Yet, it is only in our enactment of the investment, the affective embrace of its contingency, that the meaning becomes activated. It is by going fishing that I can really say that fishing matters. I take my son fishing not primarily to give him the experience of catching fish, but in order to have a relationship with him in which we fish. The same, I think, is true in our relation to God.

Nietzsche claims that he could never get on board with a God who didn't laugh. Well, I want a God who goes fishing. For what it is worth, I think that the fact that Jesus was a fisherman is perhaps the greatest apologetic for Christianity! As such, I think that philosophers of religion would do well to move from a phenomenology of *religious* life (Heidegger) to a phenomenology of a *ree*ligious life as exemplified by the narrative of Christ, expressed in Kierkegaard's notion of faithful living, and explained in Chrétien's account of the unhoped for. A phenomenology of *ree*ligious life encourages us to:

Keep fishing.
Keep praying.
Keep being who you are becoming.
Desire that which is eternally actual in order to transform historical possibility.
In other words, it encourages us to have enough hope to keep hoping.

I want to conclude by (re)turning to Anne Lamott, from whom the opening quote in this chapter is taken. In her book, *Almost Everything: Notes on Hope*, she closes the book by saying:

> We have all we need to come through. Against all odds, no matter what we've lost, no matter what messes we've made over time, no matter how dark the night, we offer and are offered kindness, soul, light, and food, which create breath and spaciousness, which create hope, sufficient unto the day.[30]

I love this. Lamott rightly notes that we already have all we need for the journey, and yet we are not yet where we are going. The kenotic logic of eschatological hope is on display as she encourages us to take solace, but to keep working.

In the end, no matter what I do while fishing, there is peace to be found in the fact that the river remains constant even as the water flows past us. It is already here and has not yet arrived. This dynamic relationship with the river offers a temporal reminder of what eschatological hope is all about. When we strive to become faithful instead of seeking to be a success, we imitate a God who kenotically meets us where we are and then invites us onward and upward, rather than a God who tells us when we are perfect enough to meet the divine. This is a God that I can take seriously because it is a God who is trouble for our accounts of self-sufficiency, a God who is trouble for our pretensions to certainty. This is a God who goes fishing and invites us to grab our rod and come along. Count me in.

Notes

1 Anne Lamott, *Almost Everything: Notes on Hope* (New York: Riverhead Books, 2018), 181.
2 I want to note that the gendered dynamics here are entirely contingent on the fact that I only have one child who happens to be a boy. None of what I am saying in this chapter should indicate any sort of gendered assumptions about the practice of fishing. Indeed, I think that resituating fishing in the way I propose here might invite us all to see it as connected to human existence, as such, in ways that productively challenge some of the sociological realities that too often attend the practice.
3 As one of the best recent philosophical discussions of this topic, see Kevin Schilbrack, *Philosophy and the Study of Religions: A Manifesto* (Malden, MA: Wiley-Blackwell, 2014). For my own contributions to these debates, see J. Aaron Simmons, "A Search for the 'Really' Real: Philosophically Approaching the Task of Defining Religion," *Bulletin for the Study of Religion* 44, no.4 (December 2015): 19–26; "Vagueness and Its Virtues: A Proposal for Renewing Philosophy of Religion," in *Philosophy of Religion After "Religion,"* ed. Michael Ch. Rodgers and Richard Amesbury, forthcoming (Tübingen: Mohr Siebeck, 2023).
4 Martin Heidegger, *Being and Time*, trans. Joan Stambaugh, rev. Dennis J. Schmidt (Albany and New York: State University of New York Press, 2010); Claude Romano, "Awaiting," in *Phenomenology and Eschatology: Not Yet in the Now*, ed. Neal DeRoo and John Panteleimon Manoussakis, trans. Ryan Coyne (Farnham and Burlington, VT: Ashgate, 2009), 35–52. See also Claude Romano, *Event and Time*, trans. Stephen E. Lewis (New York: Fordham University Press, 2014).
5 See, J. Aaron Simmons, "Living Joyfully after Losing Social Hope: Kierkegaard and Chrétien on Selfhood and Eschatological Expectation," *Religions* 8, no. 33 (2017): 1–15; see also J. Aaron Simmons and Eli Simmons, "Liturgy and Eschatological Hope," in *Philosophies of Liturgies: Explorations of Embodied Religious Practice*, ed. J. Aaron Simmons, Neal DeRoo, and Bruce Ellis Benson (London: Bloomsbury, 2023), 287–303.
6 Romano, "Awaiting," 36.
7 Romano, "Awaiting," 36.
8 John D. Caputo, *Hoping Against Hope: Confessions of a Postmodern Pilgrim* (Minneapolis, MN: Fortress Press, 2015).
9 Viktor Frankl, *Man's Search for Meaning*, trans. Ilse Lasch (Boston, MA: Beacon Press, 2006).
10 Søren Kierkegaard, *Concluding Unscientific Postscript to "Philosophical Fragments,"* vol. 1, ed. and trans. Howard V. Hong and Edna H. Hong (Princeton, NJ: Princeton University Press, 1992), 140.

11 C. S. Lewis, *The Four Loves* (New York: Harcourt Brace & Company, 1960), 137.
12 Jean-Louis Chrétien, *The Unforgettable and the Unhoped For*, trans. Jeffrey Bloechl (New York: Fordham University Press, 2002), 104.
13 Chrétien, *The Unforgettable and the Unhoped For*, 104.
14 Chrétien, *The Unforgettable and the Unhoped For*, 105.
15 Chrétien, *The Unforgettable and the Unhoped For*, 107–08.
16 See Jean-Louis Chrétien, "The Wounded Word: Phenomenology of Prayer," in *Phenomenology and the "Theological Turn": The French Debate,* by Dominique Janicaud, Jean-François Courtine, Jean-Louis Chrétien, Jean-Luc Marion, Michel Henry, and Paul Ricoeur (New York: Fordham University Press, 2000), 147–75.
17 Chrétien, *The Unforgettable and the Unhoped For*, 108.
18 Søren Kierkegaard, *Fear and Trembling and Repetition*, ed. and trans. Howard V. Hong and Edna H. Hong (Princeton, NJ: Princeton University Press, 1983).
19 For a few very good considerations of Kierkegaard's notion of faith, see Jeffrey Hanson, *Kierkegaard and the Life of Faith: The Aesthetic, the Ethical, and the Religious in "Fear and Trembling"* (Bloomington: Indiana University Press, 2017); and Merold Westphal, *Kierkegaard's Concept of Faith* (Grand Rapids, MI: Wm. B. Eerdmans, 2014).
20 Kierkegaard, *Fear and Trembling*, 29–30.
21 C. S. Lewis, *The Great Divorce* (San Francisco, CA: HarperOne, 2015).
22 I initially proposed this distinction between success and faithfulness in a TedX talk I gave in 2018, "The Failure of Success." It is available at: https://www.youtube.com/watch?v=Y4beiEp-xZ4&t. Accessed February 12, 2021.
23 Interestingly, Jacques Derrida's notion of justice articulated internal to the "democracy to come" presents precisely this structure of faithfulness such that justice, if there is such a thing, would never be just enough. Justice would be enacted only by our refusal to think that we had finished the task of becoming ever more committed to justice. See, for example, Jacques Derrida, *Rogues: Two Essays on Reason,* trans. Pascale-Anne Brault and Michael Naas (Stanford, CA: Stanford University Press, 2005).
24 Kierkegaard, *Fear and Trembling*, 41.
25 Kierkegaard, *Fear and Trembling*, 41.
26 Kierkegaard, *Fear and Trembling*, 7.
27 "I'll Fly Away," lyrics and music by Albert E. Brumley (1929).
28 "[T]o be worthy of the messianic era one must admit that ethics has a meaning, even without the promises of the Messiah." Emmanuel Levinas, *Ethics and Infinity: Conversations with Philippe Nemo*, trans. Richard A. Cohen (Pittsburgh, PA: Duquesne University Press, 1985), 114.
29 Søren Kierkegaard, *Concluding Unscientific Postscript*, 129–88.
30 Lamott, *Almost Everything*, 189.

Bibliography

Caputo, John D. *Hoping Against Hope: Confessions of a Postmodern Pilgrim*. Minneapolis, MN: Fortress Press, 2015.

Chrétien, Jean-Louis. *The Unforgettable and the Unhoped For*. Translated by Jeffrey Bloechl. New York: Fordham University Press, 2002.

Chrétien, Jean-Louis. "The Wounded Word: Phenomenology of Prayer." In *Phenomenology and the "Theological Turn": The French Debate*, by Dominique Janicaud, Jean-François

Courtine, Jean-Louis Chrétien, Jean-Luc Marion, Michel Henry, and Paul Ricoeur, 147–75. New York: Fordham University Press, 2000.
Derrida, Jacques. *Rogues: Two Essays on Reason*. Translated by Pascale-Anne Brault and Michael Naas. Stanford, CA: Stanford University Press, 2005.
Frankl, Viktor. *Man's Search for Meaning*. Translated by Ilse Lasch. Boston, MA: Beacon Press, 2006.
Hanson, Jeffrey. *Kierkegaard and the Life of Faith: The Aesthetic, the Ethical, and the Religious in "Fear and Trembling."* Bloomington: Indiana University Press, 2017.
Heidegger, Martin. *Being and Time*. Translated by Joan Stambaugh, revised by Dennis J. Schmidt. Albany and New York: State University of New York Press, 2010.
Kierkegaard, Søren. *Concluding Unscientific Postscript to "Philosophical Fragments,"* vol. 1. Edited and translated by Howard V. Hong and Edna H. Hong. Princeton, NJ: Princeton University Press, 1992.
Kierkegaard, Søren. *Fear and Trembling and Repetition*. Edited and translated by Howard V. Hong and Edna H. Hong. Princeton, NJ: Princeton University Press, 1983.
Lamott, Anne. *Almost Everything: Notes on Hope*. New York: Riverhead Books, 2018.
Levinas, Emmanuel. *Ethics and Infinity: Conversations with Philippe Nemo*. Translated by Richard A. Cohen. Pittsburgh, PA: Duquesne University Press, 1985.
Lewis, C. S. *The Four Loves*. New York: Harcourt Brace & Company, 1960.
Lewis, C. S. *The Great Divorce*. San Francisco, CA: HarperOne, 2015.
Romano, Claude. "Awaiting." In *Phenomenology and Eschatology: Not Yet in the Now*, edited by Neal DeRoo and John Panteleimon Manoussakis, translated by Ryan Coyne, 35–52. Farnham and Burlington, VT: Ashgate, 2009.
Romano, Claude. *Event and Time*. Translated by Stephen E. Lewis. New York: Fordham University Press, 2014.
Schilbrack, Kevin. *Philosophy and the Study of Religions: A Manifesto*. Malden, MA: Wiley-Blackwell, 2014.
Simmons, J. Aaron. "The Failure of Success." https://www.youtube.com/watch?v=Y4beiEp-xZ4&t. Accessed February 12, 2021.
Simmons, J. Aaron. "Living Joyfully after Losing Social Hope: Kierkegaard and Chrétien on Selfhood and Eschatological Expectation." *Religions* 8, no. 33 (2017): 1–15.
Simmons, J. Aaron. "A Search for the 'Really' Real: Philosophically Approaching the Task of Defining Religion." *Bulletin for the Study of Religion* 44, no. 4 (December 2015): 19–26.
Simmons, J. Aaron. "Vagueness and Its Virtues: A Proposal for Renewing Philosophy of Religion." In *Philosophy of Religion After "Religion,"* edited by Michael Ch. Rodgers and Richard Amesbury, forthcoming. Tübingen: Mohr Siebeck, 2023.
Simmons, J. Aaron, and Eli Simmons. "Liturgy and Eschatological Hope." In *Philosophies of Liturgies: Explorations of Embodied Religious Practice*, edited by J. Aaron Simmons, Neal DeRoo, and Bruce Ellis Benson, 287–303. London: Bloomsbury, 2023.
Westphal, Merold. *Kierkegaard's Concept of Faith*. Grand Rapids, MI: Wm. B. Eerdmans, 2014.

11

The Prescription of Liturgy for the Problem of Blindness in the Thought of Jean-Luc Marion

Christina George

In the ninth chapter of the Gospel of John, we are presented with a narrative which influenced Jean-Luc Marion's early work and which serves as an important foundation for what follows in this chapter. The account is of a man who was born blind and is subsequently healed by Jesus. This healing comes about as a result of several actions: Jesus spits on the ground and places mud on the man's eyes. He then directs him to walk to the Pool of Siloam where he is to cleanse his face of the mud. The man obeys and his sight is restored. His response extends beyond mere gratefulness for his healing to an act of belief in Jesus, whose works have been thus "displayed in him."[1] Having overheard Jesus claim that he came into the world to give sight, the Pharisees ask Jesus, "Are we also blind?," to which Jesus responds, "If you were blind, you would have no guilt, but now that you say, 'We see,' your guilt remains."[2]

From this narrative, one is given a vivid example of the self as it is faced with the other—in this case Jesus—who is sent by God into the world.[3] One senses the blind man's desire to see, and one witnesses this man's obedience to Jesus, as he goes to the pool and receives the gift of sight. In the end, the narrative concludes not only with physical sight, but with belief. Left to consider more than one species of blindness in the comparison between the once blind man and the still "blind" Pharisees, one is compelled to inquire as to whether there might also be more than one kind of sight.

This passage, which serves as the basis for Marion's early essay, "The Blind at Shiloh," provides a framework for our inquiry into Marion's examination of the self and the other, with the goal of better understanding the nature of blindness and the process by which one may progress from blindness to sight.[4] This chapter examines blindness, the possibility of sight, and the function of desire in relation to these capacities. It becomes evident that with the capacity for sight there is an attending possibility to mis-see, and liturgy as an aesthetic event is recommended as a cure for this malady of blindness. This chapter supports many of the characterizations of the self and the other as they are presented in Marion's "The Blind at Shiloh" and *In the Self's Place*, but also includes in its solution the notion of "degrees of sight," which is explored further in the conclusion.[5]

In "The Blind at Shiloh," Marion's characterization of sight is steeped in aesthetic priorities. He contrasts the ideas of image and icon and examines characteristics of visual art—Christian or otherwise—in order to demonstrate the effect of liturgy on the one who participates in it. From the outset, he also relates each of these objects of sight (image and icon) to humankind's native propensity to pursue and experience the objects of one's desire. As such, it is crucial for this chapter that we understand the nature of this desire, beginning with its relationship to the production of images and followed by its effect on our capacity for seeing (and responding to) these images.

Providing an initial framework for understanding the relationship between desire and the production of an image, Marion writes: "Desire drags its objects out from obscurity, since it is nothing more than an image that can be made visible and thus, in one sense, acceptable, or at least accepted in the circuit of distribution. The image becomes for us more than a mode—[it becomes] a world [*une mode—un monde*]. The world is made into an image [*s'est fait image*]."[6] From this we determine that desire is marked by a quality of insistence which demands that its objects be made visible. Furthermore, the image itself makes visible the desire(s) of the viewer. There is a dynamic connection between what one wants to see and what one does see, and it is this correlation which is more thoroughly explored in what follows.

The particular nature of the image in this context is the televisual screen, which is itself characterized by its pervasiveness, immediacy, and influence. Within this context, the distribution Marion speaks of refers to the dissemination of the visual image on the electronic screen, the success of which hinges not only on the desire (or even demand) of the viewer, but also on the prowess of the producer and the marketer to position the image before the viewer and satisfy this desire accordingly.[7] It is this goal of satisfaction that unites the interaction between what the viewer wants to see and what is made available for viewing. According to Marion, it is the chief aim of the marketer that "every emitted image, in order to be seen by its viewer, must precisely satisfy his desire to see . . . thus every image must reproduce in itself the measure of desire."[8] Ironically, it seems that the viewer, motivated by his innate desire and the accompanying expectation that this desire should be satisfied, occupies two contrasting positions. In one sense, he is in a place of authority, as his desire directly affects the production and perpetuation of the image. But in another sense, he is also completely beholden to his desire, heeding its insistence and pursuing its satisfaction. The images he sees are the only images he wants to see.

If this desire is so compelling, one might then ask: what is the object of this desire (other than merely its satisfaction)? Put more simply, what motivates one's longing? Marion's response to this helps us distinguish between sight and blindness insofar as either may affect the quality of one's vision. He writes: "the viewer devours the visible that is all the more available. A 'viewer' thus defined [is] one who . . . undergoes, governs, and defines the image—all under the pretext of access to information, the opening of the world, and 'connecting' on (albeit poor) current events."[9] This language of "pretext" indicates that the viewer's urge to see the screen has more to do with one's view of oneself, rather than with one's desire to access real information or apprehend a real other. Indeed, Marion admits that "the viewer watches for the sole pleasure of seeing," as well as for the ability to see whatever he desires to see.[10] The image is of great value to the viewer because it reassures the viewer that he can, in fact, see, even though the image's existence is a result of the viewer's desire in the first place.

Sight, it seems, may then be defined as the satisfaction of one's desire in a measure which is exactly proportionate to that desire.[11] If this is a true understanding of sight, then the televisual image can, indeed, accomplish the object of one's desire—assuring the viewer that he sees, and even governs, the image. Yet is this the only way to understand the nature of sight? Is it harmful to be satisfied with this image? To answer this, we must more thoroughly explore the nature of the images one demands and devours.

Marion begins his consideration of the image itself with the question, "As the image of what does this image offer itself? In other words, from what original does the image originate?"[12] It is interesting that he immediately relates the presence of this visible image to a potential corollary in an invisible original, especially given that he concludes "the image has no original other than itself and itself alone."[13] In fact, the authority and value of the image actually increases the more severed it becomes from anything original or real.[14] The image is, essentially, its own reality which is not meant to refer back to, or evoke for, the viewer any other reality. The viewer who sees the image is looking only at this single reality, a world unto itself, which prevents him from apprehending any other possible reality. This is due also to the fact that he has become satisfied, no longer desiring to see anything else, reinforcing the role of desire in an act of sight.

This two-fold nature of the image—to be simultaneously of high value to the viewer and also banal, entirely separate from an original (from what is more real)—is what constitutes its status not only as image, but as idol. The viewer is enamored with the idol, and the idol governs the viewer's desire, perpetuating the process of producing even more idols (demanding more such images).[15] Furthermore, since the relationship between viewer and image is marked by the viewer's satisfaction with the image, Marion highlights that the viewer, pleased with the idol, is also pleased with himself.[16] He confirms that here, there is a direct relationship between how one views the image and how one views oneself.[17]

Marion's characterization of the image as idol implies that one's desire is intrinsically marked by a potential capacity to truncate a more thorough task of perception, which itself implies there is another (and possibly more worthy) alternative. The sight that the viewer experiences in relation to the mere image, then, may be likened to that of the Pharisees in the opening passage from John, who believe they already see.[18] Indeed, it could be that this sight is actually blindness of two different kinds: the viewer is not able to see a real or original world, nor is he able to see himself as anything other than one who governs the image. Thus, in the case wherein the image is accepted as the sum of what is real—when it becomes its own original—the possibility of the real original is lost. This "arrogance of the image,"[19] or the image's tendency to be "closed off to its original,"[20] highlights that an alternative remains; namely, that an original may be found. This invites us to the possibility of a restoration of a kind of sight that is able to find and perceive an original.

The problem of blindness is demonstrated by way of the visual apprehending of the image and motivated by one's desire and pursuit of identity (the desire of the self to be seen and know one is seeing). The solution Marion proposes is one that is rooted in the liturgy as an aesthetic event, which similarly allows for an act of sight and a reassurance of a sense of self. One key aspect of this solution lies in the nature of that which is available for sight. In place of the total spectacle of the televisual image which encourages and results in quick satisfaction,[21] Marion suggests that the object one views ought to be marked instead by an impoverishment in order that the viewer may be prompted to consider the possibility of the other (the original which the image obscures).[22] According to Marion, this is typified not in the image, but in the icon.

Marion's description of the icon is rooted in two fundamental aspects. The first is its physical nature as an aesthetic object with a visible facade. The second has to do with the nature of the icon insofar as it allows for the possibility of sight occurring in two simultaneous directions.[23] There is first the gaze of the viewer who sees the icon. However, because the icon is not a spectacle in itself (due to its impoverishment), the viewer is not immediately satisfied by this first gaze and is instead prompted by his desire to look beyond the surface of the icon and see the "other of the visible face . . . the invisible origin of the gaze of the other upon me."[24] In this exchange, the viewer is invited to consider the possibility of Christ, "a visible lieutenant of the invisible," who does not require a love for himself, but redirects one's love to the Father.[25] Christ himself acts as the first icon, by virtue of the fact that his own impoverishment, ultimately on the Cross, yields a "transparency, in order that we might regard there the gaze of God."[26] To see Christ, then, is to see the Father who first sees us.[27] Marion writes, speaking of Christ, "If he demands I lift my eyes to him, this is not at all so that I see him only, but so that I might see also and especially the Father."[28] Thus, the icon allows for a new understanding of sight which, like our first consideration of sight, is also twofold. It includes the possibility of my gaze viewing the icon as an aesthetic object, but it also includes being seen—in the icon one "look[s] upon a gaze that envisages me,"[29] the gaze of the Father. The icon is thus meant to function as a mechanism by which one can "climb back up [*remonter*], to cross the visible image and be exposed to the invisible counter-gaze."[30] This is accomplished in the liturgy itself which serves as a paradigmatic iconic moment, achieving the "kenosis of the image for the benefit of the holiness of God."[31]

We are thus faced with two types of sight. In the context of the spectacular image, the viewer is completely driven by his desire, and demands that his desire be satisfied. This results in the production of the type of images which satisfy the viewer according to the measure of his desire. He sees the image and is kept from seeing any other original beyond the image, because the image is enough to satisfy him. Furthermore, his experience of sight reassures him that he is capable of sight, and he sees himself as such. To be sure, this framework for sight shares many similarities with the process of sight laid out within the context of the liturgy. In this latter context, the viewer is similarly motivated by his desire to see.[32] He also desires to be seen, as one does in relation to the image. The difference with respect to the liturgy, however, is that the viewer is not meant to be satisfied with the mere image (or even with the visual spectacle of the liturgy). Instead, the impoverished visibility of the icon is meant to invite the viewer beyond it, to contemplate the gaze of another, to increase one's desire. This desire ultimately leads the viewer to be seen, but not by himself. His object of sight lies beyond the physical image, and that which sees him is also separate from him. The opportunity for real sight presented in the liturgy allows us to acknowledge that the first kind of sight—the sight that demands to see the image—is in fact blindness, a condition where one thinks that he sees, which keeps him from seeing anything more real.

The role of desire in relation to both image and icon highlights the element which serves as the central crux: it is always within the self's nature to experience desire in relation to both itself and the given, and to act in a manner which pursues this desire. While we have established that at the very least the subject desires to both see and be seen, we must turn to Marion's *In the Self's Place* in order to understand why the possibility of sight offered in the liturgy is more real than the sight made possible in the context of the image. Captured uniquely by its title, which translates to "in that place where the self is found" or "in that place which is the self" (*au lieu de soi*), *In the Self's Place* is an examination of Saint Augustine's devotion to God that highlights the manner in which the approach of the self toward God is motivated by a desire to find both God and oneself. The oft-quoted selection from the *Confessions* best designates the nature of this desire: "You made us for, in view of, and in the direction of yourself, in such a way that our heart knows no rest so long as it does not rest in you."[33] This restlessness is part of the makeup of desire, and this desire is what constitutes one's movement toward the given.[34] The soul (the self), made to approach the given, longs for rest, and the soul cannot rest until its desire for selfhood has been satisfied.

This is why the function of the icon, ultimately demonstrated by way of the liturgy, is uniquely capable of engendering real sight. It centers around identifying the nature of the soul's desire—to approach and be seen by the Father. Its impoverishment—and ultimately the kenosis of Christ—allows for the participant's gaze to move beyond it and to be seen by the gaze of the Father. Even with the aid of impoverishment, however, the question remains: is it possible for one to mistake the icon for a mere image? Marion responds to this question with the conclusion that participation in the liturgy does not provide an automatic assurance that one will see God.[35] Rather, he emphasizes that the attitude of one's gaze before the liturgy is a significant part of what contributes to whether or not one is distracted by the superficial, or instead experiences the crossing of one's gaze with the gaze who first sees the self.[36] He suggests that what the self needs, and what liturgy offers, is the opportunity to choose—to make a decision: "It may be that only the liturgy summons us to such a decision: it provokes the last judgment of every gaze, which must, before it and it alone, either continue still to desire to see an idol or agree to pray. Prayer signifies here: letting the other (of the) gaze see me."[37]

Here, we detect a key correlation and corresponding question: if sight includes both the capacity to see and be seen, and prayer is "letting the other of the gaze see me," it seems that sight and prayer are akin to one other. This is perhaps the most definitive mechanism by which one can distinguish blindness from sight. Sight in relation to the image is bound by the self—the self's desire and the self's satisfaction (which itself is subject to the reality of the image). But in the liturgy, sight is given the opportunity to search after the other and to be seen—indeed, to pray. Furthermore, it seems that the opportunity—provided by the liturgy—to make this choice may be recurring, since in Marion's words, "it always remains possible to apprehend (in fact to miss) the celebration as a "grand mass . . . to be already completely absorbed by the idolatrous spectacle and certainly closed to its crossing (or being crossed) by an invisible gaze."[38] As a response to this, I would suggest that what the liturgy offers is the possibility to restore one's sight by degrees. In her *Degrees of Givenness*, Christina Gschwandtner addresses this, saying, "What consequently still seems to be missing in Marion's work . . . is an account of the transition, the development, the degrees, the in-between.... [I]f prayer is only possible when we find ourselves envisaged by the divine gaze that completely empties us of ourselves, we are in a scary position indeed."[39] Thus, it is here that we are consoled not only by the liturgy as a paradigmatic iconic event, but as one which is habitual and recurring. It doesn't simply invite one to see and believe; it *regularly* invites one grow, by degrees, in one's capacity for prayer, and thus for sight.[40]

This opportunity for decision and a gradual process of transformation through prayer recalls the opening narrative whereupon Christ, having already granted the man physical sight, asks whether or not he then *believed* in the Son of Man. The sight which was restored was not merely physical; it extended to meet the fullness of the man's desire. Thus, rather than appealing specifically to a change or impoverishment of the image, it seems that what must occur is a change within the self—a change instigated by the Giver (who gives sight and anoints), participated in by the givee (who goes to the pool and washes his eyes), and concluded with a return of the givee to the place where the Giver beckons (as the blind man returned to Jesus). This is the possibility the liturgy affords. In Marion's words, "The liturgy alone impoverishes the image enough to wrest it from every spectacle, so that in this way might appear the splendor that the eyes can neither hope for nor bear, but a splendor that love—shed abroad in our hearts [Romans 5:5]—makes it possible to endure."[41] Liturgy, which "effects the appearance of Christ and results from it,"[42] leads one regularly to the pool of Shiloh in response to the call of God.[43] It suggests that there are two kinds of sight, that vision can encourage one toward or away from belief, and that real sight, motivated by desire, is made possible by the Father who first envisages us.

To conclude, it seems the solution for the problem of blindness lies first in the beckoning of the Giver to us. But one must also be willing to walk to the pool, as Marion suggests: "In order not to remain blind—obsessed by the incessant stream of static images that wall up our eyes on themselves—in order to be liberated from the muddy tyranny of the visible, one must pray—going to wash oneself in the pool of Shiloh. At the pool of the Sent One, who was sent only for that—we are granted a vision of the invisible."[44] This examination of Marion's essay reassures us that the problem of blindness is no cause for regret; it is the very thing which makes it possible for "the works of God [to be] displayed," as described in the account of St. John.[45] But the individual must be willing to acknowledge that, left to himself, he is poorly contented with the image. Yet he is also assured that the solution lies within the continual approach of the self toward God and toward sight—the soul's place of rest.[46]

Notes

1 John 9:3 (English Standard Version)
2 John 9:41 (ESV)
3 Throughout this project, the term "other" includes multiple connotations of "otherness," at times referring to that which is different from or extended beyond the self (personal or impersonal), while at other times denoting more specifically that which relates to God. See Jeffrey Kosky's translational notes which precede *In the Self's*

Place. Jean-Luc Marion, *In the Self's Place: The Approach of Saint Augustine*, trans. Jeffrey L. Kosky (Stanford: Stanford University Press, 2012), xx.

4 Several valuable pieces of secondary scholarship consider the way in which Marion's concept of both the self (the givee) and the other (the given) deepens throughout the development of his phenomenological framework. See especially Shane Mackinlay's *Interpreting Excess: Jean-Luc Marion, Saturated Phenomena, and Hermeneutics* (New York: Fordham University Press, 2010) and Christina Gschwandtner *Degrees of Givenness: On Saturation in Jean-Luc-Marion* (Bloomington, IN: Indiana University Press, 2014), ix–24.

5 This idea of "degrees of sight" is rooted in Gschwandtner's "degrees of givenness" insofar as she accounts for what she perceives to be a discrepancy between the "excessive and utterly overwhelming" nature of Marion's phenomenological framework and the rhythms or realities which mark everyday life for the average person. See Gschwandtner, *Degrees of Givenness*, 24.

6 Marion, "The Blind at Shiloh," in *The Crossing of the Visible*, trans. James K. A. Smith (Stanford, CA: Stanford University Press, 2004), 46.

7 "Whence the efforts of announcers, programmers, producers, to target this desire, to measure it in order to satisfy it." Marion, "The Blind at Shiloh," 50.

8 Marion, "The Blind at Shiloh," 51.

9 Marion, "The Blind at Shiloh," 50.

10 Marion, "The Blind at Shiloh," 50.

11 "The viewer fixes the norm of the image without original by the demand of his desire to see merely in order to see; each image thus becomes valid, so long as and as soon as it satisfies this desire, filling it perfectly or partially; thus the image must be conformed to the expectation of this desire." Marion, "The Blind at Shiloh," 50.

12 Marion, "The Blind at Shiloh," 47.

13 Marion, "The Blind at Shiloh," 47.

14 "The image accrues [*accroît*] its authority by disconnecting itself from every original: the less gold there is, the more value the image has; so the dollar is not an image; but fortunately, the image produces dollars." Marion, "The Blind at Shiloh," 47.

15 "Doubly retaining the possibility of referring back to an original, which it should be, the image tyrannizes the world, things, and souls … It takes hold of our desire itself: the tyranny of the idolatrous image defeats us with our willing consent." Marion, "The Blind at Shiloh," 54.

16 Marion, "The Blind at Shiloh," 51.

17 "For politicians, athletes, journalists, CEOs, writers, nothing is more precious than this—'my image': I am only a self-as-image." Marion, "The Blind at Shiloh," 52.

18 "Some of the Pharisees near him heard these things, and said to him, 'Are we also blind?' Jesus said to them, 'If you were blind, you would have no guilt; but now that you say, "We see," your guilt remains." (John 9:40–41).

19 Marion, "The Blind at Shiloh," 47.

20 Marion, "The Blind at Shiloh," 49.

21 Marion, "The Blind at Shiloh," 46.

22 Instrumental here is the concept of "givenness," which is most thoroughly described in Marion's *Being Given*. Givenness is vital to this discussion of the relationship between the self and the other because one must understand what it is that comprises the original which may be detected if the image does not stop one's gaze. The original French version of Being Given, *Étant donné*, was published only one year following the original French publication of *The Crossing of the Visible* in 1996. See Jean-Luc Marion,

Being Given: Toward a Phenomenology of Givenness, trans. Jeffrey L. Kosky (Stanford, CA: Stanford University Press, 2002).
23 "I look, with my invisible gaze, upon a gaze that envisages me; in the icon, in effect, it is a matter not so much of seeing a spectacle as seeing another gaze that sustains mine, confronts it, and eventually overwhelms it." Marion, "The Blind at Shiloh," 57.
24 Marion, "The Blind at Shiloh," 56.
25 Marion, "The Blind at Shiloh," 57.
26 Marion, "The Blind at Shiloh," 62
27 Marion describes here the initiative of the Father via this first, invisible gaze which sees me. But he also details this priority of the Father as Giver in his text *Negative Certainties*, which explores the transactions of sacrifice and forgiveness, both of which are pertinent considerations for a contemplation of the transforming effect of the liturgy. Furthermore, these concepts of icon, forgiveness, and sacrifice all demonstrate various aspects of his framework of givenness explored in *Being Given*, although he does not characterize the source of the given in a theological manner within *Being Given* as he does in *Negative Certainties*. For his discussion of sacrifice and forgiveness, see Marion, *Negative Certainties*, trans. Stephen E. Lewis (Chicago: University of Chicago Press, 2015), 115–54.
28 Marion, "The Blind at Shiloh," 57.
29 Marion, "The Blind at Shiloh," 57.
30 Marion, "The Blind at Shiloh," 60.
31 Marion, "The Blind at Shiloh," 64.
32 Although it should also be noted that Marion describes more than only the sense of sight: "The liturgy proposes to demonstrate a visible spectacle, which summons and possibly fills vision, but also the senses of hearing, smell, touch, and even taste." See Marion, "The Blind at Shiloh," 64.
33 See Marion, *In the Self's Place*, 17. Marion's particular rendering highlights the image of the self progressing toward (or positioned toward) God, with implications for both the self and the other.
34 This movement toward the given, according to Marion, can be expressed in the acts of confession and praise. Marion likens praise to the movement of an object toward its place, wherein the self, giving praise, is moving toward its place, seeking rest in God: "The whole of the *Confessions* is thus framed by the double utterance of a single principle, one that we could safely say comes from physics but is applied to the spiritual life (and corrected by it): . . . 'A body is pushed by its weight toward its place. This weight is not just borne downward toward the bottom but toward its proper place.' . . . In the case where I praise God, that is to say, where I address my words to him inasmuch as I love him, my weight leads me to him as to my proper place. Praising him therefore means that I rise into my place, that I go back up there from where I am and toward him from whom I come." Marion, *In the Self's Place*, 17–18.
35 In his essay, "The Poor Phenomenon: Marion and the Problem of Givenness," Anthony Steinbock discusses the limitation of the recipient. Where I describe blindness, Steinbock articulates a poverty on the part of the beholder which is twofold: "Essentially, the gifted cannot receive the given in the manner in which it gives itself . . . the gifted in the responsal may 'want' to receive the given, but essentially (because of our finitude) cannot do so. . . In this case, poverty does not belong to the structure of the object, but to our deficiency in being ready to receive the givenness. . . We thus have two types of poverty: An essential poverty that is peculiar to every kind of seeing and about which there is nothing we can do, and a poverty of self-imposition without

reception, in which the saturated phenomenon as revelation, as call, is missed." See Anthony Steinbock, "The Poor Phenomenon: Marion and the Problem of Givenness," in *Words of Life*, ed. Bruce Ellis Benson and Norman Wirzba (New York, NY: Fordham University Press, 2010), 128–29.

36 Marion, "The Blind at Shiloh," 65.
37 Marion, "The Blind at Shiloh," 65.
38 Marion, "The Blind at Shiloh," 64.
39 Gschwandtner, *Degrees of Givenness*, 9.
40 Marion supplies another aesthetic example of this when he describes what may be called a liturgy of revisiting a work of art in *Being Given*. See Marion, *Being Given*, 48.
41 Marion, "The Blind at Shiloh," 65. Brackets original.
42 Marion, "The Blind at Shiloh," 64.
43 "... Speaking *to* God, as the confessing praise does, implies first of all turning one's face *to* God so that he can come over me, claim me, and call me starting form himself, well beyond what I could say, predict, or predicate of him starting from myself alone." Marion, *In the Self's Place*, 19.
44 Marion, "The Blind at Shiloh," 65.
45 This verse also reflects the priority of visibility which Marion places on the givenness throughout *Negative Certainties*.
46 In Augustine's words, "In your gift we find our rest. There you are our joy. Our rest is our peace." In Augustine, *Confessions*, trans. Henry Chadwick (Oxford: Oxford University Press, 1991; reissued 2008), 278. Indeed, the giving up of one conception of self in order to receive a better vision of the self as seen by God might be described with Marion's language regarding the nature of sacrifice: "I deprive myself of a good precisely in order to prove to myself that it has only a minor importance and that I remain myself even without it; hence by losing a possession that is other than me, I gain a more perfect possession of myself." In Marion, *Negative Certainties*, 118.

Bibliography

Augustine. *Confessions*. Translated by Henry Chadwick. Oxford: Oxford University Press, 2008.

Gschwandtner, Christina. *Degrees of Givenness: On Saturation in Jean-Luc Marion*. Bloomington: Indiana University Press, 2014.

Mackinlay, Shane. *Interpreting Excess: Jean-Luc Marion, Saturated Phenomena, and Hermeneutics*. New York: Fordham University Press, 2010.

Marion, Jean-Luc. *Being Given: Toward a Phenomenology of Givenness*. Translated by Jeffrey L. Kosky. Stanford: Stanford University Press, 2022.

Marion, Jean-Luc. "The Blind at Shiloh." In *The Crossing of the Visible*, translated by James K. A. Smith, 46–65. Stanford: Stanford University Press, 2004.

Marion, Jean-Luc. *In the Self's Place: The Approach of Saint Augustine*. Translated by Jeffrey L. Kosky. Stanford: Stanford University Press, 2012.

Marion, Jean-Luc. *Negative Certainties*. Translated by Stephen E. Lewis. Chicago: Chicago University Press, 2015.

Steinbock, Anthony. "The Poor Phenomenon: Marion and the Problem of Givenness." In *Words of Life*, edited by Bruce Ellis Benson and Norman Wirzba, 120–31. New York: Fordham University Press, 2010.

12

Beauty, Sacrament, and the Road to Emmaus

Wendy Crosby

When the world seems full of crises, the story of the Road to Emmaus (Luke 24:13–35) can offer hope. The two travelers are experiencing the greatest despair of their lives when, suddenly, everything looks different—brighter, more hopeful, less . . . abandoned by God. When one is riddled with fear and anxiety, that is the kind of shift in perspective that is needed.[1] How did the two travelers undergo such a transformation? How did they come to see God when God seemed absent? Jean-Louis Chrétien says that to encounter God and hear God's call one must first be wounded. The wound creates an opening for God's presence. Then, in that opening, we see the space for beauty in our response to God's call. Drawing on Chrétien's analyses of the wound opened by the call, of the gift of beauty that the call offers, and of the response to the call out of the beauty found in oneself, we may better understand the transformation of the two travelers in the story of the Road to Emmaus within the Christian tradition. This transformation is highlighted by two interpretations of the story of the Road to Emmaus: the painting *Emmaus* by Filipino artist Emmanuel Garibay and the poem "Song on the Road to Emmaus" by Dorothee Sölle. The surprising imagined responses of the travelers in Garibay's and Sölle's respective works illustrate the call of God as opening one to both the beauty found in Christ and the beauty found in oneself as described by Chrétien. I argue that the transformation the travelers undergo, and indeed the transformation which occurs from hearing a call from God, is sacramental in a Christian sense of the term in that it offers a new identity, beauty, and salvation to the travelers. The result is an aesthetic anthropology in which our vocation as humans is to recognize beauty within ourselves through sacramental participation with the divine.

The Call that Wounds

The late French Catholic phenomenologist Jean-Louis Chrétien frequently uses the story of Jacob wrestling an angel (Genesis 32:22–32) to describe the anguish and wound of hearing "the call." In this pericope, a man (the angel) battles Jacob for unspecified reasons. Come dawn, Jacob is winning but the angel makes a final blow to his hip, dislocating it. Now with the upper hand, the angel suggests they end the fight, but Jacob insists on a blessing. Here and at the end of the story we get the sense that

Jacob already knows who this man really is. The ending is as opaque as the start, but Jacob receives a new identity. He is now "Israel," the Father of the Twelve Tribes of Israel, which name he receives as a reward for his willingness to persevere against humans and God alike. But the angel does not heal his limp.

According to Chrétien, to hear a call always involves a wound, in the sense of an opening up, for otherwise we would be incapable of actually hearing something other than ourselves.[2] The literal wounds of Jacob after the fight are an effective image of the kind of wounds needed to hear a call. Jacob was called to become someone new, the Father of the Twelve Tribes of Israel, and his wound becomes a metaphor for the former self he leaves behind.

The imagery of the fight and Jacob's radical change of identity, not to mention the limp, capture the violence (Chrétien even calls it an "assault"[3]) of hearing the call quite well. The limp seems gratuitous. Was that necessary to call Jacob? Did God really need to go so far as to injure Jacob? This line of questioning serves Chrétien well by highlighting that every call always wounds. You cannot hear a call without allowing some vulnerability in yourself. So, yes, Jacob had to be wounded.

Chrétien's use of the word "wounding" eludes connotation as good or bad.[4] Capturing this ambiguity, he writes that the call and response structure "always has its origin in the wound of a joy or a distress; it always opens its lips in response to some tearing asunder."[5] To be wounded is to suffer, but Chrétien leaves open the possibility of a joyful suffering. Thus there is a tension here that cannot be fully worked out. Woundedness is like the vulnerability that opens up the possibility of intimacy—risky, but tantalizing. Or perhaps it is like when the recognition of a problem opens up the possibility of asking for help—terrifying, but also alleviating.

The Call that Reveals Beauty and Our Response

Chrétien writes that "*to kaloun*, that which calls, produces *ta kala*, beautiful things."[6] Although we must be wounded by the call in order to listen to it, the wound creates a space for what Chrétien describes as beauty and beautiful things within us. That beauty transforms us:

> In every manifestation of God, direct or indirect, there is adventure and advent: God comes to me, God happens to me, and I am affected by [God's] arrival. To speak of this beauty is to speak to it also, to respond to it and become responsible for it, just as it means becoming responsible for my own transfiguration at its hands and thus being responsible for myself more than is really possible—for it is not I who have transformed myself in this way; I would not have been capable of it.[7]

When we are drawn to the beauty of the divine, we find ourselves responding out of and responsible for the beauty that we perceive in ourselves. It was always already there, but when we find it, it seems new. Quoting Augustine, Chrétien notes that "Late have I loved you, beauty so old and so new" always describes our encounter with the beauty we find and love in ourselves.[8] Although Augustine did come to God late in life, our response to

God's gift is always late because it was always within us before we were aware. "So at whatever moment of our lives we are able to love this beauty, and however early it is placed," Chrétien writes, "it would always be possible to say 'late have I loved you.'"[9]

If we have received beauty, we will be compelled to respond. As Chrétien writes, "Beauty that is seen requires that we speak in order to respond to it and requires that we answer for it with beauty. It bestows speech and recovers speech by inspiring it to be beautiful in turn."[10] How might we respond to beauty with beauty? Where, exactly, do beautiful things come from? One might be inclined to answer that beautiful things come from God, who within the Christian tradition is often called beauty itself. However, in comparison to beauty itself, could any lesser beauty really be described as beautiful? Drawing on the poetry of Jacopone da Todi, Chrétien notes a tension between divine beauty which "seems to reduce to nothing the beauty of creation"[11] and the beauty of creation which brings us to God.[12] Chrétien asks, "Can a beauty which makes all other beauty ugly still be beauty? Is beauty a divine name?"[13] Recognizing this problem, Chrétien takes us in a different direction: God is the Source of beauty, but not necessarily as beauty itself.[14] In this way, beauty is a gift given to us. Consequently, the beauty we find in ourselves and which transforms us is an excess.[15] Reversing the quote above, Chrétien then writes, "Beautiful, *kalon*, is what comes from a call, *kalein*, which continues to call through it and in it."[16] In other words, the beauty in ourselves takes on the form of a new call. He continues: "What is beautiful is what calls out by manifesting itself and manifests itself by calling out."[17] The excess of beauty we find in ourselves is itself a call which pulls us out of ourselves.

The call emanating from our own beauty compels us to bring peace, joy, forgiveness, hospitality, justice, and so on into the world—not just for the sake of other humans, but also for creation itself.[18] As Chrétien suggests, we are tasked with creating a suitable dwelling place for plants, animals, and humans alike, and to offer the praise of creation to God.[19] These are the beautiful things we are responsible for producing; this is the task to which our own beauty calls.

In sum, the call wounds us. We are always wounded and vulnerable when we are in a position to receive something or learn something from someone else. Just to listen, whether to another human being or to God, is to allow a wound to open in us. The call also gives us a gift from God's own excess that we are hopefully able to receive if the wound is open enough. This gift is beauty. The beauty which transforms us is itself a new call that "produces beautiful things" through our participation.[20]

Reflections on the Road to Emmaus

Artist Emmanuel Garibay and poet Dorothee Sölle provide interpretations of the biblical story of the road to Emmaus that illustrate the path Chrétien describes from wound to transformative beauty, and from there to a response which produces beautiful things. Indeed, the Emmaus pericope highlights the role of beauty in the call-and-response structure better than Chrétien's own go-to story of Jacob. Jacob's wrestling and the dislocation of his hip form the center of that pericope, focusing our attention on the call that wounds rather than on the transformative gift of beauty; the wounds of the two travelers on the road to Emmaus, however, draw our attention to their moment of transformation in the recognition of Christ. Applying Chrétien's understanding of the call and response, this transformation occurs through the excess of beauty we find in ourselves, which allows us to respond to the call. In the Emmaus pericope, this is the call of God through Christ.

The Emmaus pericope is centered around hearing a call and responding to it. We begin shortly after the crucifixion of Christ with two travelers leaving Jerusalem. There are stories that Jesus is alive, but the travelers are mourning. Because of their already broken and wounded state, they are open to listening when a stranger joins them. The stranger explains how Jesus' death will fulfill the scriptures, but neither traveler recognizes the stranger as Jesus, nor fully understands his message. If Chrétien were reading this passage, he would consider the strangers' conversation a prayer despite their failure to recognize who God is. The despair the two travelers share with Jesus is a prayer of lament directed to God. Chrétien envisions prayer as a paradigm of the call and response structure which one is caught up in before one even knows how to pray.[21] The fact that the travelers do not recognize Jesus would be no obstacle for Chrétien, since for him we never know how to pray until we have started. Later the two travelers will look back and describe the walk differently. They will say, "Were not our hearts burning within us while he was talking to us on the road, while he was opening the scriptures to us?"[22] We could reword the beginning of that verse with something like, "Were not our hearts *wounded* before we recognized the stranger?"

Our travelers have been pulled into a cycle of call and response with their prayer of lament, but their own recognition of what's happening comes in the breaking of the bread. This is the point of inspiration for contemporary Filipino painter Emmanuel Garibay's depiction of the story, which illuminates the transformation from wound to beautiful thing.[23] Garibay's work regularly touches on colonialism, politics, social justice, and religion, with a particular focus on Filipino experiences as outsiders (e.g., not quite Western and not quite Asian). He shares that experience through his art.[24] When drawing on biblical narratives, his paintings never merely illustrate the story. They tell their own narrative, often challenging the viewer to become uncomfortable with what was once a familiar story. For example, his own take on Jacob wrestling with God in a painting called "Mendiola" shows protestors fighting off the police who are trying to remove them.[25]

In his colorful painting "Emmaus" from 2000, two men and one woman sit around a table at a pub laughing. Our eyes are drawn to the woman's red dress, which pops in contrast to the white t-shirts the men wear. There is an empty plate with some silverware on the table and each person has a drink. In the shadows of the background there is a man who is not paying attention, and in the foreground another man stands looking confused, like a waiter who missed the joke and only caught the laughter. The painting illustrates the moment in the story of the Road to Emmaus when Jesus breaks bread with the travelers, and Garibay's surprise for us is that Christ is the woman at the table. We the viewers are let in on the secret by the stigmata on her hands, and, though the waiter cannot see it, the travelers also recognize Christ as the provocatively dressed woman. Christ here looks like the kind of person they might desire romantically or sexually. We might describe her as beautiful, but Garibay explains that for Filipinos this woman would be seen as a one of "ill repute."[26] So, Christ here might also be the type of woman these men could take advantage of violently. (What exactly were they planning when they met this woman on the road?) However, there is no violence in this painting, only the joy of fellowship. Rod Pattenson for his part notes that the painting reveals the "human capacity for blindness."[27] We are very good at shielding ourselves and protecting ourselves from the wounds which would enable sight. Nevertheless, the travelers in this painting have removed their blindness and are now laughing at the joke that has been played on them. This is not a moment of shame or embarrassment; their laughter is *with* Christ. This woman who would normally be labeled an "outsider" does not look like the Jesus of Nazareth they remember, and yet she is in a sense that same Jesus.[28] Her surprising form, as Garibay's painting expresses, suggests that seeing God in the outsider is always possible. In this moment of transformation, the men respond to the beauty they see with their beautiful response in the form of laughter and fellowship.

In *The Call and the Response*, Chrétien notes that our response always falls short of measuring up to the call. Furthermore, we often do not know how to speak a response at all.[29] Consequently, our response starts in silence, which is not the opposite of speech but rather its source.[30] Garibay's painting offers a different take on what not knowing how to respond to a call looks like: laughter! As the travelers finally recognize Christ and hear the call, they receive the gift of an excess of beauty within themselves, and it spills out in the excess of laughter. While the men at the table may not articulate their response in words, their warm and welcoming postures in the painting exemplify how the excess of beauty in oneself becomes a response to the call.

Dorothee Sölle's poetic interpretation of the road to Emmaus similarly exemplifies how the excess of beauty within oneself becomes a response to the call. Sölle is a German theologian who was a young girl during the Holocaust. Attempting to come to terms with Christian Nazis who obeyed orders to the point of committing genocide, Sölle insists in her theology upon the necessity of our participation in bringing God into the world. Her theology leans heavily upon human responsibility and never separates the mystical from the concrete, especially when it is enacted in acts of social justice. Her poem "Song on the Road to Emmaus"[31] reflects her commitment to responsibility and justice:

> So long we have been walking
> away from the city of our hope
> to a village where life is said to be better
>
>> Hadn't we thought
>> we could overcome fear
>> the fear of the old pieceworker
>> that she'll have to take sick leave
>> the fear of the turkish girl
>> that she'll be deported
>> the fear of the haunted neurotic
>> that he'll be committed
>> forever
>
> So long we have been walking
> in the same wrong direction
> away from the city of our hope
> to the village where there's supposed to be water

Hadn't we thought
we were free and could liberate
all those poor devils
the working man's child held back and punished
in school
the adolescent on his motorbike
sent to the wrong work
for life
the deaf and dumb
in the wrong country
at the wrong time
silenced by working
a lifetime
for bread alone

So long we have been walking
in the same direction
away from the city
where our hope is still buried

> Then we met someone
> who shared his bread with us
> who showed us the new water
> here in the city of our hope
> I am the water
> you are the water
> he is the water
> she is the water

Then we turned around and went
back to the city of our buried hope
up to jerusalem

> He who brought water is with us
> he who brought bread is with us
> we shall find the water
> we shall be the water

> I am the water of life
> you are the water of life
> we are the water of life
> we shall find the water
> we shall be the water

In Sölle's poem, the travelers recall the hopes they once had for Jerusalem, but also how on the road to Emmaus they no longer believed the injustices in Jerusalem could be overcome. They had given up on Jerusalem, and perhaps on faith itself. These travelers had actively listened for God's call in Jerusalem, but they were not expecting the call to leave wounds. The road to Emmaus was a search for a new home and a new life, symbolized here in the poem as "water." Finally, the travelers recall the stranger they met who gave them "new water."[32] This water is the gift of beauty Chrétien describes which takes the form of hope for new life in the poem. Surprised by the arrival of hope, the travelers are even more surprised to recognize they are water too. The final stanzas contain a repeating phrase, "we shall find the water/we shall be the water."[33] These are dark days in Jerusalem despite the witness of a few women who claim Jesus is alive. The travelers realize that "the water of life" they had been seeking is a gift from God that they are meant to find in themselves.[34] The water now flowing out of the travelers is the transformative excess of beauty that Chrétien describes when one hears a call from God. Consequently, in this telling, the moment of the breaking of the bread was not primarily about realizing Christ could be in front of them, but about finding beauty in themselves.

Our two travelers, with their new-found hope, are now *heading back* to Jerusalem because they realize the problems of Jerusalem are their own to fix. Jerusalem cannot give them hope, but they can be hope for Jerusalem. It is a familiar pattern: leave home, discover the thing you were searching for is not what you thought, return home. We tell this story over and over because we have lived this story over and over. The call back home to do the work necessary for life to flourish is the call to make beautiful things and to find the ways God is immanent in our work for justice. The excess of beauty in Sölle's poem results in a response to the call which once again remains unspoken and is found instead in the travelers' renewed hope.

Chrétien calls the wounding of the call and our response to that call an "adventure."[35] The travelers at the end of Sölle's poem seem engaged in an adventure, having gained not only beauty but also courage, persistence, resilience, and hope. Their transformation was possible because the beauty was found, surprisingly, within themselves and not in God. If all they were able to do was gaze at the beauty of God, they would hardly be empowered to be agents of change. They might even look at themselves and their much dimmer beauty and fall further into despair: if God has new water, that is good for God, but I remain helpless; I can neither help myself nor others. God might save the world, but it will not have much to do with my efforts. Indeed, for those coming from Jerusalem, it does not look like God is going to save the world, since Jesus has died. Out of that despair, just imagine the surprise (or laughter!) to find that they actually had the beauty necessary in them already: "We shall be the water."[36] The beauty/water comes, of course, from God, but it does not leave them helpless. It makes them sufficient means for transformation and the creation of beauty. In fact, if the water really is the excess of beauty, to use Chrétien's terms, it makes them more than enough. The beauty that transforms them becomes a new call that continues the process of transformation in the world.

The Sacramental Nature of God's Call

The transformation Chrétien describes in hearing and responding to a call is not limited to calls from God, although he notes that a call from God takes on special significance. He writes, "The meaning of call and response is radically transformed when the call actually creates the respondent."[37] For the Creator, "to call is to create, to bestow being and beauty, but also to save."[38] Although Chrétien here does not use the word "sacrament," the gifts of personal identity (personal being), beauty, and salvation may be understood as sacramental. Just as the sacraments in the Christian tradition are defined as participation in the invisible reality of God's redeeming presence through visible signs, so God's call may be understood as a free gift of grace mediated through the ordinary world and the wounds of our own bodies. We are asked to participate in this gift from God that is also the advent of God's self. Beauty brings us to God and brings God to the world.

Within the Christian tradition a sacrament is transformational and grants one a new identity and salvation in Christ that becomes a vocation of sorts that in itself requires a response. In the story of the road to Emmaus, our attention is precisely on that moment of transformation—namely, when the wound becomes sacramental. By calling the opening of the wound "sacramental," I do not mean that wounding should be glorified or ritualized. The wound is sacramental because it is the place where an experience of God's grace in the ordinary material world is received and made present to us. A sacrament requires participation, since the individual must recognize and respond to God's freely given love.[39] Although, in the Christian tradition God's love is described as freely given and God's grace is always available, one's acceptance of God's grace is not forced by God. One must be intentional about noticing grace, which is why Christian churches celebrate official, communal sacraments to ritualize the reception of grace. Nevertheless, a sacrament can occur whenever one notices God's grace and that grace calls one to respond to, participate in, or celebrate the presence of the grace and beauty found in oneself or in the world.[40] Chrétien observes that whenever we hear God's call, there is a prior wound. Likewise for the Christian, to receive grace a wound or opening is necessary. When one has noticed God's grace, one has seen something one did not see before. By wounding one's narrow-sightedness and ripping one's field of vision open, a sacrament is possible.[41]

The story of the road to Emmaus lends itself to discussions of sacramentality due to its connection to the Eucharist. The breaking of bread (Luke 24:30–31), which echoes the Last Supper, is what finally opens the travelers' eyes. Despite clear connections to the Eucharist, it is, perhaps, the Catholic sacrament of Reconciliation that is most clearly reflected by Chrétien's understanding of the call and response. Reconciliation always begins with an account of one's wounds, in this case sins, although a wound need not be a sin. One approaches the priest with an attitude of remorse and regret, and the priest asks one to perform an intentional act of vulnerability, namely, declaring one's own failures. One hopes that God's mercy will overlook one's shortcomings and offer forgiveness, but reconciliation may do more than that. Absolution is not just a chance to experience God's goodness, but also a chance to be surprised by one's own goodness. The individual leaves the confessional transformed because they become newly aware of the goodness and beauty they already had as a creation called into being by God. As Chrétien notes, the beauty we find in ourselves was always already there "shining forth long before we opened our eyes to it."[42] Consequently, the wound involved in declaring one's sins simply removes the blindness to one's deeper beauty. Sölle's rendition highlights the sacramental transformation of the travelers especially well—not from bread to body, but from despair to hope and from wound to beauty.

A Theological Aesthetic Anthropology

Although Chrétien writes about beauty, he is known more for his discussions of how hearing the call wounds us. He is a thinker concerned with finitude, fragility, and vulnerability. He asks us to shed our egos in order to make room for hospitality and to listen and be changed by what we hear. Consequently, we must ask what happens to that wound when we introduce into the discussion the individual's transformation by the gift of excess beauty in a sacramental moment of participation with the divine. Is the wound erased? Redeemed? Does the wound become beautiful? A brief look at Chrétien's discussion of the beauty of Jesus can help us answer this question. In *The Ark of Speech*, Chrétien devotes several pages to the question of whether or not Jesus of Nazareth was a beautiful-looking human being. Was he beautiful because he was divine, or was he ordinary (even ugly) because he was thoroughly human? Is this even a worthwhile debate? Chrétien is not sure that it is, but he ends by returning to the way Christ's beauty gives itself away and becomes our own.[43] He writes, "Anyone who sees this beauty does not remain untouched by it but is radically transformed and renewed by it. And the very act whereby he discovers this beauty against all appearance is inseparable from the act whereby he himself, against all expectation, becomes beautiful."[44] The transfer of beauty from Christ to ourselves is suggested by the way artistic representations of Christ sometimes have elements of self-portraiture.[45] Christ is made to look like us because the beauty we would expect to find in Christ we have found in ourselves. An initial glance at Garibay's "Emmaus" would suggest he himself is an exception. Garibay does *not* look like the Christ-woman in his painting. Yet, we can imagine how Garibay's own self-identity as an outsider to both the Western world and the rest of Asia shapes his view of Christ as a woman who is an outsider. Consequently, his painting simultaneously asks us whether we can see Christ in the outsider woman and whether we can see beauty in someone like Garibay. In Sölle's poem, we do not get a literal description of Christ's appearance, but he is described as "new water." With Chrétien we may say that as soon as the travelers understand that Christ is the new water, they realize that they too are the new water. They look like Christ. One wonders if Sölle also, in writing her poem, found new water in herself. In the end, Jesus did have beauty, but far more important is how that beauty reveals our own beauty. As Chrétien remarks, beauty says *adieu*; it is always on the move making other beautiful things.[46]

The wound which opens us up to transformation and beauty ultimately remains with us, just as Christ's wounds remain after the resurrection and Jacob's wounds remain after he gains his identity as Israel. We never find the beauty within ourselves without the opening of the wound, as Chrétien shows. But when we are changed, the wound compels us forward and sends us out to God and to others. Consequently, our own woundedness can no longer be the focus of our attention. We now have a new identity, and the beauty within us calls us to produce beautiful things. In this way, Chrétien has given us the beginnings of a theological aesthetic anthropology in his discussion of beauty.[47] To be a human being is to be inherently beautiful, but it is a hidden, surprising beauty, especially to ourselves. We are blind to our own beauty and preoccupied by our finitude, vulnerability, and wounds. Our wounds seem to suggest we are broken, limping. Nevertheless, when we set aside the negative connotation of wounds (although it always exists in tension with the positive), we discover how our limitations are precisely what allow us to see something new. We find our beauty and our calling in our woundedness. To flourish as a human being is not to escape wounds or suffering, but rather to see ourselves as beautiful. This is the human vocation as suggested by Chrétien's reflections. Our beauty is not something to gaze upon, but something which commissions us. As Chrétien writes, "By calling to us, beauty moves us, in other words touches us, comes to touch us where we are, and sets us in movement, on our way and en route, so that we do not remain where we are or remain content with where we have got to."[48] Beauty must spill out in acts of love, justice, hospitality, and forgiveness. When we do not know what actions to take, it will simply spill out as laughing with God, as opposed to laughing *at* God in disbelief.

To live out the human vocation of seeing beauty intentionally we can cultivate a sacramental outlook that is similarly intentional about the learned ignorance necessary to listen and hear something new.[49] A sacramental outlook is one that is ready to be wounded and knows what Bruce Ellis Benson describes in his essay on the call that wounds:

> There is no other way of receiving the call, of being open to the other, without not merely the possibility but always the probability that we will be wounded—that is, changed or reoriented or perhaps rebuked. But one thing is certain: if we truly hear the call, we will not be the same as before we heard it.[50]

The readiness and desire to find God in the world is felt keenly and painfully by the two travelers. Recall how they describe their hearts as "burning" until they find what they desire in the stranger and themselves (see Luke 24:32). For a moment, there is a release of tension as beauty brings them to God and once again gives itself away in new calls. We are left with a beautiful woman and a beautiful laugh (Garibay), as well as a beautiful mission to redeem the lost Jerusalem (Sölle). We are left with a painting and a poem by artists known for their commitments to justice. Finally, we are left with a new perspective. Chrétien presents an understanding of the human person that is filled with hope and confidence in humanity's ability to respond out of beauty. The theological aesthetic anthropology that follows when one considers the possibility of a response out of the excess of beauty gifted to one by God suggests a potential to act even when one does not know how to speak. The beauty Chrétien describes is compelled to give itself away in acts of joy, fellowship, and justice, exactly as the travelers on the road to Emmaus experience beauty when their wounds transform them.

Notes

1   The immediate context for my own anxieties and fears was the slow emergence from the COVID-19 pandemic. What if our children are just as relentless and needy after the year of isolation as they were during it? What if we *could* interact with strangers again, but we've forgotten how to let people into our personal space, so we recoil instead? Is it possible that the world could get the virus under control, but we would all remain

broken? After all, we were broken in a lot of ways before the pandemic even started. Nevertheless, the experience of anxiety and fear transcends the pandemic as does our desire for a new perspective like that gained by the travelers on the road to Emmaus.
2 See Jean-Louis Chrétien, *The Ark of Speech*, trans. Andrew Brown (New York: Routledge, 2004), 9–10.
3 Jean-Louis Chrétien, *Hand to Hand: Listening to the Work of Art*, trans. Stephen E. Lewis (New York: Fordham University Press, 2003), 5.
4 Bruce Ellis Benson, "Chrétien on the Call that Wounds," in *Words of Life: New Theological Turns in French Phenomenology,* ed. Bruce Ellis Benson and Norman Wirzba (New York: Fordham University Press, 2010), 214.
5 Chrétien, *The Ark of Speech*, 37. Here Chrétien is specifically referring to the call and response structure as it functions in prayer.
6 Jean-Louis Chrétien, *The Call and the Response*, trans. Anne A. Davenport (New York: Fordham University Press, 2004), 7.
7 Chrétien, *The Ark of Speech*, 90.
8 Chrétien, *The Ark of Speech*, 91. See Augustine, *Confessions*, 10.27.38, trans. Henry Chadwick (Oxford: Oxford University Press, 1991), 201.
9 Chrétien, *The Ark of Speech*, 91.
10 Chrétien, *The Call and the Response*, 11.
11 Chrétien, *The Ark of Speech*, 97.
12 Chrétien, *The Ark of Speech*, 98.
13 Chrétien, *The Ark of Speech*, 98.
14 Noting a similar tension in St. François de Sales as found in Jacopone's poetry, Chrétien concludes, "The consequence of all of this is that we cannot help but think that the biblical term *glory* would be much more appropriate than 'beauty' to what St. François has in mind. When 'beauty' comes to designate the very divinity of God, it loses its community with what we can admire and praise by this name in ordinary creatures." Chrétien, *The Ark of Speech*, 99.
15 Chrétien, *The Ark of Speech,* 88.
16 Chrétien, *The Call and the Response*, 7.
17 Chrétien, *The Call and the Response*, 9.
18 "We have to speak on behalf of things, and not only on behalf of one another, as if the world was merely human. Man has a responsibility for creation, a responsibility with which God has entrusted him." Chrétien, *The Ark of Speech*, 136.
19 Chrétien, *The Ark of Speech*, 142.
20 Chrétien, *The Call and the Response*, 7.
21 Chrétien, *The Ark of Speech*, 24.
22 Luke 24:32 NRSV.
23 Emmanuel Garibay, "Emmaus" (2000) published in Emmanuel Garibay, *Where God Is: The Paintings of Emmanuel Garibay* (New Haven, CT: Overseas Ministry Study Center Publications, 2011), 15.
24 See Rod Pattenson, "Recognizing the Stranger: The Art of Emmanuel Garibay," *Image* 68 (Winter 2010/2011): 55–62. https://imagejournal.org/article/recognizing-the-stranger/. Accessed February 17, 2021. Garibay also discusses his context in Jo-Ann Van Reeuwyk, "A Conversation with Emmanuel Garibay," *Image* 65 (Spring 2010): 46–49. https://imagejournal.org/article/conversation-emmanuel-garibay/. Accessed February 17, 2021.
25 Emmanuel Garibay, "Emmanuel Garibay," interview by Daniel Nicholas, Overseas Ministries Study Center, May 2011. https://static1.squarespace.com/static/

57aa00a66a49631b242e5b6f/t/57d707f3d1758e012d349bb6/1473710069492/Emmanuel_Garibay_Describes_Paintings.pdf, 5. Accessed February 17, 2021.
26. Garibay, "Emmanuel Garibay" interview, 2.
27. Pattenson, "Recognizing the Stranger."
28. Pattenson, "Recognizing the Stranger."
29. Chrétien, *The Call and the Response*, 23.
30. Chrétien, *The Ark of Speech*, 40.
31. Dorothee Sölle, "Song on the Road to Emmaus," in *Revolutionary Patience*, trans. Rita and Robert Kimber (Maryknoll, NY: Orbis Books, 1977), 46–48. Reproduced with permission of Orbis Books.
32. Sölle, "Song on the Road," line 37.
33. Sölle, "Song on the Road," lines 48–49 and 53–54.
34. Sölle, "Song on the Road," lines 50–52.
35. "In every manifestation of God, direct or indirect, there is adventure and advent." Chrétien, *The Ark of Speech*, 90.
36. Sölle, "Song on the Road," lines 49 and 54.
37. Chrétien, *The Call and the Response*, 16.
38. Chrétien, *The Call and the Response*, 16.
39. Michael Himes, *The Mystery of Faith: An Introduction to Catholicism* (Cincinnati, OH: St. Anthony Messenger Press, 2004), 12–13.
40. Himes, *The Mystery of Faith*, 12.
41. One is again reminded of Augustine's "Late have I love you" passage, which includes, "You called and cried out loud and shattered my deafness. You were radiant and resplendent, you put to flight my blindness." Augustine, *Confessions*, 10.27.38, 201.
42. Chrétien, *The Ark of Speech*, 91.
43. Chrétien, *The Ark of Speech*, 105.
44. Chrétien, *The Ark of Speech*, 106.
45. See Chrétien, *The Ark of Speech*, 106.
46. In the chapter "Does beauty say adieu?" Chrétien writes: "What we have here is a beauty that does not keep itself to itself, but gives itself: it is impossible to distinguish in time between the moment when it is grasped and the moment when it gives itself, in other words embellishes us. This is its way of saying goodbye." Chrétien, *The Ark of Speech*, 106.
47. Thanks go to Christopher Hadley, S.J., for suggesting these connections between theological aesthetics and theological anthropology.
48. Chrétien, *The Ark of Speech*, 79.
49. Thomas Groome notes that a sacramental outlook must include a critical social consciousness that challenges Catholics to remove obstacles to recognizing God's presence in the world. Those obstacles could include things like sexism, racism, homophobia, or apathy in the face of suffering. See Thomas Groome, *Faith for the Heart: A "Catholic Spirituality"* (New York: Paulist Press, 2019), 217.
50. Benson, "Chrétien and the Call," 212.

Bibliography

Augustine. *Confessions*. Translated by Henry Chadwick. Oxford: Oxford University Press, 1991.

Benson, Bruce Ellis. "Chrétien on the Call that Wounds." In *Words of Life: New Theological Turns in French Phenomenology*, edited by Bruce Ellis Benson and Norman Wirzba, 208–21. New York: Fordham University Press, 2010.

Chrétien, Jean-Louis. *The Ark of Speech*. Translated by Andrew Brown. New York: Routledge, 2004.

Chrétien, Jean-Louis. *The Call and the Response*. Translated by Anne A. Davenport. New York: Fordham University Press, 2004.

Chrétien, Jean-Louis. *Hand to Hand: Listening to the Work of Art*. Translated by Stephen E. Lewis. New York: Fordham University Press, 2003.

Garibay, Emmanuel. "Emmanuel Garibay," interview by Daniel Nicholas. Overseas Ministries Study Center, May 2011. https://static1.squarespace.com/static/57aa00a66a49631b242e5b6f/t/57d707f3d1758e012d349bb6/1473710069492/Emmanuel_Garibay_Describes_Paintings.pdf, 5. Accessed February 17, 2021.

Garibay, Emmanuel. "Emmaus." In *Where God Is: The Paintings of Emmanuel Garibay*, 15. New Haven, CT: Overseas Ministry Study Center Publications, 2011.

Groome, Thomas. *Faith for the Heart: A "Catholic Spirituality."* New York: Paulist Press, 2019.

Himes, Michael. *The Mystery of Faith: An Introduction to Catholicism*. Cincinnati, OH: St. Anthony Messenger Press, 2004.

Pattenson, Rod. "Recognizing the Stranger: The Art of Emmanuel Garibay." *Image* 68 (Winter 2010/2011): 55–62. https://imagejournal.org/article/recognizing-the-stranger/. Accessed February 17, 2021.

Sölle, Dorothee. "Song on the Road to Emmaus." In *Revolutionary Patience*, translated by Rita and Robert Kimber, 46–48. Maryknoll, NY: Orbis Books, 1977.

Van Reeuwyk, Jo-Ann. "A Conversation with Emmanuel Garibay." *Image* 65 (Spring 2010): 46–49. https://imagejournal.org/article/conversation-emmanuel-garibay/. Accessed February 17, 2021.

13

The Saturated Flesh of Christ: Christology, Aesthetics, and Subjectivity in Jean-Luc Marion and M. Shawn Copeland

David de la Fuente

Introduction

Christology is not only about the mystery of the person of Christ, but also, in the words of Brian Daley, S.J., "about us and our salvation, about the future of *our* humanity, about the mode of God's involvement in nature and history … as the story of that involvement."[1] Thus, what is predicated of Jesus is vital for orienting the human subject. It is a matter both of the textual understanding of Jesus and the Way revealed by him, and of aesthetics, that is, of one's perception and understanding of the world in light of Christology. A sober consideration of history would recognize that Christology is a site of aesthetic struggle: some Christologies have been deployed to deleterious ends, underwriting structures of racial and cultural supremacy by idolatrously and wrongly asserting the whiteness and non-Jewishness of Christ.[2] The weight of that history takes on new significance in the present context of racial violence and resurgent white supremacy. At stake is the vision communicated by Jesus about our humanity—a vision of joining of diverse flesh in Christ's body.

Attention to Christ as "saturated" may contribute to a reconfiguration of human subjectivity by reinforcing how the experience of beauty in and through artistic depictions of Christ has the effect of transforming the subject's gaze. To see Christ aesthetically as saturated affirms that Jesus is the Beautiful One (drawing on Augustine) as well as the one who is ever greater. It also affirms that, as the Beautiful One, he reveals something about our future as humans in community by making visible the call to love and solidarity.[3] Saturation also captures the "absolute" character of self-disclosure that so overwhelms the recipient and transforms one's aesthetic vision. Since artistic depictions of Christ are not only saturated by virtue of the figure they make visible, but also by the manner in which that figure is rendered, a true turning of subjects is made possible when one takes into account the particularity of the saturated flesh of Christ.

Consider the contrasting examples of Werner Sallman's famous 1941 depiction *The Head of Christ* and the piece *China Christ* (Plate 8) by Milton Avery. Sallman's portrait of Christ with white skin, brown hair, and blue eyes has been reproduced over five hundred million times. Scholars such as David Morgan, Edward Blum, and Paul Harvey have documented the historical impact of this painting and its implications for aesthetics: Morgan's research demonstrates that for a significant number of American Christians, *Head of Christ* was taken to be a definitive portrait and even a photograph capturing the "color" of Christ. Blum and Harvey trace its widespread historical impact as part of the broader narrative of images of Jesus and the "saga" of race in America, recounting that many American soldiers carried wallet-size prints of *Head of Christ* abroad during the Second World War. Also telling was their recounting of attendees of a Billy Graham revival singing "I Surrender All" to massive billboard prints of the *Head of Christ*.[4] Evocative as *Head of Christ* may be, it makes a claim about the person of Christ that betrays his historical particularity.

By contrast, *China Christ* exemplifies a Christological work of art that deploys saturation in the two ways I mention above and will expand upon below, cautioning against the uncritical reception of *Head of Christ*. Compared with the white Jesus of Sallman's work, *China Christ* does not give a face to Jesus even though the form is recognizable. *China Christ* also renders the body of Jesus pink instead of white, suggesting a saturation to the flesh of Christ. Finally, it does not depict a generic portrait or profile of Jesus: the Christ of *China Christ* is the suffering Christ, crowned with thorns and standing bound, soon to undergo the "scourging at the pillar." Avery also includes a small multicolored cross standing over Christ's shoulder. It is not simply a beautiful depiction of Christ that the viewer encounters, but one marked by suffering—by implication, suffering at the hands of the Roman Empire ("he suffered under Pontius Pilate"). It is not simply that Christ makes a claim on the viewer in a generic way; rather, this depiction suggests that the revelation of Christ in art can evoke saturation by taking on flesh that differs from white flesh, and by pointing to a concrete message that summons the viewer to find Christ in and among those of diverse flesh who suffer.

This chapter engages the work of contemporary thinkers Jean-Luc Marion and M. Shawn Copeland on the topics of aesthetics, Christology, and their implications for subjectivity in order to argue that Christological works of art saturate the spectator's gaze in two ways. Following Marion, I argue that through beauty such works of art make a claim on the spectator by virtue of their rendering visible a "gaze" or intentionality from elsewhere. Spectators find themselves addressed by Christ through such portraits. But saturation must also be interpreted. Here, I draw on Copeland to explore how a saturation of the recipient's gaze by diverse Christological works of art can communicate the theological reality that the saturation of Christ's flesh is accomplished by taking on human flesh in its diversity, and thereby point to a way of life that acknowledges the gift of every human other. In both cases, saturation functions in an apophatic mode that reconfigures the human subject.

Christ as phenomenon does not only exceed the recipient's subjectivity, but also exceeds phenotypic whiteness. Attention to the phenomenon of Christ in this way can contribute to an "aesthetic reconfiguration" or "turning" of subjectivity towards an ethic of love and justice that concretely engages and affirms racial and ethnic differences by attending to the linkage between the saturation of Christ in the diverse bodies he embraces, and the primacy of charity he embodies.[5] I proceed by first examining Marion's treatment of subjectivity, aesthetics, and Christology and their implications for rethinking subjectivity. I then examine Copeland's analysis of subjectivity in light of race, her linkage of a Christology of liberation with new subjectivity, and finally her emphasis on aesthetics as the site of struggle. This enables a reading of diverse depictions of Christ in art.

Saturation in Marion: Decentering the Western Subject

Jean-Luc Marion's phenomenological and theological projects can be read as attempts to decenter and reorient the modern human subject from a constituting *cogito* to a subject who is instead constituted by that which is given. Such an approach to thinking the subject aims to safeguard her or him from idolatry. In terms of theological import, Marion's treatment of the subject insists on the priority of divine revelation. In *God Without Being*, for example, he argues that before God "is," God is love and loves. God therefore arrives and is manifest as sheer gift outside the bounds of a metaphysics of being, and is therefore love before all else. God's self-disclosure therefore puts the theologian in a dangerous and transgressive space. As Marion memorably observes, theology "always writes starting from an other than itself" and "renders the author hypocritical" since God alone can speak accurately of Godself.[6] The result, in Marion's estimation, is that "theology cannot aim at any other progress than its own conversion to the Word," and therefore to the love that God is.[7]

Though Marion sharply demarcates his theological works from his philosophical ones, he advances a similar argument philosophically by way of phenomenology. His methodological task is to elucidate why phenomenology should be founded not on a reduction to objectness or to being, but to a prior givenness as its first principle, according to the rule "as much reduction, as much givenness."[8] This rule builds on Marion's own reading of Husserl, for if one performs this reduction to givenness, then this means that one must be attuned to a phenomenon as it gives itself—that is, on its own terms. From here arises Marion's notion of saturated phenomena, or phenomena that give more to intention than can be "objectified" or constituted—that is, they are saturated or overwhelming in their intuitive givenness. Such phenomena include: the event, including and especially the historical event; the idol, exemplified by the work of art; the flesh, especially my own; and the icon, witnessed especially in the face of the other. Finally, there is the possibility of revelation as the saturated phenomenon *par excellence*.[9] Because these phenomena overwhelm the recipient, the self must adopt a stance of responsibility that acknowledges the priority of that which is given.

The example of painting, both in terms of the work of art itself and the creative agency of the painter, elucidates the logic of Marion's notion of saturated phenomena. The act of painting and artistic depictions both offer a fascinating play on visibility and invisibility, demonstrating that in the work of art there is a "call" elicited by and from the work of art that imposes a different subjectivity on the viewer. In *The Crossing of the Visible*, for example, Marion argues that the painting, imitating Christ, brings the unseen to light and thereby gives the painting its power.[10] It brings something new into being that makes a claim upon the viewer, it "visibly imposes itself" and "imperatively calls us." The painting "inspires the look of its visitors … it does not inhale [the look] because it exudes visibility from top to bottom … it defies us, provokes us." We visit it because it calls us.[11] In *In Excess,* Marion adds, "we cannot see a painting once and for all" but must rather revisit it. The very act of *going* to see a painting—be it a Caravaggio, a Rothko, or even a seemingly pedestrian canvas—demonstrates the call or attraction, and even the agency of the painting. It dictates the viewer's placement so that they may really see it.[12]

The act of painting also reconfigures the painter, such that in the act of creating, the painter "is characterized not by a plastic inventiveness imposing his will but rather by a passive receptivity, which, from among a million equally possible lines, knows to choose this one that imposes itself from its own necessity … the painter records, he does not invent."[13] For Marion, it is the invisible that orients the artist's agency. The painter is compelled by an invisible call from elsewhere to make the invisible visible. The end result is that, for painter and for spectator alike, the painting opens up "a pure desire to see otherwise," thereby reconfiguring one's own knowledge and desires.[14]

Marion on Christ as Saturated in Art: A Different Subjectivity

For Marion, "Every painting participates in a resurrection, every painting imitates Christ, by bringing the unseen to light."[15] Marion's Christological works of art and his writings on Christology explore this further, reinforcing that the ultimate effect of any saturated phenomenon is to reconfigure one's subjectivity. Just as a beautiful work of art addresses both artist and spectator in such a way that they are ultimately passive recipients, Christ as a saturated phenomenon of revelation makes a claim on the self. To speak of Christ in this way elicits a sense of the priority of divine revelation—one may say of the profession of Christ's Lordship, of Christ's majesty, beauty, and authority—from outside the self, imposing itself on the recipient. It also reflects the magnetism of Jesus's personality communicated in the Gospels and in many artistic renditions of the Gospel stories. Marion demonstrates this quite compellingly in his analysis of Caravaggio's *The Calling of St. Matthew*. Ultimately, this painting does not simply depict Christ's election of Matthew; rather, the whole work places the spectator under Christ's gaze as well, such that the viewer too is rendered as a gifted recipient (*l'adonné*) or a witness.[16]

This interpretation also finds credence in popular devotion. Through prayer, meditation on scripture, and contemplation of religious icons and works of art, Christians aim to encounter the "gaze" of Jesus in and through the beautiful. This is revealed in the form of a counter-intentionality or counter-gaze that summons the subject.[17] The self that results from the encounter with a saturated phenomenon is called to an ethics of the gifted, of receptivity and of an "infinite hermeneutics," precisely because it is derived from a phenomenon (Christ) who reveals his own counter-gaze that is irreducible to the subject's knowledge and understanding. Marion's reduction to givenness and emphasis on saturation thus allow one to acknowledge the priority of divine self-disclosure. Prioritizing this saturation allows the phenomenon to make its claim on the recipient in order to annul or reorient the self's desire.

Hermeneutical Challenges

For all its advances, Marion's thought gives rise to tensions: his attempt to clear conceptual space for revelation within philosophy allows for a real presence of divine revelation, but it also suggests that what shows itself in divine revelation is an unmediated, absolute, overwhelming given in terms of the content of God's self-disclosure. Revelation may overwhelm the recipient such that only an "endless" or "infinite" hermeneutics can result, but there is something that can be said about the "givenness" itself of that revelation. Christian theology asserts that God's revelation is "for us and our salvation." If we speak of divine revelation as a phenomenon, that phenomenon is not simply a disclosure of God's presence as such but a revelation of God's existence *for* ... —for us, for the world, for salvation. God's being is "being-for," as Joseph Ratzinger says, and thus truly is the manifestation of love.[18] Notably, theologies of liberation have shown how the revelation of God in scripture and history emphasizes that God's "being-for" is especially and paradigmatically for the poor, the marginalized, the outcast.[19] Depictions of Christ must attend to this dimension of divine revelation if they wish to accurately represent divine revelation.

What is needed is a hermeneutics of saturation. If an infinite or endless hermeneutics is to function at all, it needs to attend to the interpreter's pre-understanding, as well as to the roles of symbols and language in the process of interpretation. A major theme among those who critically engage and appreciate Marion's work is that it is insufficiently hermeneutical, whether in terms of phenomenological or theological methodology.[20] Richard Kearney, for example, raises questions about whether there is a pure phenomenon that can be saturated to the absolute and infinite degree that Marion supposes. Similarly, Shane Mackinlay observes that revelation only appears in a hermeneutic space that acknowledges that phenomenon as revelatory. This is in fact the thrust of Christina Gschwandtner's critique in her *Degrees of Givenness*.[21] Thus, whether the depiction of Christ appears in Caravaggio's *Calling of St. Matthew* or *China Christ* or in any icon of Jesus, one must admit that its degree of saturation may differ from one Christian to another, or from one who is differently religious or not religious at all.

This is not to say that Marion's thought completely lacks an attention to hermeneutics. His phenomenology of givenness and saturation does represent a hermeneutics of phenomena insofar as he distinguishes between ordinary and saturated phenomena. Likewise, the implications of saturation for subjectivity already constitute a key hermeneutical insight: the self is not a master but one given over to that which appears. Given the exceedingly rich character of saturated phenomena, the hermeneutical process must therefore continue endlessly since the self can never exhaust what is given. Most importantly, Marion's emphasis on love within his phenomenological and theological works functions as an important hermeneutical principle with respect to the phenomenon of revelation. He writes, "We must always consider that that which reveals itself in the saturated phenomenon of Revelation involves, as its *alpha* and its *omega*, a single and unique excess: that of charity ... Christ sets out the one element with which the phenomenon of revelation is both saturated and saturating: charity."[22] In tandem with this emphasis on charity, Marion's phenomenological focus on receptivity on the part of the human subject, now rendered as a gifted recipient, opens up a tantalizing possibility of fleshing out how the "call" of Christ as saturated phenomenon is to evoke the response of love according to the measure of what is revealed. A helpful signpost to this is Kevin Hart's phenomenology of the "kingdoms" of God. Building on Marion's reduction to givenness, Hart argues that when it comes to the phenomenon of revelation, there is a more fundamental theological "basilaic reduction" to the reign of God, a theme that is at the bedrock of the synoptic Gospels. This reduction is very much warranted in light of historical critical study of the New Testament: it is the reign of God that serves as a central theme in the synoptic tradition. Such an approach shows how Marion's phenomenological and Christological emphasis upon the primacy of charity is in response to that which is more fundamentally given and revealed by God, the reign of God. That which is saturated makes a claim and reconfigures the recipient through beauty to a new way of knowing and seeing according to the primacy of charity.

The issue, however, is that Marion does not sufficiently enter into the hermeneutical considerations that flow out of this conviction. One can look at a depiction of Christ and receive it as a saturating revelation of charity, but the question remains: in what way does this self-disclosure point to charity? Marion holds that every authentic painting imitates Christ by bringing to visibility that which is not seen. Though every Christological painting shares the same figure and ostensibly reveals the same divine charity, there are differences in each artist's rendition for interpretation. It is not enough to simply state that Jesus reveals divine love (in a beautiful painting or otherwise), for God's givenness in Christ as a saturated phenomenon appears not merely in an absolute sense, but in concrete historical and cultural circumstances—that is, in the flesh of a Palestinian Jew during the era of the Second Temple amidst the reality of the Roman Empire. Furthermore, the message of Jesus is conveyed in a series of narrative and epistolary witnesses (or interpretations!) that shed light on different aspects of the phenomenon of Christ as love and how the call to love is manifest—each with some degree of difference as to the origins of Jesus, his key teachings and actions, his friends and opponents, and the meaning (and timing) of his death. Each of these interpretive traditions reinforce that it is not simply the figure of Jesus who is beautiful, but that his life, deeds, and teachings also communicate beauty.

In this regard, a fruitful hermeneutical principle can be borrowed from Paul Ricoeur's hermeneutic phenomenology, which calls for a "thick description" of revelation as a phenomenon. This is especially true of scripture and its relation to works of art. As Ricoeur observes, in religion there is a polarity between manifestation and proclamation, and the manifestation of the divine in the Christian scriptures is inseparable from forms of discourse, such as narrative, prophetic discourse, and so on.[23] Revelation, then, is already involved in a hermeneutical process, and it requires additional hermeneutical engagement to parse out what it means to identify God's self-disclosure as love.[24] The same can be said about artistic depictions and icons of Christ: these do not arise out of a vacuum but involve an interpretive process that includes the artist or recipient of the vision. It may be true that the painter is possessed by a vision and subjected to it in a sense, but the actualization of a painting using this or that technique, color palette, medium, background, and more suggests that the revelatory nature of art also includes the agency of the artist. For example, one may compare Sallman's *Head of Christ*, Caravaggio's *The Calling of St. Matthew*, or *China Christ*. Each of these depict Christ. But understanding the saturation of Christ in each of them and in art more broadly can benefit from attending to the manner of saturation (and wherever possible the agency of the artist), for it is significant whether one chooses to render Christ as pink, brown, white, Jewish, Palestinian, Black, Asian; as a concrete figure with wounds or as abstract and ethereal, as seated in glory or as cruciform (and there, the decision to focus on dereliction or victory, light or darkness); teaching or healing, present or absent.[25] An alternative understanding of the saturation of Christ in art in terms of quality allows a fuller understanding of what is "actually" revealed in the phenomenon and how it can contribute to the turning of subjectivity towards the primacy of charity.[26]

Saturating Subjectivity: M. Shawn Copeland's Christology and Subjectivity

It is striking that despite differences in color, setting, texture, and other qualities, spectators often recognize the same figure of Christ and experience the call that emanates from that work of art. This shows that one can never exhaust the "face" of Christ in art. There is no single authoritative depiction. Instead, each portrait uniquely points to the "infinite hermeneutics" that takes place in light of the saturated phenomenon by making visible the person of Jesus in different flesh, amidst different moments in the Christ event, and through different cultural and historical settings. Recognizing these dynamics can unlock the capacity of various Christological works of art to bring about an aesthetic reconfiguration that sees Christ present in the beauty of diverse flesh.

By deploying the category of saturation in this way, I am aligning with and amplifying a trajectory within theological writing and critical race theory that names the category of whiteness as the epistemic issue with racism. As many scholars have shown, the problem with racism is never simply one of "common sense" personal bias, hostility, or rudeness. Rather, the issue is structural: constructions of race function as the norm or the condition of possibility for knowledge of and participation in life. In this system, privileges are afforded to certain people and denied to others based on imposed aesthetic standards. Many theologians and scholars working in theologies of liberation, critical race theory, and decolonial thought trace how the discipline of theology is implicated in the structures of whiteness by reinforcing arbitrary aesthetic, cultural, and epistemic norms.[27] But the normativity of whiteness is also evident in lived religion and in attitudes towards visual depictions of Jesus.[28] What is dangerous here is the risk of idolatry, which views portraits of Jesus as a white European as "purely given" and normative.

Though one may find resources in Marion's work to safeguard against such idolatry, it is Copeland who provides a fully thematic interpretation by showing how the figure of Jesus reconfigures subjectivity. She provides a theological frame for interpreting diverse Christological works and their importance in the setting of racism. Seeing Christ depicted as Black, Asian, or indigenous can contribute to a person's reconfiguration to a "new subjectivity" attuned to human others. Encountering Christ in such works of art can also reorient the recipient to embrace practices of solidarity that make Christ's body visible.[29] With this in mind, the historian and theologian Robin Jensen is correct to say that "more is better" when it comes to portraits of Christ.[30]

Subjectivity: Copeland and Seeing Otherwise

Like Marion, Shawn Copeland aims to critique the modern subject because of its inability to see rightly. In Copeland's case, her treatment of the subject overlaps philosophically with Marion's, albeit not always in the same phenomenological vein. Still, many of her insights resonate with Marion's desire to "see otherwise." Copeland seeks to reorient theological and philosophical anthropology away from the Enlightenment project of the "turn to the subject" because of its implication in the construction of racist structures.[31] Initially, Copeland does so in the terms of the philosophical and theological discourses of modernity and postmodernity. She observes that the Enlightenment turn to the subject "was intended to be emancipatory. It aimed to release humanity to dare to rely upon reason, rather than revealed truth, as the authority by which to judge, decide, and act."[32] But instead of delivering emancipation, there emerged a dynamic that restricted the norms of human subjectivity to that which is aligned with white European male normativity. This unleashed a violent and destructive form of human existence in the new world.

At issue in this understanding of the subject is its diagnosis of a flawed and destructive subjectivity rooted in racial bias. Deploying a framework that builds on the cognitional theory of Bernard Lonergan, S.J., in dialogue with critical theologies and postcolonial theories, Copeland shows how a racial formation process coincided with the development of the "modern" subject, and how in that process skin became a "horizon funded by bias." This horizon, Copeland writes, "hides the 'other' from me and renders the 'other' invisible."[33] It is, moreover, a deliberate and conscious choice to short-circuit authentic human knowing.[34] Copeland's emphasis on cognitional bias allows her to integrate critical race theories and name race not as a metaphysical given or as an objective condition, but as a social construct and as a racial formation predicated on bias. Framing race in this way allows for a better accounting of how race functions at macro and micro levels. At the macro level, racial formation allows one to attend to the shifting meanings and relevance of race; at a micro level, racial formation acknowledges the mundane reality of race: that we are taught to see it, and through sight and categorization, generate "social behavior and comfort."[35]

For the black person in a negrophobic society, the horizon of race makes it such that blackness is "so radically different that [one's] very humanity is discredited."[36] To use a concept from Marion, in such a setting the black person's face is not "saturated." To recognize the other's face as such is to recognize another as an "ethical phenomenon" whose "gaze" makes the injunction "thou shall not kill."[37] But instead, in a racist society, the other is perceived as subhuman or as threat. To be sure, the horizon of racism afflicts a whole spectrum of Othered bodies according to race and ethnicity, sexuality and gender, class and culture, but in each case there is a lack of saturation. This racial frame is the result of an impoverished and broken subjectivity in which, in Copeland's words, "a white, racially bias-induced horizon defines, censors, controls, and segregates different, other, non-white bodies."[38]

Copeland's "new anthropological subject" cuts against the totalizing Enlightenment subject by privileging the subjectivity of oppressed women of color, and by linking their subjectivity with that of Jesus of Nazareth, for, in her words, it is ultimately "the body of Jesus of Nazareth [that] impels us to place the bodies of the victims of history at the center of theological anthropology, to turn to 'other' subjects."[39] The new subject, she argues, is one whose humanness is

> [o]riented by the radical demands of the incarnation of God; it reaches its term in the dynamic realization of human personhood. Thus, to be a human person is to be (1) a creature made by God; (2) person-in-community, living in flexible, resilient, just relationships with others; (3) an incarnate spirit; i.e., embodied in race, gender, sex and sexuality, culture; (4) capable of working out essential freedom through personal responsibility in time and space; (5) a social being; (6) unafraid of difference and interdependence; and (7) willing daily to struggle against 'bad faith' and *ressentiment* for the survival, creation, and future of all life.[40]

The resonance with Marion's thought is especially evident in the first two points. To be a creature made by God is to affirm that one is the recipient of a prior, creative love. To be a person-in-community as Copeland frames it resembles the sort of openness one finds described in Marion's work with respect to the saturated phenomenon of the other, to be one who lives according to gifts and givenness. But importantly, for Copeland, love and solidarity are to be linked: "solidarity is basic to the realization of *humanum*. Inasmuch as solidarity involves an attitude or disposition, it entails recognition of the humanity of the 'other' as human, along with regard for the 'other' in her (and his) own otherness."[41] Jesus of Nazareth paradigmatically fleshes this out.

From Christology to Aesthetics

The body of Jesus becomes visible in art in such a way that each depiction makes a claim about what it means to "turn" to persons in loving solidarity. Each artistic work is ultimately tied with the scriptural witness. With this in mind, an important hermeneutical principle emerges in Copeland's identification of Christology as the hinge between subjectivity and aesthetics. In close dialogue with biblical scholarship, theologies of liberation, and critical race theory, she situates Jesus within the first-century setting of the Roman Empire. This requires that one acknowledge the impact of this context for interpreting Jesus, whose life and preaching confronted empire and reflect the "marks" of empire. Over against the imperial order of the *pax Romana*, Jesus proclaimed the *basileia tou theou*, which involved socially transgressive table fellowship, healing, and encounters with "others" that affirmed bodily and cultural difference.[42] As Copeland writes of Jesus, he "is the clearest example of what it means to identify with children and women and men who are poor, excluded, and despised," and in this way he both reveals a new way to be human and "disrupts every pleasure of hierarchy, economy, cultural domination, racial violence, gender oppression, and abuse of sexual others." Put simply, Jesus challenges empire.[43]

Recalling the anti-empire context in which divine revelation occurs can bring the "call" dimension of Christological artistic depictions into clear relief: the spectator does not merely see Christ rendered visible in art, but is also reminded that the life and meaning of Christ issue a summons to faith and to justice. Here it may be worth returning to *China Christ*. It renders the figure of Christ in the context of the "scourging at the pillar" during the Passion. Through the posture of Christ bound at the pillar and the cross that looms over his shoulder, the viewer is thereby reminded not simply of the self-gift of Jesus, but also of the way that Jesus is "marked" by empire. All four Gospels recount that it is under the authority of Pontius Pilate that Jesus is flogged (Mark 15:15, Matthew 27:26, Luke 23:16, John 19:1), and it is through crucifixion that the Roman Empire executes Jesus.

Copeland's empire-critical approach emphasizes Jesus' existence as being "with and for others[,] the poor, excluded, and despised," in a way that counters the reign of Empire. The Gospel depictions of Jesus' interaction with the marginalized have the effect of rendering visible a counter-reign, the reign of God (*basileia tou theou*) and its relation to those bodies made invisible by injustice. From here Copeland grants agency to marginalized subjects and frames theological reflection around a new "anthropological subject."[44] Though her work is not directly phenomenological, it is worth noting that her Christology resonates with the Christological phenomenological trajectory noted earlier between Marion and Hart. It is Copeland who draws out the fuller implications of an emphasis on the *basileia*. Copeland's own "basilaic reduction," so to speak, aligns with Marion's phenomenological interests. Consider one of the first instances of the *basileia* in the Gospels. At the beginning of the Gospel of Mark, the first public words of Jesus are "The time is fulfilled and the *basileia* has drawn near; repent and believe in the gospel" (Mark 1:15). What is more, the enactment of God's reign is connected with a specific type of response that prioritizes the claim that God makes upon the recipient through Christ's proclamation of the *basileia*.[45] This framework can open up the call to a different kind of subjectivity that emphasizes the lives of marginalized peoples as "saturated."

Copeland offers this reminder: all Christology is interpretation ("who do you say that I am?"). One may rightly agree with Marion that the phenomenon of revelation in Christ may be saturated in charity, but following Copeland one must also admit that divine charity takes specific forms. As many synoptic passages attest, Christ is the manifestation of a *praxis* of solidarity, liberation, and care: "the Spirit of the Lord is upon me ... to bring glad tidings to the poor" (Luke 4:18–30). For Christ, the greatest commandment is twofold: love of God and love of neighbor (Mark 12:28–31). But as Copeland shows through an empire-critical Christology, the love that Christ reveals binds humans together in diversity: "in Jesus, God manifests an eros for us *as we are* in our marked particularity of race, gender, sex, sexuality, and culture."[46]

Works of art that render Christ's body as Black, Latinx, Asian, or Jewish capture this saturation in powerful ways. They can captivate the spectator with the beauty or poignance of the depicted scene, but above all they invite the viewer to encounter different subjects as beautiful, and even an ultimate "subject" behind it all. Such paintings make visible Copeland's powerful assertion that "The only body capable of taking us *all* in as we are all with our different body marks ... is the body of Christ."[47] It is not simply Christ's flesh that is saturated, but the flesh of humanity. From this vantage point, one may return to *China Christ* and see how it points to the possibility of seeing diverse bodies in Christ's flesh, not only because it depicts Christ's flesh as saturated, but also because it depicts Christ at the moment when his flesh is marked by the Roman Empire, and at an interval that is intrinsically tied with the Christian belief in God's self-disclosure as love. To be given over to the saturated phenomenon, then, is to be an addressee to the call of that divine charity that embraces difference.

More recently, Copeland has issued a powerful call for theologians to make a further "turn," this time from subjects to persons. This semantic and conceptual shift is needed because discourse about subjects, even if decentered, gives rise to abstract considerations of human experience and thought. Subjects are "abstract, bloodless, disembodied, deracinated, and distant." By contrast, persons are "tangible and solid, flesh and blood, material and embodied; rooted in space and time, in culture and relationships. The *person* is close."[48] Persons suffer injustice and evil ranging from colonialism and genocide to sexism to racism. Perhaps most urgently, persons can be named: Trayvon Martin, Eric Garner, Breonna Taylor. From a theological vantage point, one may add that Christology is concerned with persons more than subjects: to borrow from Kevin Hart, Jesus's "phenomenological" reduction was not one intended to reconfigure subjectivity solely at a conceptual level but to bring about real conversion, repentance, and salvation. Not only do diverse Christological portraits bring the person of Christ close, but also those persons with whom he is identified. From the open-ended non-white *China Christ* to the Jewish Jesus of Chagall's *White Crucifixion* to the Black Jesus of Kehinde Wiley's *Lamentation over the Dead Christ*, to name a few examples, one can better appreciate how the encounter with Christ in art points the spectator to the fullness of divine charity as it embraces othered bodies in loving solidarity.

Confronting racism requires aesthetic reconfiguration, for, as Copeland writes, "beauty is the living up to and living out of the love and summons of creation in all our particularity and specificity as God's human creatures."[49] Saturation as beauty offers a hermeneutical and ethical principle that carries forward Marion's phenomenology by opening up a new vantage point for seeing the work of art as saturated. Since paintings imitate Christ by rendering visible what cannot be seen, and since Christological works of art thematically imitate and make visible Christ, it becomes possible to see in the work of art a summons to an ethics of love that transforms subjects into those who care for persons. Seeing Christ depicted in different flesh turns me to the persons he is identified with through that painting. Copeland helps plumb the beauty of the message and doctrine of the person of Jesus as the one who reveals the possibilities of human life authentically lived. With Copeland, one may view diverse depictions of Christ in art as instances making visible that beauty, as well as making visible the urgency of embracing a *basilaic* ethics.

Conclusion: The Saturated Flesh of Christ

This chapter began with a description *China Christ*. Compared to more classical and contemporary artistic depictions of Christ, it may appear to be a comparatively poor phenomenon. Still, *China Christ* captures the importance of saturation in several ways: by rendering Christ's flesh as nonwhite and without a face, *China Christ* resonates with Marion's assertion about the absolute character of the phenomenon. It gives too much, and in the case of revelation, it reminds us that we cannot exhaust that which is revealed. But it also points to another dimension of saturation: as nonwhite flesh, *China Christ* gestures towards many other depictions of Jesus that show that Christ is beauty incarnate in a plurality of bodily forms and phenotypes. In this way, the viewer is reminded that the person and work of Christ involve incorporation of many into one body, but always while preserving their diversity and specificity. The manifestation of Christ in art is likewise saturated in terms of color, as is evidenced by the great variety of portraits that exist.[50] Increasingly, contemporary artists are reminding and challenging Christian subjectivity by allowing Christ to become visible in paintings as Black, Asian, Latinx, Indigenous, and more. Finally, *China Christ* depicts Christ during the Passion, which further reinforces the possibility of associating this manifestation of Christ with the diverse bodies whom Jesus identifies with through suffering. Through these many depictions, the visibility of Christ makes visible the realities of those who are taken into his body so as to saturate the gaze and more fully reconfigure the viewer to the richness of what is given both aesthetically and ethically.

Notes

1   Brian E. Daley S.J., *God Visible: Patristic Christology Reconsidered* (Oxford: Oxford University Press, 2018), 26.
2   To name a few works that interrogate such historical realities, see: Edward J. Blum and Paul Harvey, *The Color of Christ: The Son of God and the Saga of Race in America* (Chapel Hill: University of North Carolina Press, 2012); J. Kameron Carter, *Race: A Theological Account* (Oxford: Oxford University Press, 2008); James Cone, *A Black Theology of Liberation*, fortieth anniversary edition (Maryknoll, NY: Orbis Books, 2010), and idem, *The Cross and the Lynching Tree* (Maryknoll, NY: Orbis Books, 2011); Jeannine Hill Fletcher, *The Sin of White Supremacy: Christianity, Racism, and Religious Diversity in America* (Maryknoll, NY: Orbis Books, 2017); Susannah Heschel, *The Aryan Jesus: Christian Theologians and the Bible in Nazi Germany* (Princeton, NJ: Princeton University Press, 2008); Willie James Jennings, *The Christian Imagination: Theology and the Origins of Race* (New Haven, CT: Yale University Press, 2010).
3   Augustine, "Exposition on Psalm 44," in *Exposition of the Psalms: 33–50, vol 3/16*, trans. Maria Boulding, *The Works of Saint Augustine: A Translation for the 21st Century* (Hyde Park, NY: New City Press, 2000), 283.
4   David Morgan, *Visual Piety: A History and Theory of Popular Religious Images* (Berkeley: University of California Press, 1999), 40.
5   The emphasis on "turning" is drawn from M. Shawn Copeland, *Enfleshing Freedom: Body, Race, Being* (Minneapolis, MN: Fortress Press, 2010), where she articulates a new

anthropological subject by giving precedence to the historical practices of solidarity of women of color, and by explicating how the dangerous memory of Jesus of Nazareth contributes to a turning of subjects. See also Copeland, "Turning Theology: A Proposal," in *Theological Studies* 80, no. 4 (2019): 768–69.

6 Jean-Luc Marion, *God Without Being: Hors Texte* (Chicago, IL: University of Chicago Press, 2012). 1–3.
7 Marion, *God Without Being*. 158.
8 Marion cites this rule variously throughout his works. See, for example, Marion, *Reduction and Givenness: Investigations of Husserl, Heidegger, and Phenomenology*, trans. Thomas A Carlson (Evanston, IL: Northwestern University Press, 1998), 203; Marion, *Being Given: Toward a Phenomenology of Givenness*, trans. Jeffrey Kosky (Stanford, CA: Stanford University Press, 2002), Book I; and Marion, *In Excess: Studies of Saturated Phenomena*, trans. Robyn Horner and Vincent Berraud (New York: Fordham University Press, 2002), 17–18.
9 Marion, *Being Given*, 234–36.
10 "Every painting participates in a resurrection, every painting imitates Christ, by bringing the unseen to light." Jean-Luc Marion, *The Crossing of the Visible*, trans. James K. A. Smith (Stanford, CA: Stanford University Press, 2004), 27.
11 Marion, *The Crossing of the Visible*, 30.
12 Marion, *In Excess*. 70–72.
13 Marion, *The Crossing of the Visible*, 36.
14 Marion, *The Crossing of the Visible*, 33.
15 Marion, *The Crossing of the Visible*, 27.
16 Marion, *Being Given*, 283–85. Pope Francis's own remarks about this work resonate with this point. "That finger of Jesus, pointing at Matthew. That's me. I feel like him. Like Matthew." Antonio Spadaro, S.J., "A Big Heart Open to God: An Interview with Pope Francis." *America Magazine* 209, no. 8 (September 30, 2013), 15–38, at 16.
17 Marion, *Being Given*, 240.
18 Joseph Ratzinger, *Introduction to Christianity*, trans. J. R. Foster (San Francisco, CA: Ignatius Press, 2004), 129.
19 M. Shawn Copeland, "Poor is the Color of God," in *The Option for the Poor in Christian Theology*, ed. Daniel G. Groody (Notre Dame, IN: University of Notre Dame Press, 2007), 216–27.
20 Marion has developed and responded to hermeneutical critiques in Jean-Luc Marion, *Givenness and Hermeneutics*, trans. Jean-Pierre Lafouge (Milwaukee, WI: Marquette University Press, 2013), and in idem, "The Hermeneutics of Givenness," in *The Enigma of Divine Revelation: Between Phenomenology and Comparative Theology*, ed. Jean-Luc Marion and Christiaan Jacobs-Vandegeer (Cham, Switzerland: Springer Nature Switzerland AG, 2020), 17–48. In "The Hermeneutics of Givenness," for example, Marion cautions against resorting to hermeneutics as the self-evident universal solution for interpreting the given, for it can well be infected by ideology. See "The Hermeneutics of Givenness," 33. Instead, Marion argues, hermeneutics must be determined by the given according to the call-and-response framework he develops elsewhere, including in *Givenness and Hermeneutics*.
21 Jean-Luc Marion and Richard Kearney, "Hermeneutics of Revelation," in *After God: Richard Kearney and the Religious Turn in Continental Philosophy*, ed. John Panteleimon Manoussakis (New York: Fordham University Press, 2006), 319; Shane Mackinlay, *Interpreting Excess: Jean-Luc Marion, Saturated Phenomena, and Hermeneutics* (New York: Fordham University Press, 2010), 176–178; Christina

Gschwandtner, *Degrees of Givenness: On Saturation in Jean-Luc Marion* (Bloomington: University of Indiana Press, 2014), 8–9.
22 Marion, *Givenness and Revelation*, trans. Stephen E. Lewis (New York: Oxford University Press, 2016), 60.
23 The concept of "thick description" comes from Gilbert Ryle and was employed and developed in Clifford Geertz, *The Interpretation of Cultures* (New York: Basic Books, 2017). Ricoeur demonstrates the impact of Geertz on his thinking on several occasions. See Paul Ricoeur, "Philosophical and Biblical Hermeneutics," in *From Text to Action: Essays in Hermeneutics, II*, trans. Kathleen Blamey and John B. Thompson (Evanston, IL: Northwestern University Press), 90–91. Furthermore, Ricoeur argues that phenomenology rests on a hermeneutical presupposition in *From Text to Action: Essays in Hermeneutics II*.
24 Paul Ricoeur, *Figuring the Sacred: Religion, Narrative, and Imagination*, trans. Mark Wallace (Minneapolis, MN: Fortress Press, 1995).
25 One thinks of the intentional differences in Marc Chagall's *White Crucifixion* and Kehinde Wiley's *Lamentation over the Dead Christ*, and even differences between Christ as Good Shepherd in the Roman catacombs and the imperial depiction of Christ in the Basilica of San Vitale in Ravenna.
26 The recent publication *Saturation: Race, Art, and the Circulation of Value* draws on the concept of saturation in color theory as an interpretive lens for the politics of race and representation in the realm of fine arts, and it has indirectly informed my argument. However, one must acknowledge that for the editors, C. Riley Snorton and Hentyle Yapp, saturation seems to be an ambivalent term that names the tensions of racial representation. They note that, since in color theory saturation is defined as the intensity of a color's difference from white, it can be employed to increase racial representation in art institutions. It can do so in a way that is problematic, since color theory can perpetuate institutional life without achieving a true reconfiguration. C. Riley Snorton and Hentyle Yapp, ed., *Saturation: Race, Art, and the Circulation of Value* (Cambridge, MA: MIT Press, 2020).
27 For the distinction of common-sense definitions of racism versus a fuller cultural/structural analysis, see Bryan Massingale, *Racial Justice and the Catholic Church* (Maryknoll, NY: Orbis Books, 2010). For important treatments of whiteness, see Joe R. Feagin, *The White Racial Frame: Centuries of Racial Framing and Counter-Framing* (New York: Routledge, 2013); George Yancy, ed., *Christology and Whiteness: What Would Jesus Do?* (New York: Routledge, 2012); and Willie James Jennings, *After Whiteness: An Education in Belonging* (Grand Rapids, MI: Wm. B. Eerdmans, 2020).
28 Morgan, *Visual Piety*, 47. See also Blum and Harvey, *The Color of Christ*, 208–12.
29 Copeland, *Enfleshing Freedom*, 105.
30 Robin Jensen, *Face to Face: Portraits of the Divine in Early Christianity* (Minneapolis, MN: Fortress, 2005), xii.
31 A number of influential works have identified the Enlightenment and Western Christian imperialism as major culprits in the generation of racist structures. See Emmanuel Chukwudi Eze, ed., *Race and the Enlightenment: A Reader* (Cambridge, MA: Blackwell, 1997); J. Kameron Carter's *Race: A Theological Account;* and Theodore Vial, *Modern Religion, Modern Race* (New York: Oxford University Press, 2016).
32 Copeland, *Enfleshing Freedom*, 85. Also relevant are Copeland, "Racism and the Vocation of the Christian Theologian," *Spiritus: A Journal of Christian Spirituality* 2, no. 1 (Spring 2002): 15–29; Copeland, "Poor is the Color of God"; and Copeland, "The Black Subject and Postmodernism," *Bulletin of Ecumenical Theology* 18 (2006): 93–110.

33 Copeland, *Enfleshing Freedom*. 18. Similarly, Lonergan was soberly aware of the problem of bias, noting that authentic insights can be unwanted. Bernard J. F. Lonergan, *Insight: A Study of Human Understanding* (Toronto: University of Toronto Press, 1992), 214.
34 Copeland, *Enfleshing Freedom*, 13
35 Copeland, "The Critical Aesthetics of Race," in *She Who Imagines: Feminist Theological Aesthetics*, ed. Laurie Cassidy and Maureen O'Connell (Collegeville, MN: Liturgical Press, 2012), 73–85, at 79.
36 Copeland, *Enfleshing Freedom*, 19–20.
37 Marion, *In Excess*. 116–17.
38 Copeland, *Enfleshing Freedom*, 15. Also instructive here is Frantz Fanon's exploration of the phenomenology of perception as experienced through race in his chapter "The Fact of Blackness." Frantz Fanon, *Black Skin, White Masks*, trans. Charles Lam Markmann (London: Pluto Press, 1986). 82–107.
39 Copeland, *Enfleshing Freedom*, 84.
40 Copeland, *Enfleshing Freedom*, 92.
41 Copeland, *Enfleshing Freedom*, 94.
42 Willie James Jennings evocatively refers to such encounters as a "revolution of the intimate." Willie James Jennings, *Acts: Belief—A Theological Commentary on the Bible* (Louisville, KY: Westminster John Knox, 2017), 1.
43 Copeland, *Enfleshing Freedom*, 65.
44 M. Shawn Copeland, *Enfleshing Freedom*. 78. See also 57–64 for an empire-critical reading of New Testament Christology.
45 Kevin Hart, "For a Phenomenology of the Kingdom," *Louvain Studies* 39 (2015–16): 364–76, at 371. See also Hart, *Kingdoms of God* (Bloomington: Indiana University Press, 2014), 139–40.
46 Copeland, *Enfleshing Freedom*, 80.
47 Copeland, *Enfleshing Freedom*, 83.
48 Copeland, "Turning Theology," 768–69.
49 Copeland, "The Critical Aesthetics of Race," 75. See also Copeland, "Turning Theology," 772.
50 Though space does not permit a treatment of icons, it is worth noting the popularity and impact of icons and devotions to Christ with dark flesh such as the *Cristo Negro*, the *Black Nazarene*, and the *Santo Niño de Cebú*.

Bibliography

Augustine. *Exposition of the Psalms: 33–50*, vol. 3/16, *The Works of Saint Augustine: A Translation for the 21st Century*. Translated by Maria Boulding. Hyde Park, NY: New City Press, 2000.
Blum, Edward J., and Paul Harvey. *The Color of Christ: The Son of God and the Saga of Race in America*. Chapel Hill: University of North Carolina Press, 2012.
Carter, J. Kameron. *Race: A Theological Account*. Oxford: Oxford University Press, 2008.
Cone, James. *A Black Theology of Liberation*, fortieth anniversary edition. Maryknoll, NY: Orbis Books, 2010.
Cone, James. *The Cross and the Lynching Tree*. Maryknoll, NY: Orbis Books, 2011.
Copeland, M. Shawn. "The Black Subject and Postmodernism. *Bulletin of Ecumenical Theology* 18 (2006): 93–110.

Copeland, M. Shawn. "The Critical Aesthetics of Race." In *She Who Imagines: Feminist Theological Aesthetics*, edited by Laurie Cassidy and Maureen O'Connell. Collegeville, MN: Liturgical Press, 2012.

Copeland, M. Shawn. *Enfleshing Freedom: Body, Race, Being*. Minneapolis, MN: Fortress Press, 2010.

Copeland, M. Shawn. "Poor is the Color of God." In *The Option for the Poor in Christian Theology*, edited by Daniel G. Groody. Notre Dame, IN: University of Notre Dame Press, 2007.

Copeland, M. Shawn. "Racism and the Vocation of the Christian Theologian." *Spiritus: A Journal of Christian Spirituality* 2, no. 1 (Spring 2002): 15–29.

Copeland, M. Shawn. "Turning Theology: A Proposal." *Theological Studies* 80, no. 4 (2019): 753–73.

Daley, S. J., Brian E. *God Visible: Patristic Christology Reconsidered*. Oxford: Oxford University Press, 2018.

Eze, Emmanuel Chukwudi, ed. *Race and the Enlightenment: A Reader*. Malden, MA: Blackwell, 1997.

Fanon, Frantz. *Black Skin, White Masks*. Translated by Charles Lam Markmann. London: Pluto Press, 1986.

Feagin, Joe R. *The White Racial Frame: Centuries of Racial Framing and Counter-Framing*. New York: Routledge, 2013.

Fletcher, Jeannine Hill. *The Sin of White Supremacy: Christianity, Racism, and Religious Diversity in America*. Maryknoll, NY: Orbis Books, 2017.

Geertz, Clifford. *The Interpretation of Cultures*. New York: Basic Books, 2017.

Gschwandtner, Christina. *Degrees of Givenness: On Saturation in Jean-Luc Marion*. Bloomington: University of Indiana Press, 2014.

Hart, Kevin. "For a Phenomenology of the Kingdom." *Louvain Studies* 39 (2015–16): 364–76.

Hart, Kevin. *Kingdoms of God*. Bloomington: Indiana University Press, 2014.

Heschel, Susannah. *The Aryan Jesus: Christian Theologians and the Bible in Nazi Germany*. Princeton, NJ: Princeton University Press, 2008.

Jennings, Willie James. *Acts: Belife—A Theological Commentary on the Bible*. Louisville, KY: Westminster John Knox, 2017.

Jennings, Willie James. *After Whiteness: An Education in Belonging*. Grand Rapids, MI: Wm. B. Eerdmans, 2020.

Jennings, Willie James. *The Christian Imagination: Theology and the Origins of Race*. New Haven, CT: Yale University Press, 2010.

Jensen, Robin. *Face to Face: Portraits of the Divine in Early Christianity*. Minneapolis, MN: Fortress, 2005.

Lonergan, Bernard J. F. *Insight: A Study of Human Understanding*. Toronto: University of Toronto Press, 1992.

Mackinlay, Shane. *Interpreting Excess: Jean-Luc Marion, Saturated Phenomena, and Hermeneutics*. New York: Fordham University Press, 2010.

Marion, Jean-Luc. *Being Given: Toward a Phenomenology of Givenness*. Translated by Jeffrey Kosky. Stanford, CA: Stanford University Press, 2002.

Marion, Jean-Luc. *The Crossing of the Visible*. Translated by James K. A. Smith. Stanford, CA: Stanford University Press, 2004.

Marion, Jean-Luc. *Givenness and Hermeneutics*. Translated by Jean-Pierre Lafouge. Milwaukee, WI: Marquette University Press, 2013.

Marion, Jean-Luc. *Givenness and Revelation.* Translated by Stephen E. Lewis. New York: Oxford University Press, 2016.
Marion, Jean-Luc. *God Without Being: Hors Texts.* Chicago, IL: University of Chicago Press, 2012.
Marion, Jean-Luc. "The Hermeneutics of Givenness." In *The Enigma of Divine Revelation: Between Phenomenology and Comparative Theology,* edited by Jean-Luc Marion and Christiaan Jacobs-Vandegeer, 17–48. Cham, Switzerland: Springer Nature Switzerland AG, 2020.
Marion, Jean-Luc. *In Excess. Studies of Saturated Phenomena.* Translated by Robyn Horner and Vincent Berraud. New York: Fordham University Press, 2002.
Marion, Jean-Luc. *Reduction and Givenness: Investigations of Husserl, Heidegger, and Phenomenology.* Translated by Thomas A. Carlson. Evanston, IL: Northwestern University Press, 1998.
Marion, Jean-Luc, and Richard Kearney. "Hermeneutics of Revelation." In *After God: Richard Kearney and the Religious Turn in Continental Philosophy,* edited by John Panteleimon Manoussakis, 318–39. New York: Fordham University Press, 2006.
Massingale, Bryan. *Racial Justice and the Catholic Church.* Maryknoll, NY: Orbis Books, 2010.
Morgan, David. *Visual Piety: A History and Theory of Popular Religious Images.* Berkeley: University of California Press, 1999.
Ratzinger, Joseph. *Introduction to Christianity.* Translated by J. R. Foster. San Francisco, CA: Ignatius Press, 2004.
Ricoeur, Paul. *Figuring the Sacred: Religion, Narrative, and Imagination.* Translated by Mark Wallace. Minneapolis, MN: Fortress Press, 1995.
Ricoeur, Paul. *From Text to Action: Essays in Hermeneutics II.* Translated by Kathleen Blamey and John B. Thompson. Evanston, IL: Northwestern University Press, 1991.
Ricoeur, Paul. "Philosophical and Biblical Hermeneutics." In *From Text to Action: Essays in Hermeneutics II,* translated by Kathleen Blamey and John B. Thompson, 89–101. Evanston, IL: Northwestern University Press, 1991.
Snorton, C. Riley and Hentyle Yapp, eds. *Saturation: Race, Art, and the Circulation of Value.* Cambridge, MA: MIT Press, 2020.
Spadaro, SJ, Antonio. "A Big Heart Open to God: An Interview with Pope Francis." *American Magazine* 209, no. 8 (September 30, 2013), 15–38.
Vial, Theodore. *Modern Religion, Modern Race.* New York: Oxford University Press, 2016.
Yancy, George, ed. *Christology and Whiteness: What Would Jesus Do?* New York: Routledge, 2012.

List of Contributors

Thomas Breedlove is a postdoctoral research fellow in the Institute for Studies of Religion at Baylor University in Texas. His current research examines relationships between conceptions of human nature and human flourishing and the role and importance of embodiment in the doctrine of the divine image.

Wendy Crosby is an associate professor of religious studies at Siena Heights University in Michigan. Her research is in the area of contemporary Catholic theology and incorporates insights from feminist theology and Continental philosophy of religion.

David de la Fuente is a doctoral candidate in systematic theology at Fordham University in New York. His research interests are in Trinitarian theology, philosophical and theological hermeneutics, and Christian spirituality.

Christina George is an assistant professor of music at Sterling College in Vermont, where she teaches courses in musicology and philosophy of aesthetics. Her research centers around linguistic and conceptual changes surrounding aesthetic taste, as well as music's place within a Great Books education.

Jake Grefenstette is a doctoral candidate in the Faculty of Divinity at the University of Cambridge. His current research examines the legacy of Romanticism in the twentieth century, particularly in Catholic theology and the arts.

Kevin G. Grove, CSC, is an assistant professor of theology at the University of Notre Dame in Indiana. His research interests include memory, Christology, and the thought of St. Augustine. He is the author of *Augustine on Memory* (2021).

Tyler Holley is a doctoral candidate at the University of Aberdeen in Scotland. His research explores how perspectives on desire contribute to differing construals of subjectivity within French philosophy.

Richard Kearney holds the Charles Seelig Chair of Philosophy at Boston College and is author of twenty-five books on philosophy and literature, including three novels and a volume of poetry. His most recent books are *Touch* (2021), *Radical Hospitality* (2021), and the novel *Salvage* (2022).

Joseph G. Kickasola is a professor of film and digital media at Baylor University in Texas. He is the author of *The Films of Krzysztof Kieślowski: The Liminal Image* (2004), as well as numerous essays on film theory, film aesthetics, and religion and film.

Daniel Adam Lightsey is a doctoral candidate at Southern Methodist University in Texas. His current research focuses on the overlapping worlds of Sergii Bulgakov, a theology of beauty, the metaphysics of the person, and theologically inflected literary speculation.

Taylor J. Nutter holds a PhD from the University of Notre Dame in systematic theology. His research employs the thought of Augustine to interrogate the relationship of theological method to modern and postmodern philosophy.

Nathan D. Pederson holds a PhD in theology and ethics from Loyola University Chicago and is a lecturer in theology at Fordham University. His research takes up a hermeneutical phenomenology of whiteness and examines how racial and colonial discourses were constructed and are maintained through theology and lived religion.

Martha Reineke is a professor of religion emeritus at the University of Northern Iowa. Recent books include *Intimate Domain: Desire, Trauma, and Mimetic Theory* (2014) and *Ana-María Rizzuto and the Psychoanalysis of Religion: The Road to the Living God*, edited with David Goodman (2017).

Christopher C. Rios holds a PhD in systematic theology from the University of Notre Dame. His research interests lie at the intersection of phenomenological aesthetics and theology, with a particular specialization in the thought of Mikel Dufrenne and the theological turn in French phenomenology.

J. Aaron Simmons is a professor of philosophy at Furman University. Among his authored or edited books are *Christian Philosophy: Conceptions, Continuations, and Challenges* (2018) and *The New Phenomenology* (with Bruce Ellis Benson; Bloomsbury Academic, 2013).

Férdia J. Stone-Davis is the director of research at the Margaret Beaufort Institute and an affiliated lecturer at University of Cambridge. She is the author and co-editor of several books, including *Musical Beauty: Negotiating the Boundary between Subject and Object* (2011).

Index

Abraham, 155
Absence, 19
aesthetic experience, 5
aesthetic object, the, 2
aesthetic reconfiguration, 188–9
aesthetic struggle, 187
aesthetics, 4, 87, 103–5, 125–6
affective becoming, 93
Agamben, Giorgio, 50
agency, 108
Alberti, Leon Battista, 46, 51, 51–2, 52
Albertson, David, 106
Alhasen, 46
analogia entis, the, 3
Anderson, Jonathan, 60, 65–6n5
animality, 30–1
anxiety, 152
apophatic anthropology, 13, 21–2
Aquinas, Thomas, 3
Aristotle, 30
art, 3, 89, 91–2
    phenomenology and, 119–20
Augustine, St., 1, 3, 8, 63, 74, 75–6, 77, 78, 81–2n24, 167, 171n46, 174–5
autonomy, 134
Avery, Milton, *China Christ*, 187–8, 191, 196, 197, 198

Bal, Mieke, 6, 103, 105–6, 113–4n29
Baldwin, James, 7, 134–9, 141n25, 142n30, 142n31
Balthasar, Hans Urs Von, 4, 104–5
Barbaras, Renaud, 4
baroque art, 105–6, 107, 111–2
    theological aesthetics, 103–5
Bauman, Zygmunt, 14–5
beauty, 1–2, 7, 173, 174–5, 175–6, 179, 180, 181–2
becoming, 31, 93
becomingness, 3
being, 33–7

Belting, Hans, 52
Benedict XVI, Pope, 4
Benson, Bruce Ellis, 139n2, 182
Bergson, Henri, 33
Bernard of Clairvaux, 107, 121
Bernini, Gian Lorenzo
    art historical perspective, 105–6
    criticism, 112n1
    The Ecstasy of St. Teresa, 6, 103–12
    eucharistic symbolism, 110–1
    and scandal, 103–5
    staging, 106–7
    Teresa's hidden form, 107–10
    theatrically, 106–7, 112
Betz, John, 3
Biran, Maine de, 33, 34
blackness, 194
blindness, problem of, 163–8
Bloom, Molly, 124
Blue (Kieslowski), 6, 87, 93–6, 97, 99n45
Blum, Edward, 188
bodily sensations, 33
body, the, 29, 30–3, 93
    and being, 33–7
    spread, 30-3, 37–9
breath and breathing, 142–3n37
Breedlove, Thomas, 7
Brunelleschi, Filippo, 46
Bulgakov, Sergius, 61
Butler, Judith, 109
Byzantine empire, iconoclastic controversies, 1

Cabasilas, Nicholas, 1–2
Calhoun, David, 71
call and response, 17–9, 173–82, 192
Caputo, John, 153
Caravaggio, *The Calling of St. Matthew*, 190, 191, 193
Careri, Giovanni, 108
Carman, Charles, 45

Carnes, Natalie, 5, 59, 63–5, 68n43
cataphatic imagery, 106–7
Catherine of Siena, 104
Catholic Reformation, 6
Cavell, Stanley, 78–9
Chagall, Marc, *White Crucifixion*, 197
Chrétien, Jean-Louis, 4, 5, 7, 13, 16–7, 18, 131–2, 132–4, 134, 136, 137–9, 140–1n17, 141n18, 141n24, 143n41, 150, 153–4, 158, 173, 173–4, 174–5, 175–6, 177, 179, 179–80, 181–2, 194–5
Christology
  aesthetic reconfiguration, 188–9
  aesthetic struggle, 187
  and aesthetics, 195–7
  Copeland, 193–8
  empire-critical approach, 195–6
  hermeneutical challenges, 191–3
  as interpretation, 196
  Marion, 189–93
  and racism, 193–4, 194–5, 197
  saturation, 187–98
  and subjectivity, 190, 193–8
cinematic form, 6, 87–97
  aesthetic energies, 97
  auditory dimensions, 92, 93–4, 99n45
  Blue (Kieslowski), 93–6
  and the body, 93
  intensity, 93
  and movement, 93
  phenomenological aesthetics, 87
  prophetic role, 96
  representational, 92
  sight, 92
  and time, 93
cognitional theory, 194
colonial desire, 51–2
color, 92
color theory, 200n26
conceptual art, 61
conceptual mysticism, 63
conceptualist theory, 5
confession, 170n34
consciousness, 2, 33
Constas, Maximos, 64, 68n41
consumer culture, 15
consumption, 15
contingency, 158

Copeland, M. Shawn, 7–8, 188, 193–8
Cornaro Chapel, 103, 106–7, 110–1. *see also The Ecstasy of St. Teresa* (Bernini)
Courtine, François, 132, 140n10
COVID-19 pandemic, 182–3n1
creation, 37
creative capacity, 31
creativity, 36
critical race theory, 193, 194, 195
critical theologies, 194
Crosby, Wendy, 7
crucifixion, the, 196
Cusan perspective, 43–53
  ambiguity in, 49
  and colonial desire, 51–2
  and linear perspective, 43, 44, 45–7
  and the mirror, 46–7, 48–9, 49–51, 52
  and mystical darkness, 44–5, 50
  phenomenological stakes, 47–59

Daley, Brian, 187
Damascene, John, 1
Damisch, Hubert, 46
Davenport, Anne, 140n15
Davis, Joshua, 133, 140–1n17, 141n24
de Certeau, Michel, 13, 17–9, 45, 49
De visione Dei (Nicholas of Cusa), 5
  and colonial desire, 51–2
  and linear perspective, 43, 44, 45–7
  and the mirror, 46–7, 48–9, 49–51, 52
  and mystical darkness, 44–5, 50
  phenomenological stakes, 47–59
de-centering, 45–6, 189
Deleuze, Gilles, 4, 6, 31, 39, 103, 107, 109
Denby, David, 74
dependence, 136
DePrun, Jean, 109
Derrida, Jacques, 160n23
desire, 6, 7, 62
  ambiguity of, 63
  colonial, 51–2
  commodified, 22
  experience of, 2
  and memory, 71–9
  need-based, 15
  networks of, 43–4
  pain of, 135
  politics of, 134–7

power of, 136
  Ravaisson and, 34, 35
  sacred, 119–27
  and sight, 163–8
despair, 176
detachment, 21
disenchantment, 13–4, 22, 23n5
divine descent, 35
divine love, 103
divine mind, the, 36–7
Dufrenne, Mikel, 4, 9n8
Dupré, Louis, 50

Ebert, Roger, 71, 74, 75
Eckhart, Meister, 21
The Ecstasy of St. Teresa (Bernini), 6
  art historical perspective, 105–6
  criticism, 112n1
  eucharistic symbolism, 110–1
  evocation of the erotic, 103
  illumination, 111
  and scandal, 103–5
  spiritual agency, 114n29
  staging, 106–7
  Teresa's hidden form, 107–10
  theatrically, 106–7, 112
embodied experience, 134–7
embodied life, 132
enchantment, 22
Enlightenment, the, 104, 194–5, 195
ennui, 31
ephemeral memory, 75–8
eros, 6, 32, 104, 123, 124, 127
erotic experience, 122
  embodied, 106
  evocation of, 103
  and religion, 103–5
  and spirituality, 104
  transformative power of, 32
erotics of sight, 59, 63–5
eschatological hope, 149, 151, 152–3, 156–7, 157–8, 159
eucharistic symbolism, 110–1
Evdokimov, Paul, 1
everyday life, 7
existential hope, 149, 151, 152, 154
existentiell hope, 149, 151–2, 152–3, 154
expectation, 151, 152
external forces, 37–9

faithfulness, 7, 154, 155–7, 158, 160n23
Falque, Emmanuel, 4, 5, 29–33, 33, 34, 37, 38, 39–40, 43, 47, 48–9, 53
Fanon, Frantz, 201n38
Farrer, Austin, 64
fear, 152
feelings, Chaos of, 31
female mystics, 104
Fénelon, François, 34–5
film theory, 91
finality, refusing, 154
flesh/body dualism, 29
Foligno, Angela da, 104
Foster, Hal, 61
Francis, Pope, 4
Frankl, Victor, 153
Friedrich, Caspar David, 75
Fuente, David de la, 7–8
future, the, hope for, 152, 154

Gallagher, Sheila, 121, 124–7
Garibay, Emmanuel, "Emmaus", 7, 173, 175, 176–7, 181, 182
Garner, Eric, 197
gaze, 167, 170n27, 188, 190
Genesis, 173–4
genocide, 177
George, Christina, 7
Gesamkunstwerk, 99n35
Girard, René, 103
givenness, 169n22
Glenstal Abbey, 125
God
  absolute sight, 47–8
  beauty of, 179
  call of, 173–82
  in Christ, 37
  connection to, 21
  darkness of, 44–5
  desire for, 104, 149–50
  desire to find, 182
  experience of, 2
  gaze, 43, 44, 47–8
  grace, 180
  Heidegger and, 2–3
  hidden within nature, 35, 36
  and hope, 154
  immanence, 3
  and life, 88, 97

redeeming presence, 180
reign of, 192
response to, 174–5
revelation, 140n11
self-disclosure, 189, 191
Source of beauty, 175
Godard, Jean-Luc, 72
grace, 29, 180
Grefenstette, Jake, 5–6
Groome, Thomas, 184n49
Grove, Kevin, 82n26
Gschwandtner, Christina M., 7, 167–8, 169n5, 191

Hafiz, 125, 127
Hamilton, Julie, 71, 81n19, 82n36
Harries, Karsten, 44, 52, 53n2
Hart, Kevin, 192, 196, 197
Harvey, Paul, 188
Haxthausen, Charles, 67n27, 67n32, 69n51
Heidegger, Martin, 2–3, 4, 43, 52, 78–9, 120, 138, 151
Henry, Michel, 4, 6, 32, 33, 87–97, 132, 140n11
   Blue (Kieslowski), 93–6
   dismissal of representation, 91
   focus, 90–2
   and the internal, 89
   phenomenological aesthetics, 87
   phenomenological life, 88–9
   Seeing the Invisible: On Kandinsky, 88–9, 91
   theological language, 96
   theological trilogy, 97
hermeneutical challenges, 191
hidden wisdom, 151
Hildegard of Bingen, 107
Hills, Helen, 105, 107, 109
Hindu aesthetics, 125–6
Holley, Tyler, 5
hollowing out, 22
holocaust, the, 153
homophobia, 142n30
hope, 149, 150–4, 156–7, 159
hopelessness, temptation to, 156
human growth, 113n26
human vocation, the, 182
humility, 154

Husserl, Edmund, 119–20, 132, 138, 152–3, 189

iconoclasm, 1
icons, 1, 166–7
identity, 165, 180
Ignatius, 104, 106
image, the, nature of, 164–6
incarnate subject, the, 1
incarnation, the, 1–2, 39
infinite, the, 132–4
Ingarden, Roman, 4
intensity, 93
intentionality, 88
internal, the, 89
intimacy, power of, 136

Jacob wrestling an angel, 173–4, 175–6
Janicaud, Dominique, 132
Jesus Christ, 97, 111, 163, 168
   aesthetic reconfiguration, 188–9
   beauty, 181
   call of, 192
   context, 195–6
   depictions of, 7–8, 187–98
   gaze, 190
   God in, 37
   as icon, 166
   incarnation, 1–2
   on the Road to Emmaus, 176–7
   saturation, 187–8, 187–98
   subjectivity., 190
   transcendent sublimity, 3
   wounds, 181
John, Gospel of, 163, 165, 168
John Paul II, Pope, 4
justice, 160n23, 177–9

Kandinsky, Wassily, 89, 91, 92, 99n35
Kearney, Richard, 6, 191
kenosis, 158
Kickasola, Joseph, 6
Kierkegaard, Søren, 122, 150, 153, 154, 155–7, 157, 158
Kieslowski, Krysztof, *Blue*, 6, 87, 93–6, 97, 99n45
kinetic sculptures, 37–9
Knauss, Stefanie, 81n15
knight of faith, the, 155–7, 157

Index

knowledge, pursuit of, 45
Kristeva, Julia, 123

Lacan, Jacques, 4, 113–4n29
Lagerlöf, Margaretha Rossholm, 109–10
Lamott, Anne, 149, 158
language, 30
Lash, Nicholas, 13
Leavis, F. R., 79
Leibniz, Gottfried, 97
Levinas, Emmanuel, 4, 15, 22, 157
levitation, 111
Lewis, C. S., 78, 153, 156, 157
LeWitt, Sol, 5, 59–65, 66n14
    Serial Project #1, 62
    Wall Drawing #65, 62–3
Lightsey, Daniel, 5
linear perspective, 43, 44, 45–7
liquid modernity, 5, 13, 13–5, 22
listening, 16–7, 17–9
liturgy, effect of, 163–8
lived experience, 2, 29
lived flesh, 30, 31–2, 33, 39
Lloyd, Vincent, 142n31
Lonergan, Bernard, 194
Lubac, Henri de, 8n6
luck, 150
Luke, Gospel of, 173, 180, 182, 196

McIntosh, Mark, 112
Mackinlay, Shane, 191
Malick, Terrence
    aesthetic concern, 79
    on art and the divine, 77–8
    and ephemeral memory, 75–8
    A Hidden Life, 81n16
    influence, 82n35
    phenomenological context, 78–9
    and silence, 73–5
    storytelling, 81n15
    visual poetics, 82n36
    To the Wonder, 5–6, 71–9
Manetti, Antonio, 46
manifestation, 140n15
Marion, Jean-Luc, 4, 5, 7, 7–8, 29, 43, 47–8, 49, 52, 132, 133, 163–8, 188, 189–93, 194, 196
Mark, Gospel of, 196
Martin, Trayvon, 197

meaning, 20
meditation, 190
memory, 5–6, 152
    Augustinian theology of, 71, 75–8
    and desire, 71–9
    ephemeral, 75–8
Merleau-Ponty, Maurice, 4, 6, 33, 73, 103, 107, 109, 133, 137
metaphysics, 3, 4, 29
Meyer, James, 61
mind, the, as a mirror, 50–1
mind, the divine, 36–7
minimalism, 59–60, 61, 66n14
mirror, the, 46–7, 48–9, 49–51, 52
modernity, 43, 50
monumental art, 92–3, 99n35
Morgan, David, 188
Mormando, Franco, 113n15
Morris, Robert, 59–60
motion, 37–9
movements of, 93
Murdoch, Iris, 64
musical experience, 5, 16, 19–20
    apophatic anthropology, 13, 21–2
    Chrétien and, 16–7
mystical darkness, 44–5, 50
mystical experience, 5, 13, 16, 17–9, 21–2

nature, 35
    fulfillment of, 35–6
    mastery of, 51–2
    movements of, 37–9
Nederman, Cary, 52
Nelstrop, Louise, 105
Neo-Platonism, 35
Neo-Scholasticism, 2
Nicholas of Cusa, 53n2
    ambiguity in, 49
    and colonial desire, 51–2
    De visione Dei, 5, 47–59
    and linear perspective, 43, 44, 45–7
    and the mirror, 46–7, 48–9, 49–51, 52
    and mystical darkness, 44–5, 50
    perspective in, 43–53
    phenomenological stakes, 47–59
Nietzsche, F., 31, 34, 158
nocturnal identity, 140n11

optics, 46

passivity, 30, 30–1
Paul, St, 88
Pawlikowski, Paweł, 73
peace, 158–9
Pederson, Nathan G., 5
perspective
    and colonial desire, 51–2
        Cusan, 43–53
        linear, 43, 44, 45–7
        and the mirror, 46–7, 48–9, 49–51, 52
        and mystical darkness, 44–5, 50
        phenomenological stakes, 47–59
Pfau, Thomas, 60
phenomenological life, 88–9
phenomenology, 2–8, 137–8, 189
    art and, 119–20
    limits of, 139
Pieper, Joseph, 4
Plato, 74
Porete, Marguerite, 121, 124, 127
postcolonial theories, 194
praise, 170n34
prayer, 153–4, 168, 176, 190
Presence, 19
Przywara, Erich, 2, 3–4
public space, 43–4, 53

race and racism, 8, 142n30, 193–4, 194–5, 197, 200n26
Rahner, Karl, 4
rationality, 30, 31
Ratzinger, Joseph, 1–2
Ravaisson, Félix, 5, 30, 33–7, 37, 38, 39, 39–40
reality, 165
reconciliation, 180
Reineke, Martha, 6
representational art, 91–2
responsibility, 177–9
revelation, 140n11, 140n15, 191–3, 196
revelatory experience, and touch, 109–10
Rickey, George, 5, 30, 37–9, 39
Ricoeur, Paul, 6, 62, 121–3, 192
Rivera, Joseph, 140n11
Roman Empire, 195–6, 197
Romano, Claude, 151, 152
Rosa, Hartmut, 24n23
Rousseau, Henri, 91

sacrament, 179–80
sacred depiction, 1
sacred desire, 119–27
sacrifice, 171n46
Sallman, Werner, *The Head of Christ*, 187–8, 193
salvation, 110, 180, 187
Sartre, Jean-Paul, 4
scandal, 103–5
Scruton, Roger, 25n56
seeing oneself seen, 47–9
seeing otherwise, 194–5
self, the, 167
    apophatic anthropology, 21–2
    de-centering, 13–22
    and liquid modernity, 13–5
    and musical experience, 16, 16–9, 19–20
    and mystical experience, 16
    transformation, 17, 18
self-affectivity, 132
self-consciousness, 34
selfhood, 53, 134
self-knowledge, 78
self-preoccupation, 21–2
self-realization, 90
self-revelation, 88
sensation, 33, 37, 37–9, 93
sensory experience, 89, 90
sensory thresholds, 20
sexual desire, 104
sexual love, 105
sexuality, 32, 103, 112
sight, 163–8, 169n5
Sigurdson, Ola, 60
Silentio, John de, 155–7
Simmons, J. Aaron, 7
Sloterdijk, Peter, 45
Socrates, 75
Sölle, Dorothee, "Song on the Road to Emmaus", 7, 173, 175, 177–9, 181, 182
Solovyov, Vladimir, 68n46
Song of Songs, 6, 119–27
soul, the, 21, 143n41, 167
soul/body dualism, 29
sound, 92, 93–4, 99n45
Soviet cinema, 78
spiritual agency, 113–4n29

spiritual transformation, 97
Spiritualism, 33
spirituality, 104, 124
spread body, the, 30, 30–3, 37–9
staging, 106–7
Stein, Edith, 4
Steinbock, Anthony, 170–1n35
Stella, Frank, 59, 61, 65n1
Stone-Davis, Férdia, 5
story, power of, 95
suffering, 31, 95, 138
Swenson, Kirsten, 66n18
synoptic tradition, 192

Taylor, Breonna, 197
Taylor, Charles, 14
television, 90, 164–6
Teresa of Avila, 104, 107, 110–1, 112, 114n42, 121. *see also The Ecstasy of St. Teresa* (Bernini)
theological aesthetic anthropology, 181–2
theological aesthetics, 4, 103–5
theological tradition, 4
theologically oriented criticism, 60
theology, backlash, 29
thresholds, 19, 20
time, 93
To the Wonder (Malick), 5–6, 71–9
    aesthetic concern, 79
    arcs, 71
    on art and the divine, 77–8
    and ephemeral memory, 75–8
    the Lady and the Unicorn, 81n19
    literary resonances, 83n43
    opening, 71–2
    phenomenological context, 78–9
    plot, 72–3, 77
    scholarship, 83n45
    score, 72
    secondary arc, 77–8
    sex scenes, 74
    and silence, 73–5
    theological dialectic, 73
Todi, Jacopone da, 175

Toscanelli, Paolo, 52
touch, 7, 109–10, 131–9
trace, 19
transcendence, 140–1n17
transformation, 17, 18, 167–8, 170n27, 173, 175–6, 179, 181–2
transperspectival subjectivism, 51–2
transubstantiation, doctrine of, 111
transverberation, 107–10, 114n42
trout fishing, 7, 149–59
    contingency, 158
    and faith, 155–7
    and hope, 150–4, 159
    and humility, 154
    joy of, 157–9
    limiting out, 150
    and religion, 151
truth, 45
Turner, Denys, 21

ungraspability, 65

value, 20
van Eyck, Jan, 48–9
Viladesau, Richard, 4
vision, 5, 47–8, 59–65, 68n41, 92, 163–8, 169n5
voices, plurality of, 18

Wagner, Richard, 99n35
Warwick, Genevieve, 106, 108
Weber, Max, 23n5
whiteness, 193
Wiley, Kehinde, *Lamentation over the Dead Christ*, 197
will to power, 31, 34, 36
Williams, Rowan, 67n24
women, mystic spirituality, 104
wonder, sense of, 31
world-building, 43
worldly embodiment, 156
wounds, wounding and woundedness, 7, 131–9, 173, 174, 180, 181–2

Žižek, Slavoj, 16